Coalitions of Convenience

Coalitions of Convenience

United States Military Interventions after the Cold War

Sarah E. Kreps

UNIVERSITY PRESS

2011

OXFORD
UNIVERSITY PRESS

Oxford University Press, Inc., publishes works that further
Oxford University's objective of excellence
in research, scholarship, and education.

Oxford   New York
Auckland   Cape Town   Dar es Salaam   Hong Kong   Karachi
Kuala Lumpur   Madrid   Melbourne   Mexico City   Nairobi
New Delhi   Shanghai   Taipei   Toronto

With offices in
Argentina   Austria   Brazil   Chile   Czech Republic   France   Greece
Guatemala   Hungary   Italy   Japan   Poland   Portugal   Singapore
South Korea   Switzerland   Thailand   Turkey   Ukraine   Vietnam

Copyright © 2011 by Oxford University Press, Inc.

Published by Oxford University Press, Inc.
198 Madison Avenue, New York, New York 10016

www.oup.com

Oxford is a registered trademark of Oxford University Press.

Library of Congress Cataloging-in-Publication Data
Kreps, Sarah E. (Sarah Elizabeth)
Coalitions of convenience : United States military interventions after the Cold War / Sarah E. Kreps.
p. cm.
Includes bibliographical references and index.
ISBN: 978-0-19-975379-6; 978-0-19-975380-2 (pbk.)
1. United States—Foreign relations—1989- 2. United States—Military policy. 3. Intervention (International law). 4. Coalitions. I. Title.
E840.K74 2010
355'.033073—dc22   2010009170

9 8 7 6 5 4 3 2 1
Printed in the United States of America
on acid-free paper

Acknowledgments

Military historian B. H. Liddell Hart famously said, "If you wish for Peace, understand War." My goal in studying the causes and conduct of war has been to locate the conditions suited to peace. I started that study in 1994, when I first put on a military uniform. In the mid-1990s, Air Force Reserve Officer Training Corps had something of a detached textbook feel, almost a casualty of the post–Cold War "peace dividend." Sure, I learned about military strategy, how to pitch a tent, and why waking up for PT (physical training) at 4:50 A.M. is a bad idea, but actually going to war seemed remote. The closest thing to combat I encountered was riding my bike through Central Square on my way from Harvard to MIT.

From there, peace rather than war began to seem more elusive. I spent the year at Oxford between 1998 and 1999, and as I traveled through Europe and the Middle East, I experienced both the effects of conflict and the American role in it. During that year, I traveled through Gaza and the West Bank, saw American flags burned in Geneva, and was asked by a Serbian in Prague why my country was bombing her family in Belgrade.

I put on the uniform full-time in late 1999, somehow feeling like I had missed out on my classmates' migration to Silicon Valley. It took a burst tech bubble but especially the 9/11 attacks to realize that I was in the right place. Fresh doubts arose in the run-up to the Iraq War, however, when my Royal Air Force counterparts' questions about the decision to go to war were met with silence on this side of the Atlantic. I began to wonder in earnest not just why countries go to war, but why they have tighter alliances with some countries than others and whether international institutions and norms actually constrain powerful militaries such as that of the United States. These are the questions I have tried to answer by writing this book.

In the course of my research and writing about international institutions, alliances, and military intervention, I have incurred a number of debts. I thank Professors Roger Porter and William Clark of Harvard and the late Professor Stephen Meyer of MIT; they unwittingly convinced me to pursue political science and shelve my misguided attempts to become a surgeon. I would also like to thank Dr. Barbara Polla, who invited me to join her environmental science labs in Paris and Geneva during college, inspired me with her volumes of publications, and fortified me with French culinary delights.

Several individuals shaped the questions I asked in the book. Professors Dan Byman and David Edelstein rightly insisted that I write on something that would both interest me *and* get me a job. They read numerous drafts of the dissertation and book manuscript and provided helpful comments along the way. Professor Jeffrey Legro posed questions that challenged my assumptions and improved the book's argument. Professors Jonathan Kirshner and Peter Katzenstein carefully reviewed drafts of the manuscript and offered extensive feedback that improved both the argument and the coherence of the book.

My thanks also go to those who graciously responded to my research queries and requests for interviews: Colonel John Agoglia, Richard Betts, Stephen Biddle, Conrad Crane, Lieutenant General Johann-Georg Dora, Karl Eikenberry, Doug Feith, Martha Finnemore, Francisco Flores, Colonel Mike Fleck, Marc Grossman, Colonel Dave Greco, Colonel Mike Greer, Rian Harris, Lieutenant Colonel Walter Kretchik, Matthew Kroenig, Tony Lake, Robert Lieber, Brigadier General H. R. McMaster, Meghan O'Sullivan, General David Petraeus, Kalev Sepp, Jamie Shea, Colonel Steve Sklenka, Colonel Hans Wiermann, Abiodun Williams, and Colonel Isaiah Wilson.

The research for this book would not have been possible without support from a number of institutions: The University of Virginia's Miller Center for Public Affairs, Harvard University's Belfer Center for Science and International Affairs, the Deutscher Akademischer Austausch Dienst (DAAD), and the German Marshall Fund.

I would like to thank a number of friends and colleagues who have been helpful sounding boards along the way: Michael Allsep, Alexander Downes, Dan Drezner, Matt Kreps, Alexander Lennon, Sean McGraw, Andrew Mertha, Tom Pepinsky, Tige Stading, and Jessica Weeks.

My gratitude goes to Oxford University Press's acquisitions editor Dave McBride and his team for making the publication of this book possible and to Kendra Bartell for her assistance in the final stages of edits.

Finally, I would like to thank my family, without whom life's pursuits would have been impossible and uninspired. My grandfather, Benjamin Roseto, served in North Africa and Europe during World War II, an example that prompted me to join the military, which was a life-changing experience. My parents provided endless opportunities, love, and support from day one, a model I can only hope to replicate with my own family. Gustavo has been a truly invaluable partner, not just in the evolution of this book but in life. This book is dedicated to them.

Ithaca, New York

Contents

Coalitions of Convenience

1

Introduction

In 2002, the perennial pessimist of American power, Paul Kennedy, made a remarkable reversal. He boldly declared that "in global military terms only one player on the field now counts—the US." Having been stunned by the 9/11 attacks, he wrote, the United States went on to wreak "appropriate oblivion" on the foes in Afghanistan. More impressive yet is that the United States intervened with allied contributions described as "mere tokenism."[1]

The lesson was instructive: American military power was unrivaled by friend and foe alike. Unilateralism appeared to be a logical by-product of unipolarity, a world in which all power indicators favored the United States. In this world, allies would be less meaningful than they were in shifting the balance of power during the great wars of the previous century. Moreover, relying on multilateral institutions, their most strident critics had pointed out, was tantamount to "reacting to events or passing the buck to multilingual committees with fancy acronyms."[2] Even defenders of multilateral institutions had to admit that multilateralism in a unipolar world meant less autonomous decision making, leading them to wonder "why multilateralism might ever be preferred to an architecture where the hegemon could more directly exercise dominance?"[3] Put another way, why would the most powerful states need help from their friends?

Despite its power advantages, the United States has generally sought allies and international organization authorization for its military interventions. In eight of the ten interventions in the post–Cold War period, the United States used force multilaterally even though the outcomes did not appear to be in doubt. For example, in 1994, the United States intervened multilaterally against a Haitian army derided because it did not "have the skill and dedication to fight its way out of a retirement home."[4] Why did the United States seek allies to intervene in a situation with such sharp power disparities?

This book asks why powerful states such as the United States intervene multilaterally more often than not. When does the United States instead sidestep multilateral channels and intervene alone? When it sticks with multilateralism, how does it choose from the menu of multilateral institutions, whether a formal institution such as the United Nations (UN), the North Atlantic Treaty Organization (NATO), or an informal coalition of the willing?

To answer those questions, this book looks at instances of American military intervention after the Cold War. The combination of theoretical and empirical analysis shows why multilateralism often prevails even for the one player on the field that counts. It clarifies why unilateralism is desirable in some cases but why these are exceptions. Finally, it spells out why multilateralism can take many forms and how lead states choose among them.

THE ARGUMENT

At its most basic level, state behavior has often been modeled as a duality: states either cooperate or are in conflict.[5] In reality, they can do both at once. For example, they might cooperate with allies to plan and undertake a military intervention against another state. States might also cooperate with an international organization whose members authorize and partake in the conflict. Sometimes, however, a lead state goes into conflict unilaterally, having given little effort to cooperating either with allies or with international organizations.

Structural arguments expect that the last option, unilateralism, will be tempting for the most powerful states. Robert Jervis summarizes the view as follows: for the United States, "the great ability to act on its own will militate against its being bound by impartial justice and meaningful standards of appropriate behavior."[6] In other words, he writes elsewhere, unilateralism "is the logical outcome of the current unrivaled U.S. position in the international system."[7] Scholars such as William Wohlforth and Stephen Brooks agree that with such overwhelming power disparities, unilateralism might just be an inevitable consequence of unipolarity.[8] Author Max Boot has similarly written that "any nation with so much power always will be tempted to go it alone. Power breeds unilateralism. It's as simple as that. Oh, sure, American presidents may pay lip service to allies, but when push comes to shove, we just don't need anyone else's help very much."[9] This argument has tremendous intuitive appeal: powerful states go it alone because they *can*.

By contrast, normative arguments expect that material power has little to do with the choice of whether to cooperate on the way to conflict. According to this view, even powerful states intervene multilaterally because doing so is considered an appropriate means of using force. The legitimacy conferred by international organizations and a multinational force becomes a worthy end in itself, even if it introduces inconveniences along the way. That a powerful state such as the United States nonetheless intervenes multilaterally is testimony to the power of multilateral norms.[10] As a result, this argument goes, powerful states go multilaterally because they *should*.

Besides being diametrically opposed in their expectations of U.S. cooperation in the post–Cold War period—suggesting that they cannot both be right—normative and structural arguments face challenges from the post–Cold War empirical record. The normative explanation cannot account for the ostensible "unilateralist turn"[11] in American foreign policy with the Iraq War. Nor can it explain variation in the form of multilateralism states used, for example, between the UN-authorized, multinational force in Bosnia, the UN-authorized but U.S.-led intervention in Haiti (1994), and the NATO-led peacekeeping operations in Afghanistan. On the other hand, the structural account is convenient in explaining the Iraq War but is entirely inconsistent with the large number of multilateral interventions in the post–Cold War period—a time of unrivaled American power.

The argument of this book reaches out to elements of both camps.[12] It agrees with normative arguments that states would rather have more legitimacy than less when they use force abroad. It challenges the motivation behind wanting legitimacy, however. According to my argument, states do not act out of a sense of "appropriateness," as some normative arguments would suggest, but rather out of cunning and consequence. As the study of nineteenth-century European history tells us, powerful states stay powerful only if they are guided by a sense of limit and the claim of legitimacy. The Austrian statesman Metternich understood that the durability of his country's position required that its actions be "legitimized by a doctrine of conservatism and stability, and brought about, if possible, in the name of existing treaties rather than by their rupture."[13] When given the chance, the statesman wisely chose not to "impose a vengeful peace" on Napoleon, instead setting up a system of alliances that solidified Austrian hegemony throughout central Europe.[14] Legitimacy and the preservation of a status quo that favored Austria came from acceptance by other great powers, not by imposition.

That lesson had been learned in part through the demise of Napoleon, who favored universality, assertion of power, and governance by force. Of this contrasting tale, Henry Kissinger writes that "whatever else the events of 1812 had proved, they had demonstrated that the game could no longer be won by pulverizing either the antagonist or the pieces; that it had to be played according to its own rules which placed a premium on subtlety and not on brute strength. The longer Napoleon hesitated in recognizing this truth, the more certain his ultimate defeat."[15] Brute force had its limitations, which Napoleon eventually discovered with his ignominious defeat in Russia.

As this historical vignette shows, legitimacy is not strictly the province of idealists. It was long the instrument of realpolitik statesmen who favored the status quo and understood that the way to prolong state power was to work within the international order rather than disrupt it. Wise statesmen of the nineteenth-century knew this, and it is no less the case today that a sense of restraint and a willingness to work within the established international order are power-conserving strategies.[16] The appropriate question is therefore not "why cooperate?" but rather "why not cooperate?"[17] Powerful states have more reasons to act within the established international order than they do to contravene it. But from time to time, states do sidestep that order, and the question is when and why they do that.

The answer is sympathetic to classical realist concerns about power. As E. H. Carr tells us, "It is as fatal in politics to ignore power as it is to ignore morality."[18] Sometimes states can get what they want only by using power. Those times should be a matter of national exigency to warrant force over the order-preserving benefits of self-limitation, however. They are not determined by the underlying structural or social environment but rather by the specific security context that surrounds the intervention. The two main factors are (1) a state's time horizon, which is a function of the directness of threat, and (2) the operational commitment, or how resource-intensive the intervention is expected to be. Both factors affect the willingness to intervene alone, with allies, with international institutions, or a combination thereof.

The argument proceeds from the straightforward observation that even if a multilateral coalition confers legitimacy and creates opportunities for burden-sharing, pursuing a multilateral response is more time-consuming, less reliable, and more limiting than operating alone. Organizations that bless the intervention and states that share in the burden do so at some cost to the lead intervening state. For example, the UN-authorized 1991 Gulf War coalition took five months to assemble. States that reluctantly agreed had some voice in decisions on how long to leave economic sanctions in place before starting the intervention (Russia preferred more time), command structure (the French insisted on not being under American command), and goals (the UN did not authorize going into Baghdad to remove Saddam Hussein).

Multilateralism is essentially a pay-to-play scheme in which the actors that contribute—whether in the form of troops, financial resources, or institutional authorization—have a say in decision making. Since actors' interests inevitably diverge, multilateralism means less expediency, independence, and flexibility than had the lead state intervened alone. As Robert Keohane points out, even "advocates of multilateralism have difficulty claiming that the UN or other multilateral organizations are more efficient than states." He goes on to say that the bureaucratic process of multilateralism ensures that "it will respond slowly and often partially to rapidly changing events."[19]

The slow and partial response may not be a problem for states with long time horizons, that is, those who value the future versus the present and therefore prize long term investments. Even if it must pay the up-front costs of seeking international organization authorization and assembling a multi-lateral coalition, multilateralism promises payoffs in the long term, since the costs of intervention—troops, finances, and opportunity costs—add up over time. With longer time horizons, the lead intervening state will welcome the opportunity to be seen as acting multilaterally and will gladly share the burden, whatever the inefficiencies attendant to cooperative decision mak-ing. Longer time horizons are associated with less direct threats to security, whether in terms of the nature of the threat (political instead of military), target (a third party versus the homeland), and time (long term versus immediate). An evolving political threat to a third party, for example, Haiti in the early 1990s, means a greater willingness to take the time to assemble a multilateral response and relinquish some decision-making autonomy. States that are able to take the long view will see these cooperation costs as worth the price.

But faced with direct threats—for example, a military attack on the home-land or an ally—short-term security concerns will dominate. Uncertainty about the future will create short time horizons and temptations to scoop the short-term gains of unilateralism, even if it means forgoing the longer-term benefits of multilateralism. If the future looks threatened, why con-serve power resources for tomorrow? As chapter 3 will show in more detail, the shortest time horizons and least likely scenario for multilateralism are associated with immediate, military attacks on the homeland, a Pearl Harbor or 9/11 style of attack.

With less direct threats to security and longer time horizons, states are likely to pursue a multilateral strategy, either international organization (IO) authorization or authorization *and* a robust participatory coalition. The form of multilateralism it pursues depends on the second factor: operational com-mitment. Even an advanced military power such as the United States, which accounts for 45 percent of the world's defense spending, has "contested zones" that challenge its dominance. For example, the Chinese military, the North Korean People's Army, and possibly the Iranian military have more men under arms than the American military. The "sheer expense of [U.S.] uniformed personnel"[20] required to confront an adversary of this size means that battle-field victory is far from certain. In this zone, the United States has incentives to aggregate resources with allies and form a sizable coalition that can, together, confront the "adversity"[21] likely to accompany this kind of challenger.

Leading up to the Gulf War, for example, Chairman of the Joint Chiefs Colin Powell warned that the war would be "harder than Panama and Libya...it would mean a major confrontation...the ratio is weighted in his [Saddam's] favor."[22] The predicted battle of attrition would be a costly proposition, and intervening alone would be a losing proposition, warned President George H. W. Bush.[23] The United States undertook an impressive effort to obtain UN authorization and recruit a sizable multilateral coalition.

In contrast, conflicts where the lead state is uncontested—in which it thinks it can win quickly or on the cheap—create fewer incentives to assemble a broad multilateral coalition. With long time horizons, the lead state may have opportunities to produce IO authorization but may reach out to fewer allies, such as in the Somalia intervention, which was expected to be a manageable food aid mission, and the early phases of Haiti in 1994, where the United States expected it could take over the island in a day.

To summarize the argument, states would rather have more legitimacy than less. They would also rather have more ways than fewer to share what are often the costly burdens of military intervention. Despite these general preferences, the expediency of unilateralism may be attractive under some circumstances. Short time horizons associated with direct threats will make the immediate payoffs of unilateralism more attractive. With short-term challenges to security, a state with an outside unilateral option will instead intervene on its own terms rather than waiting for authorization and playing the coordination game with allies. Longer time horizons create a space in which the lead state can assemble a multilateral response. The form of that multilateral response depends on whether the challenger is a "contested zone" for the lead state and is thought to require a large operational commitment.

Outcomes are rarely monocausal, of course, particularly on complex decisions about how to deploy a state's resources, manpower, and prestige. In some cases, alternative explanations such as international norms on the use of force, domestic politics, and regional power influence the decision on whether to intervene unilaterally or with some form of multilateralism. These alternative accounts do not explain variation across cases but do contribute insights in particular cases.

Norms on the use of force suggest that "appropriate" intervention behavior is multilateral. States act multilaterally not out of instrumental calculations about how to get what they want but because it is considered legitimate. The very need to justify an action in norm-compliant terms—the Bush administration touting the 47-state "Coalition of the Willing" for a largely unilateral intervention into Iraq—could be considered evidence of normative pull.[24] The United States would want to be seen as multilateral because it is consistent with social norms on the use of force.

Domestic politics—in this case, American political institutions such as Congress and the public itself—create legislative and electoral constraints around the executive's freedom of action. Since Congress authorizes and funds military interventions, and public opinion is a key source of the executive's political capital, going against domestic preferences can come at a cost, both narrowly to the success of the intervention and broadly to the leader's political agenda. According to this argument, domestic-level preferences for multilateralism over unilateralism should give the executive strong incentives to pursue multilateral strategies. The 1994 case of Haiti, in which the American domestic audience was overwhelmingly opposed except under the condition that the United States intervene multilaterally, is evidence of these incentives.

Last, the regional power thesis—which suggests that regional powers constrain U.S. freedom of action for interventions in their spheres of influence—would explain why the lead state intervenes unilaterally in some cases and multilaterally in others. In regions with major powers, the United States would be less likely to intervene unilaterally. At best, incorporating powerful regional partners helps pool resources and offset the costs of intervention; at worst, a coalition that does not include these powerful regional actors could cause them to interfere unproductively (balance) against U.S.-led interventions. According to this account, multilateralism would be more likely in Europe and Asia, where the forgone assistance or cost of balancing would be high, than in Latin America.

As these brief examples suggest, the "alternative" explanations are not always alternative or contradictory to the argument I advance. Different explanations can have the same analytical expectations. In these cases, the only way to tease out which explanation is dominant is through tracing the causal mechanism. For example, my account of time horizons and operational commitment and the explanation about multilateral norms both expect multilateral cooperation under most circumstances; process tracing is therefore the only way to discern whether behavior was motivated by a logic of consequences (support for my argument) or appropriateness (support for norms). Chapter 3 develops that distinction in more detail.

BRIEF PLAN OF THE BOOK

Chapter 2 introduces and defines the key terms of the book, including *unipolarity*, *intervention*, and *multilateralism*. Chapter 3 develops the argument, drawing on theories of cooperation to develop the two main factors critical to whether states cooperate in times of war: time horizon and operational commitment. It assembles the argument's key assumptions from two types of historical examples—contrasting cases of great powers that have acted with and without restraint, as well as from historical challenges of fighting wars with allies. Chapter 3 goes on to illustrate the basic contours of the argument with reference to post–Cold War cases of intervention.

To test the arguments and trace the causal mechanisms, I turn to several case studies. Chapter 4 looks at the 1991 Gulf War because it was unusually multilateral. This case of multilateralism is an exemplar for the conditions particularly suited to multilateralism; it provides a heuristic for understanding when multilateralism is more likely.

Chapter 5 examines the multilateral 1994 Haiti intervention, an unlikely case of multilateralism for both the operational commitment and regional power explanations. The vast power disparities between the U.S. and Haitian militaries and the absence of regional powers should have meant an interest in minimal multilateralism; the UN-authorized intervention and allied support challenge these explanations.

Chapter 6 is a before-and-after study[25] in which the cooperation strategy in Afghanistan changed from unilateral to multilateral over time; it controls for many factors that do not change—norms, domestic politics, and regional powers—and helps to isolate how changes in time horizon and operational commitment affect cooperation decisions.

The last case, the 2003 Iraq conflict, would seem to contest the time horizon and operational commitment argument, because long time horizons and low operational commitment would predict multilateral strategies. Instead, we saw minimal cooperation, a strategy best explained by the overestimated threat (and flawed time horizons) and underestimated operational commitment.

Each case tests the central argument of the book and alternative accounts of cooperation behavior. These cases and the post–Cold War empirical record show that while the United States would prefer to intervene multilaterally, this preference is based not on lofty normative principles but on narrow utility considerations: if the United States can produce UN authorization and collect allies relatively easily, it proceeds along a multilateral path, which reassures other states of its intentions and helps shoulder the costly burden of intervention. In the post–Cold War world, the United States generally had the power that allows it to cajole allies and trade UN votes to generate support for its intervention at little cost. When time horizons were short and expectations about operational commitment low, however, the United States was more likely to circumvent multilateral institutions. It might still give a nod in the direction of the UN and cloak its unilateral intervention in multilateral language, both relatively cost-free propositions, but would intervene largely alone.

In some cases, domestic politics affected whether to pursue a resolution authorizing force, such as in Iraq, but the United States barely genuflected in the direction of the UN before carrying out its intervention in the way that short time horizons and expectations of low operational commitment would have predicted. Norms helped explain why the states put on a good political show about multilateralism, but they look more circumspect when compared with unilateral actions that were incongruent with its words and with an unwillingness to make costly compromises for cooperation. Regional powers might have explained which states the United States sought to incorporate in certain ventures, but in most cases the United States was more interested in a permissive environment than in pooling regional actors' resources per se. Despite lending some insights in particular cases, none of these alternative accounts explains cooperation behavior across episodes of intervention.

In addition to assessing the empirical record of past interventions, this analysis looks to the future of security cooperation. It shows that critics who bemoaned the end of multilateralism with the unilateral invasion of Iraq may have spoken too soon.[26] There are at least three reasons that American cooperation with allies and institutions continues to look likely. First, its power will endure longer by working within a legitimate, multilateral order than if it dismisses the same system from which it has profited handsomely. Second, the number of U.S. international interests means that it would also face overstretch without pursuing its actions multilaterally. Third, there are some circumstances—particularly against adversaries with large numbers of military-age troops—in which American military power is simply insufficient. With these constraints in mind, it becomes clear that all but the most pressing circumstances make some form of multilateralism a wiser strategy and one that the United States will continue to pursue.

Nonetheless, the multilateral declinist camp may be right if their skepticism is limited to *formal* multilateralism. In the early post–Cold War period, the UN operated as its charter had envisioned; no longer paralyzed by power politics, it became the go-to institution for authorizing the use of force. Vetoes plummeted, Chapter VII authorizations for actions to "restore international peace and security" increased, and with enough time, quid pro quos, and side payments, the United States was able to gain authorization for its interventions. That permissive UN Security Council dynamic is likely to change as China rises and Russia becomes resurgent. Rather than the UN being a one-stop shop for coalition-building, changing distributions of power will mean greater "forum shopping,"[27] as the United States seeks multilateral institutions that can accommodate its interests more efficiently. The United States may still start but not stop with the UN. Ad hoc coalitions of the willing, much pilloried after the Iraq War, may actually be the multilateral way ahead if, as during the Cold War, going through the UN becomes untenable.

What may remain the same—or, if this analysis is any guide, should increase—are hybrid approaches to intervention. As the last chapter concludes, discussing cooperation strategies as either unilateralism or multilateralism presents policy makers with a false choice. Approaches may be layered, or one may follow another. Afghanistan has demonstrated both. The United States intervened largely unilaterally until the fall of the Taliban. It then turned peacekeeping over to a UN-authorized, NATO-led force while it operated a mostly unilateral offensive counterterrorism operation outside the multilateral peacekeeping mission. The advantage of this hybrid approach is that the lead state gains relative autonomy in the combat phases, where differences in technological capability—in which one state is more advanced than another—may create more acute interoperability challenges. It then receives multilateral assistance in the peacekeeping and reconstruction phases that can last indefinitely and pose high opportunity costs if the lead state has to commit large numbers of troops for peacekeeping missions. Cooperation choices are therefore not binary but rather may be used in conjunction with each other over different phases of an intervention.

Why Study the United States?

This book may strike some critics as too U.S.-centric. This is a self-conscious choice made for two reasons. First, the United States intervenes more often and farther afield than any other state.[28] Arthur Stein is correct to point out that "the choice between unilateralism and multilateralism exists not only for the U.S., but for others...the choice of going it alone...is open to all."[29] By virtue of intervening more than other states, however, the United States makes this choice more often than any other state. And because it is the most powerful state, these choices have more profound impacts on international institutions, allies, and target countries.

Second, American power has remained relatively stable in the post-Cold War. If a state's relative power does affect cooperation decisions, then we would want to examine a period where power fluctuated little. The post-Cold War span of American dominance provides this environment. An added advantage of this period is that the post–World War II multilateral institutions such as the UN have functioned reasonably well after the Cold War. Largely inert during the Cold War, unilateralism was less of a choice than the outcome of an implicit or explicit veto. In contrast, any unilateralism after the Cold War is less the product of paralysis by power politics than the choice that a great power has made to circumvent multilateral institutions. A study of why great powers pursue particular institutional strategies is far less interesting if the choice is limited—as was largely the case during the Cold War—and the outcome a foregone conclusion. Thus, the post–Cold War period, with post–World War II multilateral institutions in place *and* functioning, is the subject of this study.

The implications, however, go far beyond questions of how the United States intervenes. Rather, they speak to unanswered questions about how the world works when capabilities are concentrated in the hands of one state. The field of international relations already has well-developed theories of how states behave when there are two superpowers (bipolarity) or three or more (multipolarity). It is still relatively bereft of theories that speak to the conditions of unipolarity.[30] Of the still-unanswered questions about unipolarity, this book focuses on the specific question of whether international rules, institutions, and cooperation are more or less difficult to sustain under these circumstances.[31] This book shows that unipolarity may create more opportunities for the lead state to act alone, but that the incentives are stacked against doing so. After all, it is the status quo order—one of multilateral cooperation, often organized through international institutions—that elevated the United States to its position of unipolarity in the first place. The way to maintain that position is not to violate that order but to work within it.

2

Defining Cooperation under Unipolarity

This research turns on concepts that are central to international politics—polarity, intervention, cooperation—but ones that remain loosely defined in the literature. What does *unipolarity* mean, and why does the distribution of power matter? What is an intervention? When does a particular use of force constitute an intervention? How do we know whether a particular coalition is multilateral or whether it is stacked with states that provide more window dressing than any real decision-making influence? Those are the questions this chapter answers.

Despite the rise of China, American missteps in Iraq, and an economic crisis, the international distribution of power remains unipolar. According to William Wohlforth, "unipolarity is a structure in which one state's capabilities are too great to be counterbalanced."[1] This does not imply that other states will not try to balance power; rather, it means that the distribution of capabilities resides overwhelmingly in the hands of one state so that if other states tried, at least in the near term, they would fail.[2] Put more simply, an "international system is unipolar if it contains one state whose share of capabilities places it in a class by itself compared to all other states."[3] The last few years have seen the "rise of the rest"—the term Fareed Zakaria uses to refer to states such as India and China—but the United States remains the "materially preeminent" state across all dimensions of power. Its share of defense spending is 66 percent of the world total—compared to 47 percent in 1991[4]—its share of the world economy was almost 21 percent in 2008,[5] and it is an unrivaled leader in technology innovation, research and development, and higher education.[6] Taking these measures into account, the world, John Ikenberry and colleagues conclude, is a "one superpower world."[7]

Though this distinction is already superlative, others have gone even further. Christopher Layne calls the United States a "hegemon."[8] Hegemony, according to this definition, is more than the simple distribution of power. It involves not just preponderant power but a state that "purposefully exercises its overwhelming power to impose order on the international system"; essentially, it uses its power to create a hierarchy in the international system. This definition of *hegemony* takes as a given—the imposition of power—what the analysis of this book suggests may depend on circumstance. Unipolarity is a subset of hegemony; the United States is unipolar but not hegemonic.

Having clarified these terms, I turn to intervention, the activity that is the subject of this book. Intervention is the foreign deployment of combat-ready, regular military troops (ground, air, or naval) across international borders to engage in coercive action in or against the target country.[9] The definition includes conflicts such as the Gulf War, since the United States and its allies deployed regular troops to force Iraq out of Kuwait after the 1990 invasion. It is inclusive of coercive airstrikes such as the 1998 response to the embassy bombings, since they were designed to undermine Sudan and Afghanistan's support for terrorism.[10] It also includes humanitarian military actions such as the one in Somalia since it involved the imposition of military forces to coerce the warlords to allow humanitarian relief efforts into the country.[11] In each of these cases, the lead state seeks to make the status quo costlier for the target than making concessions.[12]

The definition excludes noncoercive measures such as routine troop maneuvers, training exercises, disaster relief, logistics support, protection of embassies, and activities of diplomatic personnel or international observers, since these do not intend to use force to change the behavior of the target. Also excluded is covert action because such commitments do not risk large military losses, are conducted without any domestic debate, and therefore do not raise issues of domestic mobilization, international cooperation, sovereignty norms, and authorization, as do larger scale uses of force.[13]

This definition also seeks to make a distinction between wars and interventions. Wars are typically fought over territory between states. Intervention is less about conquest of territory and more about influencing behavior—whether it be the nature or goals of the regime—and often through the assistance of a local ally.[14] Thus, I include conflicts that are often casually referred to as wars, such as the 1991 Gulf War and the 2003 Iraq War, as interventions.

COMPETING DEFINITIONS OF MULTILATERALISM

Existing definitions of *multilateralism* tend to gather around two camps. The quantitative definition focuses on the number of actors involved, "the practice of coordinating national policies in groups of three or more states, through ad hoc arrangements or by means of institutions."[15] By this account, the "coalition of the willing" that intervened in Iraq[16] could qualify as multilateral, even though most of those states did not have any say over decision making. The qualitative definition emphasizes elements such as the institution's legitimacy; "socially constructed indivisibility," in which an attack on one is perceived to be an attack on all; "generalized organizing principles," meaning that all parties must be treated similarly; and diffuse reciprocity, in which members do not exact quid pro quo exchanges but rather may expect a longer term assurance that benefits will distribute equitably over time.[17] The Concert of Europe, in part because it considered peace to be indivisible among its members, qualified as multilateral during the eighteenth century, as do the contemporary examples of the United Nations (UN) and the North Atlantic Treaty Organization (NATO).

Where the quantitative definition is too easily manipulated by unilateralism masquerading as multilateralism, the other is overly restrictive and ambiguous in a world in which states may plausibly shop among issue-specific multilateral fora.[18] Given this reality of proliferating, multilateral institutions, a reasonable definition of multilateralism must not be restricted to formal institutional choices such as the UN.

I therefore stake out a middle ground between the overly restrictive qualitative definition and the too easily manipulated quantitative definition. I define *multilateralism* as "policy coordination of multiple actors that have influence over decision making." Such coordination resides either at the institutional level, which requires authorization by an international or regional organization, or at the participatory level, which requires a substantive set of actors that have influence on the operation's decision making.

According to the first level, an intervention is multilateral if it engages and gains authorization from an international organization (IO). Acquiring IO authorization requires that the lead state coordinate policy preferences, distribute side payments as necessary, and negotiate differences on the resolution's language and the intervention's objectives. As Alexander Thompson suggests, "Channeling coercion through the Security Council entails costly constraints—even a superpower usually must modify its policy and may be blocked altogether."[19] Because of the heterogeneity of interests, the process of generating IO approval and avoiding a veto requires a good deal of policy coordination. Moreover, once a UN resolution has authorized the use of force, it acts as a guidepost for decision making and indeed has influence over the expansiveness and conduct of the intervention.

On the basis of its number and heterogeneity of actors, the United Nations Security Council (UNSC) is the most obvious institution to qualify as formal multilateralism,[20] but regional organizations, whether the Organization of American States (OAS) or NATO, may also constitute formal multilateralism under two important conditions. First, the organization must have a voting mechanism in which a member state brings forth an initiative and other members pass (or veto) the measure according to some preestablished set of voting rules. What would therefore not qualify is the 1983 behavior of the Organization for Eastern Caribbean States (OECS); three of the seven members of the organization sent a letter to President Reagan requesting military assistance in Grenada. Not only did not all members lodge the request but also the issue was never brought to a formal vote in the OECS.[21] The United States was keen to cast its Grenada intervention as multilateral because of the OECS request, but the Grenada intervention does not qualify as multilateral because of the unofficial, informal role the OECS played in the intervention.

Second, the authorization may not occur *ex post* and still qualify as multilateral. For example, in 1965 President Johnson authorized army and marine troops to intervene in the Dominican Republic to prevent a leftist regime from assuming office. Anticipating that the OAS would oppose his plan to use force for regime change in the Caribbean, Johnson undertook the plan first, then later asked the OAS for permission. Only once the intervention was under way did the administration ask the OAS to authorize an inter-American peace force, to which the states reluctantly agreed, in part as a way to gain some agency over an intervention that all states including the United States knew was entirely unilateral and out of their control otherwise.[22] But the *ex post* request and authorization did not constitute multilateralism because it did not grant the permission to use force prior to the intervention; formal multilateralism requires that the authorization come before the use of force commences.

Defining and measuring participatory multilateralism requires some means by which to assess whether members of a coalition have influence over decision-making outcomes. Applying the theoretical literature on institutional design—how various organizational arrangements affect decision-making procedures—to the specific practice of military coalitions, I advance five relevant dimensions by which to measure the coalition robustness:

- Number of states
- Percentage of lead state's troops relative to the coalition
- Percentage of lead state's financial resources relative to the total
- Power (a)symmetries in the coalition
- Presence of key regional actors

The first dimension of participatory multilateralism is the number of states in the coalition. The number of countries participating in a coalition is not sufficient as an overall measure of multilateralism, but it is *one* important indicator. Assembling and holding together a coalition of 30 countries necessarily takes more coordination and compromise than a coalition of three countries. Transaction and information costs increase since the number and diversity of interests increase, on average, as the number of participants increases. Finding and achieving common goals becomes considerably harder with larger groups than with smaller groups.[23]

The second and third dimensions address whether those participants have a shallow investment in the coalition. A large coalition of members who are participants in name only will be easier to coordinate than a coalition of participants who have a material stake in the outcome. In a battlefield context, that stake comes if they have contributed either troops or financial resources. These are both proxies for state interest, which Stephen Krasner has argued "condition[s] both regime structures and related behavior."[24] In exchange for their contributions, states that have a greater material interest—measured through either troops or financial resources—will "demand more sway over the institution."[25]

In the run-up to the 1991 Gulf War, Thomas Friedman described the trade-offs between state interest (participation) and decision-making autonomy as follows: "The coalition is also confining because, as anyone who has raised money will attest, the minute you accept money or a political endorsement you have to take the donor's opinions into account."[26] The United States may have sent planes, tanks, and marines to the Gulf War, but others provided the funds or political cover for their use, which means they cannot be used at will. This quid pro quo—states offering resources in exchange for a say over decisions—applies both to troop and financial contributions.

The fourth is the power status or symmetry of the states that constitute a coalition, or what Koremenos, Lipson, and Snidal refer to as "asymmetrical distribution of actors' capabilities."[27] The basic argument is that "powerful actors will be more likely to get their favored institutional outcome."[28] The more actors with rough power parity, the more difficult it will be to coordinate preferences because each strong actor will have more decision-making clout than an actor with less relative power. On the contrary, a coalition led by one dominant state will require fewer compromises from the lead state since smaller states will have less bargaining power and will have to cede decision-making power to the more powerful state. A coalition of the United States, the United Kingdom, and France, for example, requires more policy coordination than a coalition of the United States, Micronesia, and Mongolia.

The fifth measure of participatory multilateralism is the presence of key regional actors.[29] States with geographical advantages relative to the intervention have disproportionate bargaining power. For example, in the Gulf War, Saudi Arabia's location conferred decision-making power because of its proximity to Kuwait and Iraq. Its support in the form of basing access to almost a half million U.S. troops had more obvious utility than had the same support come from a state outside the region; as the co-commander of the operation (alongside the United States), its influence on decision making was more commensurate with the value of its strategic location than with its aggregate national power.[30]

The more state participation along these dimensions, the more constraints on the lead state's decision making. What made the Persian Gulf War coalition potentially fragile is that it had 24 state participants that provided two-thirds of the financial resources and one-third the troops, and these states included major powers such as the United Kingdom, France, Germany, and Japan and all the major regional powers except Israel, since the Arab states would not participate in a coalition that included Israel. As the lead state, the United States could not undertake major shifts in strategy without first coordinating with the other coalition members.

In contrast, less participation along these parameters in the Iraq War meant fewer constraints, though less help. The United States did bring 47 countries into its coalition of the willing, but consider the other four dimensions: many of the states in the coalition did not have large standing armies and therefore contributed no troops. Unlike the Gulf War, no state provided financial resources. Other than the United Kingdom and Australia, there were no other major state powers in the coalition. Last, there were no regional powers such as Saudi Arabia, Turkey, Syria, and Egypt, as there had been in the Gulf War. Overall, the degree of multilateralism was anemic, even if a couple of states such as the United Kingdom and Australia participated. It did mean that the United States had a good deal of autonomy, however; coordination largely took place along an axis of a few like-minded states.

To this point, pure unilateralism—in which the United States is the only state participating—is relatively uncommon. Because of its institutionalized practice of intelligence sharing, training, and undertaking military operations with the United Kingdom and Australia, the theoretical concerns about cooperation costs apply far less to working with these states. And as Greg Sheridan of the *Australian* quipped, "If the Americans wanted to invade the moon, we would be right there behind them."[31] These states are likely to be part of almost any U.S.-led intervention and unlikely to impose considerable decision-making constraints. Thus, since pure unilateralism is rare and, despite these indicators, multilateralism can be difficult to measure, the more useful way to think about cooperation is along the two levels discussed previously. First, did the lead state obtain authorization from a multilateral organization? Second, was state participation highly multilateral along these dimensions outlined here, or did few if any states provide broad, material sanction? Taken together, an intervention that is both IO authorized and has broad state participation is considered fully multilateral. On the other end of the spectrum are those interventions that are neither authorized by a multi-lateral organization nor have broad state participation; these are considered unilateral, bilateral, or minilateral interventions. Unilateral refers to a policy pursued by just one state, bilateral is cooperation between two states, and minilateral is cooperation of small numbers (but at least three) and often on an ad hoc, issue-specific basis (see figure 2.1).[32]

In between are the IO-authorized interventions undertaken without broad participation by states (formal multilateralism) and those with broad

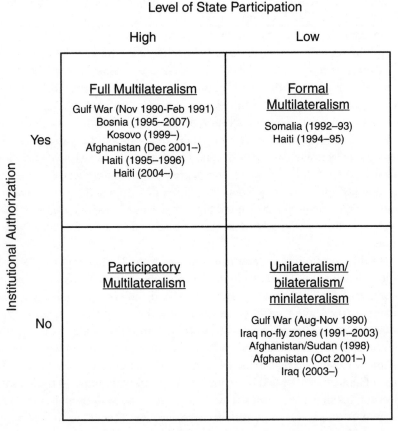

Figure 2.1 Forms of cooperation. Multilateralism may result either through institutional authorization (e.g., an international or regional organization) or through broad state participation in a coalition. The two-by-two matrix shows the various forms of cooperation and which phases of post–Cold War interventions fall under each heading.

state sanction but no IO authorization (participatory multilateralism). Of these two middle categories, one is not necessarily *more* multilateral than the other. Rather, they are different forms of cooperation, and one of the goals of this research is to understand the conditions in which we are likely to see one form over another, both among the types of multilateralism and the less constraining paths of unilateralism, bilateralism, or minilateralism.

THE EMPIRICAL RECORD OF POST–COLD WAR INTERVENTIONS

Defined by these criteria, there were ten U.S.-led military interventions from 1990 to 2009. While the unit of analysis is an intervention, some of these cases are notable for the shift in cooperation strategy over time. The Gulf War, Haiti, and Afghanistan began with one form of cooperation and then shifted to multilateral strategies—the Gulf War for the start of operations and Haiti and Afghanistan for postconflict operations—over the course of the intervention. Thus, there are 10 interventions but 13 observations (see table 2.1).

In this period, there are no cases of participatory multilateralism. In no instance did the United States lead an intervention that did not have IO authorization but did have broad participation from states. The main reason has to do with structural changes that accompanied the end of the Cold War. In the first four decades of its founding, the Security Council had been paralyzed by explicit or implicit vetoes by the Soviet Union.[33] With the end of the Cold War, the number of vetoes plummeted, and the number of resolutions passed, including Chapter VII "threats to the peace" authorizations, soared, from 8 resolutions in the first four decades of the charter to 105 in the next decade.[34] Without a peer competitor, the United States became "the principal driver of the Council's agenda and decisions, passively and actively."[35] Cast more cynically but probably as accurately, Samuel Huntington wrote that with "the collapse of the Soviet Union, the United States was often able to impose its will on other countries,"[36] a dynamic brought into sharp relief with authorization for the 1994 Haiti intervention (chapter 5). Low likelihood of vetoes and preponderant assets available to cajole reluctant allies conferred opportunities to gain IO authorization for interventions that would have gone unauthorized during the Cold War.[37]

With UN authorization relatively forthcoming during this period, there was less need to intervene with ad hoc coalitions *outside* the UN, meaning that once the United States decided against unilateralism, its real choice was between full and formal multilateralism, and it decided between these two based on whether it expected a costly burden of intervention. With UN authorization workable in the immediate post–Cold War world, participatory

Table 2.1 Variations in Cooperation Strategy in Post–Cold War U.S. Military Interventions

Intervention	Year	International Organization Authorization	State Participation	Cooperation Strategy
Persian Gulf War	August 1990–November 1990	None	Low	Bilateral
	November 1990–February 1991	UNSC	High	Full Multilateral
Somalia	1992–1993	UNSC	Low	Formal Multilateral
Iraq no-fly zones	1993–2003	None	Low	Bilateral
Bosnia	1993–2007	UNSC	High	Full Multilateral
Haiti	1994–March 1995	UNSC	Low	Formal Multilateral
	March 1995–1996	UNSC	High	Full Multilateral
Afghanistan/Sudan	1998	None	Low	Unilateral
Kosovo	1999–	NATO	High	Full Multilateral
Afghanistan	October 2001–	None	Low	Unilateral
	December 2001–	UNSC	High	Full Multilateral
Iraq	2003–	None	Low	Minilateral
Haiti	2004	UNSC	High	Full Multilateral

multilateralism was a less obvious multilateral choice. As I suggest in later chapters, the rise of China and the resurgence of Russia could mean that participatory multilateralism, absent in the immediate post–Cold War period, would become an increasingly useful multilateral vehicle. As such, it is worth theorizing not only the pattern of cooperation behavior that was pursued in this period but also the pattern that might be likely under distributions of power where other states have more influence. It is to the former question that the next chapter turns.

3

Explaining Cooperation in Post–Cold War Military Interventions

Perceived American decline in the 1970s and 1980s prompted concern about the demise of international cooperation out of fear that without U.S. leadership, cooperation might not be possible.[1] It might seem surprising, then, that the sense of fear returned early in the twenty-first century, though for the opposite reason: American strength might now mean the United States would not need institutions and opt out, making those institutions less relevant.[2] As Robert Kagan seemed to advocate the view: "We are in a novel situation in world history where one nation has such overwhelming power and the capacity to act unilaterally ... it's not the UN Security Council that is the key force; it's really what the United States decides to do."[3]

Even though the United States *can* exercise its power unilaterally does not mean it does, and for good reason. Classical realist E. H. Carr suggests that political actions typically couple morality and power. Quoting Thomas Paine, he further writes that governments do not arise either "out of the people or over the people, the answer is that they do both. Coercion and conscience, enmity and good will, self-assertion and self-subordination, are present in every political society."[4] States that rely solely on coercion, enmity, and self-assertion pay a price.

The contrasting consequences of France's Napoleon's and Austria's Klemens von Metternich's approaches to power are instructive.[5] For Napoleon, "Domination was his deity."[6] His ambitions knew no bounds, and his disposition knew no humility. Having advanced his Grande Armée throughout Europe, defeating a series of European coalitions, Napoleon met Metternich in 1813 and promised that "I have annihilated the Prussian army ... I have beaten the Russians. Now you wish your turn to come. Be it so; we shall meet in Vienna."[7] The combined impact of audacious words and actions exercised throughout Europe triggered strong counterbalancing across the continent and eventually led to the overextension of France's power. Napoleon's ultimate defeat in Russia made manifest the lessons of governing by force and without a "recognition of limits."[8] In the short term, his expansionist, scorched-earth strategy succeeded, in part because of the uncoordinated response of the opposing coalitions and the force behind the large, conscript army. In the long term, however, a coalition of European great powers—many of which had sat on the sidelines in the short term—overcame earlier coalition failures and marshaled enough manpower and unity to bring down Napoleon.[9]

In contrast, the Austrian statesman Metternich acted as the "custodian" of legitimacy, working within an informal "international agreement about the nature of workable arrangements and about the permissible aims and methods of foreign policy."[10] Blunt force could silence adversaries temporarily but did not automatically produce the legitimacy necessary for a stable, durable order.[11] What would bring legitimacy and indeed powerful allies was a sense of restraint, an appreciation for the status quo, and "voluntary submission" to an international order rather than one foisted upon other states. The crafty establishment of order and "sense of limit," held together by savvy diplomacy, led to a prolonged period of stability that favored Austria's interests.[12] The goal was not legitimacy for legitimacy's sake, however. Rather, acting legitimately within the established international order rather than contravening it was considered to be a more successful long-term strategy.

The divergent approaches and outcomes produce a set of compelling lessons. The general point is that states "that have most successfully navigated their rise to power and established an order consistent with their objectives have been those that most clearly recognized limits of power as a basis of rule."[13] The statement can be disaggregated into a few parts. First, a wise state conserves its resources and prolongs its power by acting within established rules rather than flagrantly circumventing them and provoking others to impose costs on its actions. It is not power maximizing and crusading, but rather reassuring, cautious, and cognizant of being seen as legitimate in its actions.[14] Second, supplanting legitimacy with force is, of course, possible but foolish, even suicidal, Kissinger observed.[15] Third, success requires that other states "believe that its [a powerful state's] leadership is benign."[16] Substituting cooperation and legitimacy for brute force does not make a convincing case for benign leadership.

The benefits of cooperation go beyond these strategic, long-term advantages of preserving one's position in the international system. Using military force is costly. It produces financial, personnel, and opportunity costs. Going alone means carrying the lion's share of the costs, whereas cooperating with institutions and allies offers a way to share the costly burden of intervention. The 1991 Gulf War showed how a multilateral approach could help the lead intervening state avoid some of those costs. Allies contributed about two-thirds of the financial costs, with Saudi Arabia, Kuwait, Germany, and Japan picking up much of the financial burden.[17] By contrast, the United States underwrote almost the entire cost of the Iraq War, the second most expensive military engagement in U.S. history.[18] Francis Fukuyama contrasted the financial implications of the two approaches as follows: "Multilateralism means the difference between the $70 billion contributed by foreign powers to pay for the Gulf War and the $13 billion they have pledged for reconstruction" in the later conflict.[19]

An intervening state also typically pays a high price in casualties and general wear and tear on deployed troops, particularly for long-enduring conflicts. Allies can help here as well. The contrasting experiences of Afghanistan and Iraq point to the consequences of having internationalized the former but been unilateral in the latter. As of 2009, the United States had had 24 times the fatalities of the state with the second highest number of fatalities for the Iraq war (the United Kingdom) but only 5 times in the case of Afghanistan.[20] Further, the size and duration of Iraq rotations prevented the military from reaching recruiting goals, retaining soldiers, and maintaining its equipment at high levels of "readiness."[21]

Over time, these deployments create opportunity costs.[22] High numbers of troops in one location are unavailable to deploy elsewhere. Those costs are particularly salient because of the open-ended nature of many post–Cold War interventions. Of the 10 post–Cold War U.S.-led interventions, 5 were ongoing as of 2006.[23] Had the United States not had allies in Haiti, Bosnia, and Kosovo, its commitments in each of these interventions would have lasted considerably longer. In each of these cases, the United States was able to leave the country or dramatically reduce its presence well before the intervention came to a close. For example, whereas U.S. forces were 23 percent of the original Bosnia deployment, by 2003 U.S. forces were 16 percent of the total, and just 2 percent by 2004.[24] By 2007 the United States was able to redeploy its own forces, turning over control to the European Union which assumed responsibility from NATO in 2004 and has remained in Bosnia since then.[25]

For states such as the United States with a number of international commitments, these costs of international engagements accumulate. As Robert Gilpin points out, "As a state increases its control over an international system, it begins at some point to encounter both increasing costs of further expansion and diminishing returns from further expansion."[26] A powerful state such as the United States has more international interests; the world, Robert Jervis writes, "is its neighborhood."[27] Policing the world neighborhood by itself is costly; policing it with help is more manageable. Enlisting allies helps shoulder the onerous burden that comes with managing the international system.

Taken together, these factors suggest that the United States has much to gain from multilateralism. Its default preference, contrary to structural arguments that couple unilateralism with unipolarity, is therefore likely to be multilateralism. Multilateralism is not a foregone conclusion, however. In a telling comment to one of his World War II generals, Prime Minister Churchill once opined that "there is only one thing worse than fighting with allies—and that is having to fight without them."[28] That the British prime minister would carp about allies after begging for their help for two years speaks to just how much they can complicate operations.

One main problem, as he discovered, is that the process of initiating conflict as a coalition can take time. It involves bargaining efforts that often resemble a war of attrition in which the other sides hold out for better terms—whether less expansive war aims, better side payments, perhaps a longer period of sanctions—a negotiating process that can produce "costly delays" or sometimes no agreement at all.[29] Daniel Poneman, who helped mediate the North Korean nuclear crisis in the mid-1990s, summarized the challenges of multilateral cooperation: "Multilateralism is a hassle. It takes a lot of time and energy for a government to coordinate its objectives, strategies, and tactics with other governments, each seeking to advance its own—sometimes widely divergent—interests and objectives."[30]

Diplomatic bargaining leading up to the 1991 Gulf War illustrates these constraints. The United States expended almost four months persuading the Soviet Union and other holdouts on the Security Council that economic sanctions had run their course and that military force would be necessary. The six-month diplomatic effort, undertaken largely by President George HW Bush and his Secretary of State James Baker, consisted of daily diplomatic attempts to persuade foreign allies to join the coalition. Between 2 August 1990 and 15 January 1991, Secretary Baker alone undertook 10 foreign missions, conducted 200 meetings with foreign leaders, and traveled 100,000 miles in an impressive, extended act of shuttle diplomacy. President Bush was given the moniker "mad dialer" for the amount of telephone diplomacy he undertook to recruit reluctant allies.[31] Even when states agreed to the principle of intervention, they differed on the timing. The Soviets, for example, asked the United States to extend the period of sanctions. Thus, rather than beginning on 1 January 1991, the United States waited two additional weeks to accommodate Soviet preferences and instead began operations on 16 January 1991.[32]

In addition to time, the diplomatic efforts also required nontrivial amounts of side payments. Romania, for example, sought $80 million in humanitarian assistance in exchange for its support in the Gulf War, Zaire was interested in the restoration of foreign military aid that Congress had previously terminated, the Soviet Union sought a $4 billion transfer from Saudi Arabia, and the Ivory Coast sought debt forgiveness.[33] Though a modest amount for the United States, these bargains did take time and coordination—for example, the Soviet request required coordination with Saudi

Arabia, and the Ivory Coast and Zaire required that Baker return and coordinate with his Congress for debt forgiveness and foreign aid—that complicated the move toward intervention.

Last, the United States had to moderate its goals in exchange for UN authorization. Malaysia, a rotating member on the Security Council, did not want the resolution to mention "force" or "military," and the Soviet Union (USSR) also preferred more moderate language than the United States had proposed. In the end, the UN settled on the more limited goal of removing Saddam from Kuwait rather than removing him from power altogether. Although there were other reasons for not going into Baghdad, President Bush and National Security Advisor Brent Scowcroft cited the "stated mission, as codified in UN resolutions, was a simple one,"[34] and this did not involve going into Baghdad to remove Saddam Hussein. As this example illustrates, diplomatic transactions, even when states generally agree that they must "do something," take time, resources, and compromises on goals.

The previous discussion suggests that all things being equal, multilateralism is desirable even for a state with great power. Being seen as legitimate and sharing the burdens of managing the international system are both ways to conserve power over the long term. Hans Morgenthau's assertion that "a nation will shun alliances if it believes that it is strong enough to hold its own unaided" gives short shrift to the many reasons that even powerful states would benefit from multilateral approaches. His insight that "whether a nation shall pursue a policy of alliances is a matter not of principle but of expediency"[35] *is* more consistent with these instrumental motivations for multilateralism, but it is indeterminate. What factors enter into calculations of expediency? To answer this question, we need a more specific set of parameters.

TIME HORIZON

As the earlier discussion makes clear, multilateralism involves a complex and mixed set of trade-offs. The most fundamental obstacle is that multilateral payoffs accumulate inconsistently over time. Multilateralism pays in the long run because it is the way to prolong the lead state's position in the world. Moreover, the financial, personnel, and opportunity costs increase over time, sometimes nonlinearly, as in the case of Iraq and Afghanistan, where the least costly years were the first year or two of operations.[36] For a state with a number of international interests, shouldering the entire burden alone can become debilitating over time.

In the short term, however, multilateralism may be costly as a state embarks on the often onerous task of recruiting allies, bargaining on the language of a

UN resolution, and identifying and resolving the necessary side payments to lure states into acquiescence. Because of the way these incentives accrue over time, it follows that short-term challenges to security will make unilateralism an attractive short-term strategy. As Stephen Brooks writes, "A rational state will always seek first to maximize its short-term military security from potential rivals, even if this has negative long-term repercussions for other state priorities."[37] Uncertain about its security position tomorrow, a state is more likely to privilege gains today, even if it means compromising future payoffs.[38] In other words, "If there's no tomorrow, why save today?" questioned two scholars writing about intertemporal tradeoffs.[39] In the case of tradeoffs about whether to cooperate or not, sense of uncertainty about tomorrow may create temptations for the immediate gains of unilateralism.

The challenge is in explaining a priori the conditions under which a state will feel more immediate security threats and experience shorter time horizons. Scholars whose work has referenced time all admit in various ways that "time horizons are an undertheorized and understudied question of international relations" that warrants further study.[40] Thomas Risse agrees that "there is no deductive theory available to decide under which conditions great powers should behave in a farsighted way."[41] The problem is similar in the economics literature from which the term *time horizon* draws: "there is no single definition of time horizon, as it can manifest in many different ways with different implications."[42] Despite it being undertheorized, there is general agreement that time horizon refers to the way actors value the future versus the present, or the period of time that actors take into account when making decisions.[43] It is different from calendar time. It is a reaction to the strategic environment rather than a constant.

The length of an actor's time horizon is a function of the actor's expectations about the "future behavior of the environment" and about the agent himself. When economic, social, or political conditions are changing slowly and are subject to few exogenous shocks, time horizons are longer, expectations are more stable, and forecasts are likely to converge with realizations. With rapidly changing conditions, time horizons shrink, and expectations are likely to change often, be more erratic, and perhaps diverge from realizations.[44] In his study of spending patterns among professions and societies, nineteenth-century Scottish economist John Rae found that "when engaged in safe occupations, and living in healthy countries, men are more apt to be frugal than in unhealthy, or hazardous occupations, and in climates pernicious to human life. Sailors and soldiers are prodigals."[45] Those in safe occupations or healthy countries would be less averse to delaying gratification, knowing with greater certainty that they would be able to enjoy consumption in the future. Sailors and soldiers, whose futures were more precarious, were more apt to spend their resources frivolously in the near term.

States considering military force face similar choices about how to use resources. At the moment of decision, a state has a fixed amount of economic, military, and political capital. It can choose to expend a large share of it in that one intervention if it uses force alone, or it can use its capital more sparingly, intervening multilaterally, reassuring other states, and drawing on their capital rather than using just its own. Does the intervening state act like a sailor who expends his resources today or like someone in a "safe occupation"?

The answer depends on the security environment. A relatively safe, predictable security environment makes it a reasonable bet that if the intervening state conserves its resources by acting multilaterally, it will be in a position down the road to enjoy the fruits of those conserved resources; thus, time horizons are long. An environment with more security hazards creates shorter time horizons; with the future looking more uncertain, the lead actor may be tempted to act like a sailor, reaping the benefits of resources today even if doing so makes those resources less plentiful tomorrow.

The relative predictability or uncertainty of the security environment—the key determinant of time horizon—depends on the directness of threat. Working off the insights of Thomas Christensen,[46] I organize the security environment around three main inputs: the target of a particular challenge, whether that challenge is immediate or distant, and whether it is military or economic. This typology illustrates the strategic environment to which leaders respond; the most direct challenges create the most uncertainty about the future and lead to the shortest time horizons:

- The Target of a Challenge: Home versus Away
  - Threats against the homeland are considered the most direct and make it less likely that powerful states will respond to those threats within a multilateral order. Threats against third parties are the least salient and most likely to produce status quo, multilateral strategies. Threats against allies or friendly states fall somewhere in between and will tend toward multilateralism, depending on the two additional factors.
- Time: Immediate versus Distant
  - Immediate attacks challenge the target state most directly and make it less likely that the target will respond with the default, multilateral strategy. The more distant that threat becomes, the more likely the state will pursue status quo, multilateral strategies.
- Type of Challenge: Military versus Political or Economic
  - Military challenges are considered the most direct threat and are therefore more likely to shorten a state's time horizon, particularly compared with political or economic challenges. (See figure 3.1.)

	Three Measures for Directness of Threat			Time Horizon
	Target of Challenge	Time Frame	Type of Challenge	
High	Home Country	Immediate	Military	Short
Medium	Allied Nation/ Friendly Power	Short-term	Political/humanitarian	↕
Low	Third Party	Long-term	Economic	Long

Figure 3.1 Typology of threat and time horizon outcome.

In this typology, time is just one input to time horizon. Target and type of challenge also affect whether actors look and plan long term or whether they are more shortsighted. At one end of the spectrum, the shortest time horizons would be the result of the most direct threats and cause actors to search for immediate payoffs; these conditions favor unilateralism. Conversely, at the other end, indirect threats such as political or economic challenges to a third party create longer time horizons and encourage cooperation behavior that may create costs in the short term but that preserves power in the longer term.

OPERATIONAL COMMITMENT

Longer time horizons make multilateralism more likely, but time horizons do not say much about the *form* of multilateralism a state will pursue. Whether it seeks (1) a broadly sanctioned state response alongside international organization (IO) authorization or (2) a small coalition that is IO authorized but undertaken by a small group of states depends on a second factor: operational commitment, which refers to the level of resources directed toward the particular intervention.[47] If multilateralism requires that states "sacrifice substantial levels of decision making flexibility … and resist short term temptations in favor of long term benefits,"[48] then a conflict that is expected to be short, easy, and inexpensive—low operational commitment—will only accentuate those short-term temptations.

This part of the argument turns on the idea that while a powerful state such as the United States has "command of the commons"—superiority in the air, sea, land, and space—its resources are not infinite. Whereas some states *need* international assistance to provide security (e.g., Kuwait in 1990), the motivation for great powers to seek assistance returns to the idea of power preservation. Only by conserving its resources can it maintain a position of dominance in the international system. A large, substantive coalition means the lead state has to assume fewer costs. If it were so easy, of course, the lead state would assemble a Gulf War–size coalition for every intervention. Yet there are many cases, such as Somalia in 1993 and Haiti in 1994, in which the United States undertook a UN-authorized intervention largely alone. The reason is that there are costs to intervening with large coalitions. Each additional player and each contribution brings more voices into the decision making. Coalitions have been brought to their knees, undermined, or at least brought to uncomfortable compromise because of divergent interests among the contributing parties.

In a best case, coalitions may present challenges but ultimately prove successful, as in World War II. What, in Churchill's eyes, made fighting with allies hard was that they had different interests and notions about how to win the war. The Americans were eager to invade occupied France in 1943 but were nonplussed about the threats of Stalin. The British wanted to pause on invading France but were zealously attuned to the ambitions of Stalin.[49] As Churchill, Roosevelt, and their generals found—and international relations theorist Kenneth Waltz later observed—"since the interests of allies and their notions of how to secure them are never identical alliance strategies are always the product of compromise."[50] The more powerful the contributing states and the more substantive the contributions, the more those states will expect a voice in decision making and the more difficult it will be to arrive at an outcome that is anything but the lowest common denominator of states' interests.

In a worst-case scenario, the travails of coalition operations can produce disastrous outcomes. History is rife with examples, but the series of coalition wars against Napoleon is illustrative. Though Napoleon's army was no doubt large and well trained, one reason for his early successes in the 1800s was the incoherence and uncoordinated nature of the opposing coalitions, what a Metternich biographer called the "cumbrous machine of the Coalition."[51] In the Third Coalition, for example, Austria and Russia deployed more manpower than the French but suffered yet another coalition defeat. Smugly, the Grande Armée's official bulletin recorded the victory in this way: "Never have victories been so complete and less costly."[52]

Working in favor of the French military was the homogeneity of its training behind the strategic vision of one leader, Napoleon. The opposing force, by contrast, was a hodgepodge of aristocratic, poorly supplied, and most of all, badly coordinated militaries. Despite Austrian expectations to the contrary, Russian forces arrived late in Ulm, leaving the Austrians without reinforcements and causing a series of defeats that ultimately led to Napoleon's advance on Vienna and the dismal outcome at Austerlitz. As historian David Chandler observes, Austria's "fatal miscalculations concerning the proximity of their Russian allies had made the catastrophe practically inevitable."[53] Ultimately, France forced Austria's withdrawal from the coalition, leaving Russia to fight the French alone and effectively ending the Third Coalition until the Prussians joined the next incarnation, the Fourth Coalition, whose outcome was hardly more favorable.[54]

Though technology and communications have smoothed some of the difficulties of coalition operations (and made others worse),[55] the difficulty amid success of World War II and the assembly and failure of a multiple coalitions against Napoleon illustrate the challenges of coalition operations. These are just a couple of historical examples among many that show why states that do not need the help of allies might sidestep the challenges of coalition operations. These cases show the tensions between wanting to share the burden of conflict, on the one hand, and realizing the difficulty of coordinating and winning with genuine coalitions, on the other.

Reconciling that tension depends on how the lead state sees the operational commitment. If the lead state thinks it can win quickly or on the cheap, there will be fewer incentives to aggregate resources, and a robust coalition of states will be less likely. A short, even if intensive mission (such as the Panama intervention, which lasted two weeks), missions in which long stability operations are either not anticipated or not contemplated, or air strikes will also reduce constraints on a state and make participation from other states less likely.

However, even the most powerful states face contested zones that challenge their dominance. According to Barry Posen, contested zones are "arenas of conventional combat where weak adversaries have a good chance of doing real damage to U.S. forces."[56] What many of these contested zones have in common is a large inventory of military-age men. Iran, for example, has 20 million males between the ages of 16 and 49, of which almost 18 million are fit for service. North Korea has more than 6 million available for military service, of which 4 million are fit for service. Both exceed the size of the all-volunteer American military and would impose considerable operational commitment in a force-on-force conflict.[57]

From his analysis of these contested zones, Posen concludes "that the U.S. must avoid lengthy military operations that require a large number of ground troops."[58] While the conclusion that the U.S. military "must" avoid lengthy military operations against states with large, conscript armies is debatable, it is clear that this type of adversary will create incentives for collecting allies whose resources the United States can pool with its own. During the first Gulf War, for example, Bush administration leaders expressed concern for the number of troops Saddam Hussein had quickly stationed in Kuwait: 200,000 compared to the 20,000 U.S. troops in theater. "As the U.S. brought in heavy armored forces, two of the world's large armies eventually would be facing off. If there was conflict, it would be major land warfare. This was nothing like the liberation of Grenada or Panama."[59] The Iraqi military was thought to have 1 million well-trained soldiers, compared with an active-duty U.S. Army size of about 800,000 soldiers.[60] Secretary of State James Baker weighed the cooperation decision as follows: "There are times when great powers must forswear even trying collective action and go it alone in the first instance, as we had done in Grenada in 1983 and Panama in 1989. This was definitely not one of them."[61]

A related challenge to an intervening state refers less to the intensity and more to the duration of conflict. The longer the intervention endures, the greater the financial and personnel commitment from the lead inter-vening state, and the higher the opportunity costs. Commitments that are open-ended, irrespective of the nature of the foe, create incentives to share the burden. Asymmetric threats—for example, in the form of insur-gencies or guerrilla warfare—fall under this heading, as do stabilization and reconstruction = operations, which create long-term commitments of resources.

WHEN TIME HORIZONS AND OPERATIONAL COMMITMENT CONFLICT

While these two factors—time horizon and operational commitment—may be interdependent in practice, time horizon tends to dominate.[62] The most direct threats and shortest time horizons are likely to favor immediate and unilateral response. Pausing to negotiate UN resolutions, collect allies, and bargain on side payments produces costly delays for a state with pressing security concerns. The temptation is therefore to address those threats uni-laterally, even if doing so makes it more difficult to achieve longer term goals,[63] such as addressing security problems that may arise elsewhere. Since time horizon dominates, high operational burdens for the most direct secu-rity threats will still favor unilateralism. A direct military attack on the homeland such as 9/11, for example—the most direct of threats according to this typology—was a most likely case for unilateralism despite Afghanistan having a history of bankrupting its conquerers.[64]

If, however, a state faces no immediate threat and has a long time horizon, it can then choose an institutional strategy among formal and informal alter-natives. Here the lead state can have its legitimacy cake and eat it, too. With indirect threats and longer time horizons, it can pursue the reassuring path of IO authorization in a way that is interest compatible; threats are less direct, time horizons are long, and delays are not costly. Whether the lead state intervenes with a substantive multilateral coalition or goes through the UN

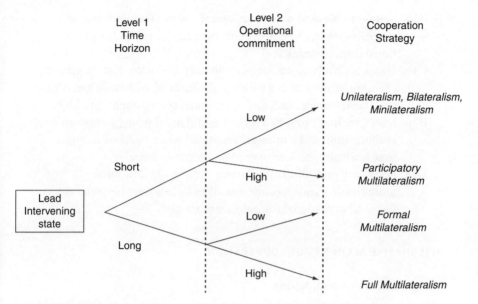

Figure 3.2 The effect of time horizon and operational commitment on cooperation strategy.

and conducts the operation without allies depends on operational commitment. High operational commitments, as discussed earlier—those that are large force-on-force operations, for example—provide incentives to create a substantive coalition. Long time horizons and low operational commitment—which might seem to point in different directions—find a compatible outcome in formal multilateralism: one that is IO authorized but undertaken by a small coalition of states. (See figure 3.2.)

This framework helps explain why the United States would "limit" its power by cooperating with allies and institutions rather than acting alone.[65] The reason is that going alone is often costly; multilateralism offers a way to reassure other states, share what are often costly burdens, and conserve power over the long term. Moreover, multilateralism in the form of coalitions is comparatively less limiting than a fixed alliance. Arguments about cobinding in which states "tie one another down by locking each other into institutions that mutually constrain one another" do not apply to a system in which coalitions are often fluid rather than sticky and change composition for each new intervention.[66] Nonetheless, under some circumstances, unilateralism will look attractive as an expedient answer to security challenges. The preceding analysis provides the following expectations about the conditions in which a lead intervening state may be more likely to favor one path over another:

H1a. States are likely to pursue unilateral , bilateral, or minilateral strategies when faced with short time horizons and low operational commitments.

H1b. States are likely to pursue participatory multilateral strategies—a coalition of allies acting without institutional authorization—when time horizons are short and operational commitments are high.

H1c. States are likely to seek a formal multilateral strategy—institutional authorization and a minimal coalition—when faced with longer time horizons and low operational commitments.

H1d. States will seek a full multilateral strategy—institutional authorization and a coalition of allies—when time horizons are long and operational commitments are high.

ALTERNATIVE ACCOUNTS OF COOPERATION

The Effect of Multilateral Norms

Multilateralism in the post–Cold War period is no puzzle at all for normative accounts of cooperation. The tendency toward multilateralism is easily accounted for by the emergence of a multilateral norm. During the Cold War, the two superpowers operated in a spheres-of-influence system in which the United States and the Soviet Union dominated their spheres ideologically, militarily, and economically. According to this Cold War norm of cooperation, the two "superpowers were entitled under the rules of this system to intervene unilaterally to put down revolutions in their sphere."[67] In their own spheres, these two states could intervene unilaterally with impunity. If a state needed allies for material support, it would seek a multilateral approach to an intervention, but its strategies were not conditioned by any normative pressures to intervene multilaterally.

Those use-of-force norms changed at the end of the Cold War. The "beliefs shared by a community about who they are, what the world is like" went from approving of unilateralism to censuring it.[68] No longer was it acceptable to circumvent the UN; states were expected to go to "great lengths" to obtain UN blessings for their interventions and to assemble coalitions of strategically "disinterested" states.[69] Great lengths meant that states would "adhere to them [multilateral norms] even when they know that doing so compromises the effectiveness of the mission.... That UN involvement continues to be a central feature of these operations, despite the UN's apparent lack of military competence, underscores the power of multilateral norms."[70] The multilateral norm was regulative, in that it would "specify standards of proper behavior."[71] Proper behavior, according to this formulation, would trump effectiveness, telling states that when they engage in foreign military intervention, they should go through international organizations and with allies.

This normative argument—"most closely related to...'constructivism' in political science"—challenges the assumption that states make decisions based on utility calculations grounded in terms of material payoff.[72] It assumes that "the pursuit of purpose is associated with identities more than with interests, and with the selection of rules more than with individual rational expectations."[73] Actors are guided by a sense of "appropriateness"—or shared beliefs about how they should act—rather than expectations of behavioral consequences.[74] Put another way, states do not pursue multilateralism because it works, but because that is just what states are expected to do when they use military force.[75]

The strongest evidence for the dominance of this norm is that even the United States appeared to adhere to these social expectations of intervention behavior after the Cold War. "Such strong multilateral norms are not what one would expect from a distribution of material capabilities so overwhelmingly unipolar."[76] Implicit is that the United States would not need allies to shift the balance of power in its favor. That it nonetheless sought allies was evidence of a strong multilateral norm. The reason the United States would still seek allies, according to this argument, is that they grant the unipolar power what a large defense budget and advanced military equipment cannot: legitimacy. Interested in appearing legitimate in its interventions, the United States would then want to intervene multilaterally. Even when narrow utility imperatives might prescribe a unilateral outcome, powerful states such as the United States would go multilaterally because they *should*.

In the specific case of cooperation and the use of force, knowing that a state pursued a multilateral strategy is less helpful than discerning whether it was for reasons of consequence (the rationalist argument) or appropriateness (the constructivist argument), a distinction I develop more carefully later in this chapter. The norm on the use of military force would say that when states intervene, they should do so multilaterally not because it produces material gains but because international society expects states to use force multilaterally. The preceding discussion produces the following analytical expectation:

> H2 *States will be expected to act on the basis of "appropriateness" when they intervene; they will go to great lengths to obtain IO authorization and assemble a multilateral coalition.*

The Effect of Domestic Politics on Cooperation

Domestic-level accounts of foreign policy explain why "states similarly placed in a system behave in different ways."[77] Under this heading are factors such as regime type, type of democratic institutions (presidential versus parliamentary, majoritarian or proportional), and strong states versus weak states. These distinctions might be useful in explaining variation across

states, but not why one state might behave differently across different episodes of force, since these factors typically do not vary within one state.
More important for these purposes are domestic-political institutions that
might vary across episodes of intervention. In particular, two sets of actors
are likely to affect the flexibility of the executive in the way he or she wages
war: (1) Congress, which has war-making and war-funding powers under the
U.S. Constitution, and (2) the American public, whose preferences create
electoral risks for an executive who acts in opposition to those preferences.

In considering how a state uses or sidesteps domestic audiences on its way
to war, domestic preferences can matter in two ways: either directly in their
specific preference for using institutions over going it alone or indirectly in
how their general position on the war influences the leader's range of institutional options. The logic is that since both the Congress and the public
affect the executive's ability to implement a broader agenda—one through
legislative oversight, the other through electoral accountability—the executive has incentives to accommodate these domestic-level preferences before
using force abroad. Congress technically authorizes and funds conflicts,
which should give their preference some weight. The public reelects and
provides political capital, so the claim that "a mounting body of evidence
suggests that the foreign policies of American presidents—and democratic
leaders more generally—have been influenced by their understanding of the
public's foreign policy views"[78] is not surprising.

The first category of "policy views" deals with whether either set of
domestic actors has registered a preference for multilateralism. For example,
Senator Joseph Biden critiqued the multilateral approach to Bosnia in the
early 1990s and urged stronger American leadership, deriding multilateralism as a way to "blame one another for inaction, so that everyone has an
excuse. It does not mean standing together; it means hiding together."[79]
Several years earlier, he and other members of Congress had urged greater
multilateralism in the Gulf War, saying that otherwise "if there's a war,
95 percent of the casualties ... will be American."[80] According to the domestic
politics account, the executive would have incentives to use force in a way
that is consistent with prevailing congressional preferences on how to
intervene.

Whereas the legislature registers its preferences on the floor of Congress, the
American public does so through polls. The public also votes, of course, but it
can be difficult to discern which particular issue had the largest effect on why an
individual voted as he or she did. A poll, by contrast, tends to be more targeted.
According to the public opinion variant of the domestic politics argument, strong
domestic preferences for one cooperation strategy over another should affect
incentives for leaders to use force multilaterally or unilaterally. If the conventional wisdom is correct and the public tends to view multilateral interventions

more favorably than those that are unilateral—whether for purposes of burden-sharing or legitimacy—[81]then an executive would risk electoral retribution for going against these public preferences. If, on the other hand, "public preferences are not for multilateralism over unilateralism as a general disposition, but rather it depends on the principal policy objective (PPO),"[82] then the public might exert fewer constraints on *how* the United States intervened but rather on the intervention's goals more generally, whether the intervention was designed to address humanitarian goals, implement regime change, or to stop aggression against the United States or an ally.

Such general attitudes toward whether to intervene at all, the second category of policy views, could nonetheless have an indirect influence on how a leader undertakes the operation. Strong opposition may not stop the intervention but may give the leader reasons to pursue multilateral channels. In the case of Congress, IO authorization, according to Kenneth Schultz, "puts legislators in the politically risky position of having to put the brakes on an ongoing operation," which might be seen as undercutting national commitments, particularly U.S. troops.[83] International organization authorization effectively ties the hands of Congress. Having lobbied for IO authorization presumably for months, this becomes a powerful signal to Congress that the U.S. executive is unlikely to back away from intervention once it has been authorized.[84] Congress can either be seen as standing in the way at a time when the public is starting to rally around the flag, a politically untenable position, or it can throw its support behind the intervention. IO authorization pushes Congress toward the latter option. Thus, IO authorization becomes a backdoor way to reduce domestic opposition, even if it does not elicit outright authorization.

For the public, general levels of support for intervention may affect incentives to pursue a particular cooperation strategy in somewhat different ways. Under certain conditions, public support may soar, giving the executive a window of opportunity in which to act. Hetherington and Nelson define such a public rally in the following way: "the rally effect is the sudden and substantial increase in public approval of the president that occurs in response to certain kinds of dramatic international events involving the United States."[85] An international event such as the attacks of 9/11 gives the president a surge of popular support and political capital. Rarely is that rally effect of a lengthy duration, however. Its ephemeral nature means a leader has a fleeting opportunity to act. The effect can be to limit the extent to which he or she pursues multilateral channels, the reason being that the time needed for international consultation may cut into the domestic license that the rally has granted. A similar logic might apply to the legislative branch, eager to be seen as patriotic during an international crisis but likely to revert to politics as usual after the crisis subsides.

These arguments suggest that an executive has both legislative and electoral incentives to listen to the domestic audience. The analytical predictions that follow are:

H3a: Domestic preferences for multilateralism create legislative and electoral incentives for decision makers to pursue a multilateral cooperation strategy.

H3b: Domestic opposition and support for war more generally have indirect effects on cooperation strategy; domestic rallies create fewer incentives for multilateralism than opposition, which creates incentives for IO authorization as a way to tie the hands of a reluctant domestic audience.

Regional Power Dynamics

The last alternative account of cooperation behavior suggests that power dynamics within a particular region affect the intervening state's approach to cooperation. Regions without major powers act as a permissive environment for unilateralism, whereas the presence of major powers constrains freedom of action. The general argument is that unilateralism can trigger counterbalancing and create political and military costs, but that prospect is less likely if the potential counterbalancers are small states in Latin America, for example, than if they are major powers in Europe or Asia.[86]

At worst, the regional power can materially support the target state, making it costlier to reach the same goals. For example, during the Korean War, Stalin committed "fully the arms, tanks and other military equipment for 2 divisions, 2 tank brigades and 12 battalions" to support the North Koreans and shore up their ability to fight against the South.[87] China contributed hundreds of thousands of troops, further adding to the North's strength and creating considerably higher costs and casualties for the United States.[88]

At best, the intervening state forgoes an opportunity to benefit from the resource pooling that attends cooperation. As David Lake argues, "The pooling of resources by two polities produces more security than the sum of their individual efforts."[89] These potential benefits are considerably higher when the lead intervening state is using force in a distant region with powerful states. By definition, regional powers are associated with high levels of political, economic, and military capital. Cooperating with these states is an attractive way to create "joint production economies," or cost savings created by sharing assets. Forward operating bases, for example, become invaluable not just for cost savings but as a technological imperative when projecting force across long distances.[90] Thus, multilateral strategies would accordingly be more likely when the lead state intervenes in the backyards of major powers at long distances.[91] Intervening in the Balkans without the major European military powers, for example, would unwisely ignore the potential benefits of their local resources.

Therefore, when intervening in areas with regional powers, the lead intervening state would be expected to pursue a multilateral strategy because of the potential costs of balancing and the opportunities that those powers offer for sharing the high costs of conflict. The inverse of this argument would suggest that a region without powerful states is a permissive environment; the low risk of countervailing balancing costs and little opportunity for those states to help the lead state avoid costs would contribute to less robust multilateralism. The following predictions follow from this discussion of regional power dynamics:

H4. *The propensity toward unilateralism or multilateralism depends on the presence of regional powers.*

  a. A region without major powers (e.g., the Western Hemisphere) is
     likely to be the most permissive environment for unilateralism,
     lacking regional partners for pooling resources or for materially
     challenging the intervention.
  b. Interventions in regions with major powers (e.g., Europe and Asia)
     will create the most likely conditions for cooperation, as the lead state
     seeks regional partners for sharing costs and for minimizing
     countervailing influence.

The Individual, Learning, and Supply Side Accounts of Cooperation Behavior

In addition to the explanations already outlined, there are three standard accounts of cooperation behavior that bear brief consideration. One is an individual-level account of behavior that locates the preference for unilateralism or multilateralism "in the nature and behavior of men."[92] According to this argument, states pursue one strategy over another because some leaders are more predisposed toward collective security than others. Stephen Walt, for example, suggests that the George W. Bush administration may have had similar goals of U.S. primacy and the global promotion of liberal U.S. ideals as the administrations of George H. W. Bush and Bill Clinton but pursued a different set of vehicles for advancing those goals. Whereas Presidents George H. W. Bush and Bill Clinton had been reflexively multilateralist, the George W. Bush administration was more willing to "go it alone," unilaterally exercising power more than his predecessors.[93] According to this individual-level account, leaders would come in two forms: those with unilateral preferences and those with multilateralist (or collaborative) preferences.[94]

This argument, while intuitively appealing, is inconsistent with the evidence. Although the George W. Bush administration indeed showed a propensity toward unilateralism, other seemingly multilateral presidents were also clearly willing to use unilateral force. The invoker of the new world order, George H. W. Bush, unilaterally sent 28,000 American troops into Panama to expel Manuel Noriega and only suggested that they make the "necessary calls" to allies after undertaking the intervention. In addition to alarming allies with a series of unilateral airstrikes against Iraq in 1993 and 1998, the seemingly strong multilateralist Bill Clinton took tough stands on several multilateral treaties that were considered to be singularly rejected by George W. Bush. Referring to the International Criminal Court, Clinton said, "I will not, and do not recommend that my successor submit the Treaty to the Senate for advice and consent until our fundamental concerns are satisfied."[95] Similarly, the Clinton administration symbolically signed the Kyoto Protocol but used no political capital to push the treaty through Congress, and the vote failed by 95–0. His rhetoric and tone were certainly more multilateralist—though even his administration had its hints of arrogance as it referred to itself as the "indispensable nation"[96]—but his actions were at times quite unilateral.

Even President George W. Bush, who earned a reputation as a unilateralist in his first term, was "multilateral to a fault" in the second term, according to Deputy Assistant Secretary of State for East Asian and Pacific Affairs Thomas Christensen (2006–2008). Deferring to multilateral fora on North Korea, Iran, Darfur, and Myanmar, the second term of the administration, Christensen has suggested, was one of the most multilateral in American history.[97] Thus, individual-level explanations are unable to account for why the same leaders confronted security challenges in different ways.

Another dominant account of cooperation behavior is that actors learn from previous experiences of intervention, leading to changes in beliefs about whether a particular cooperation strategy will work. According to the learning thesis, positive experiences with multilateralism might lead to multilateral strategies in a subsequent intervention, whereas negative experiences with one of the two approaches would produce the opposite strategy in the next intervention.[98] The George W. Bush administration was more inclined toward unilateralism or loose coalitions of the willing, the argument goes, because of their observations of what appeared to be NATO's onerous collective decision making in Kosovo.[99]

Though it may seem persuasive on its face and for particular episodes of force, the learning thesis also suffers upon inspection. It does not explain why the same leaders who conducted the Panama operation unilaterally and by most accounts successfully in 1989 would then seek a robust multilateral coalition for the Gulf War. The logical lesson to learn from Panama is that unilateralism works; it allowed freedom of action in quickly and secretively pursuing Manuel Noriega in Panama, without having to pause and ask allies for approval. Yet the subsequent major operation was one in which the same Bush administration built an impressive multilateral coalition that intervened in Iraq with UN authorization. A similar problem arises in the case of Somalia or Rwanda. Despite their obvious multilateral failures, the subsequent intervention in Bosnia was also highly multilateral, suggesting either that those lessons did not determine subsequent cooperation outcomes or that the foreign policy establishment internalized the lessons differently;[100] neither offers a satisfactory accounts.

A third possible challenge to the explanations previously examined suggests that multilateralism is not a choice at all. Whether multilateralism results depends not just on whether a lead state wants it, but on whether other states are willing to grant it. Multilateralism, in other words, is the product of an interaction between the lead state's *demand* for it and other actors' willingness to *supply* their endorsement. An argument that focuses primarily on the demand side of alliances misses the important supply side and the interaction between demand and supply. Despite this claim, there are two reasons to focus on whether and when a powerful state seeks (demands) allies.

The first is the veritable cottage industry associated with the study of why states agree to ally (or bandwagon) with a lead state, when they seek to balance against that state's actions, or how allies are important in shifting the balance of power.[101] The most powerful states have little need to shift the balance of power, however. This is particularly true for the kinds of interventions that have characterized the post–Cold War period. In these, the United States has intervened against far less powerful states, making balance of power considerations applicable as explanations for why it would seek allies. There has been comparatively little work on why powerful states pursue multilateral strategies in these settings and when they are willing to go it alone.[102]

Moreover, just as actors who might supply their assistance get a vote, so does the lead state. With enough time and compromise, some form of multilateral consensus is almost always possible. For powerful states, however, defecting from multilateral negotiations is also almost always an option. The question is when a lead state is willing to take that time and make the necessary compromises. Once it decides to go it alone, there is no longer a bandwagon on which to jump. Thus, supply-side considerations are only part of the story. To understand cooperation on the way to conflict, we need to understand not just the supply of allies—which has been studied at length—but why a lead state would pursue a path of cooperation and provide a bandwagon rather than defect and intervene alone. This research offers a theoretical and empirical account of when powerful states will seek cooperative approaches to conflict and when it will exercise its unilateral option and go it alone.

METHODS AND CASE SELECTION

To understand the trade-offs among different cooperation strategies and the conditions under which one form of cooperation is more likely than another, this book focuses on U.S. intervention after the Cold War. It does so because according to structural expectations of power and cooperation, the United States should be a most likely case for unilateralism; the United States has had more opportunities for unilateralism than any other state, and security cooperation is thought to be the most demanding issue on which to generate international cooperation.[103] Multilateralism on the part of the U.S. would cast doubt on the validity of a theory that predicts cooperation strategies on the basis of material power.[104] The advantage of restricting the analysis to the post–Cold War period is that it holds power fairly constant since there have not been major shifts in the distribution of power during this time.[105]

Since the number of post–Cold War interventions is small, the analysis is organized around the qualitative method of structured, focused comparison. In each case, I ask why the United States pursued the particular cooperation strategy it chose; this structures the collection of information in a standardized way, "thereby making systematic comparison and cumulation of the findings of the cases possible."[106] By looking at specific aspects of a case—at decision making, specifically the decision to pursue a particular cooperation strategy, rather than the success of that strategy, for example—the study is focused. This approach enables a controlled comparison across cases.

The analysis becomes complicated in cases where the various explanations do not actually compete but rather overlap. In more cases than not, the rationalist argument about time horizons and operational commitment would expect multilateral outcomes, which is the standard expectation of normative accounts. The key difference is that the rationalist argument expects a multilateral outcome because it pays, that is, because it is seen as the effective means by which to achieve the goals. Decision makers acting on the basis of consequences seek a "positive stream of benefits. Actors are constantly recalculating the expected payoff to remaining in the system and stand ready to abandon it should some alternative promise greater utility."[107] They determine their optimal strategy based on whether there are "gains to coordinated action,"[108] specifically whether intervening multilaterally ("doing X") helps them stay powerful or reach political goals ("achieve Y").[109]

Evidence for consequences as a motivation for behavior would include remarks like those of former Director of Policy Planning Richard Haass, who said that "for all of our power, we can't meet most of the challenges we face on our own."[110] In other words, it behooves the United States to operate multilaterally because many of the problems the United States faces are transnational in nature or would overextend American resources. Acting multilaterally under these circumstances derives more from instrumental, means-ends calculations than from principled stances on multilateralism that would tell states how they *should* intervene.

In contrast, constructivist accounts go more like this: norms tell states "do X, don't do X" or that "if you do Y, then do X." Decision makers would say that if they decide to intervene ("do Y"), then they must do so multilaterally ("do X"). These arguments expect a multilateral outcome on the basis of appropriateness, in which states act according to socially constructed rules and practices. Accordingly, "compliance [is] no longer motivated by the simple fear of retribution, or by calculation of self-interest, but instead by an internal sense of moral obligation: control is legitimate to the extent that it is approved or regarded as 'right.'"[111] States follow what they think is appropriate, not simply what is likely to produce the highest material payoffs.

One form of evidence for normative accounts would consist of "multilateral talk," since a "sign of an international norm's domestic impact is its appearance in the domestic political discourse."[112] Leaders justifying their behavior in terms of existing rules, precedents, or standards of behavior would be evidence of normative salience.[113] The difficulty is in discerning sincere justification from cheap talk. As the cases show, leaders almost always frame their behavior in the language of legitimacy; this is certainly some form of normative pull, but it looks disingenuous and impugns the normative thesis if the multilateral talk diverges from actions or intentions. The 47-state "coalition of the willing" that intervened in Iraq, for example, was a rhetorical charade for an intervention that was decided, planned, and undertaken almost entirely by the United States.

Thus, beyond rhetoric, it is important to look at actions. What was the depth of cooperation, that is, how much did it part with what states would otherwise have done?[114] Cooperation depth is defined by "the extent to which it requires states to depart from what they would have done in its absence."[115] Counterfactual analysis that points to shallow cooperation, in which cooperation behavior deviated little from how the United States would have sought to intervene anyway, would tend to support instrumental calculations. Deep cooperation, in which instrumental calculations would have expected a limited form of cooperation and the United States instead pursued a more robust form of cooperation, would offer strong evidence for normative arguments. This line of evidence compares actual intervention behavior with how the state would have intervened in the absence of that norm.

Though this discussion has focused on how to discern evidence for the rationalist argument from that for the normative argument, counterfactual reasoning also applies for domestic politics and regional power dynamics arguments. How did the cooperation behavior resulting from domestic influences or regional powers diverge from what might be expected if narrow utility calculations—the length of time horizon and the amount of operational commitment required—had determined the cooperation strategy? Evidence that the intervention strategy shifted because of an election cycle or because the president went out of his way to obtain congressional authorization would support a domestic politics account. Evidence that the United States went to great lengths to accommodate selective, powerful actors in the region to gain their assistance or avoid their counterbalancing would support the regional account of cooperation.

This book probes several sources for evidence. One set of sources consists of dozens of personal interviews conducted with individuals who were associated with post–Cold War military interventions. Those individuals include military officers who planned or participated in interventions throughout the post–Cold War period, as well as civilians in the Departments of State and Defense, NATO, and the National Security Council. A second set of sources includes unclassified and declassified government documents about security threats (e.g., National Intelligence Estimates, the British Joint Intelligence Committee assessments) and military plans for intervention (e.g., the Office of the Secretary of Defense or Central Command's planning documents for Iraq, some of which are now declassified). A third set consists of sources such as memoirs of key decision makers (e.g., George H. W. Bush and General Brent Scowcroft, UN weapons inspector Hans Blix), secondhand accounts from journalists and scholars, and newspaper articles. Together, these sources contribute evidence on why key leaders pursued a particular cooperation strategy when undertaking military intervention.

CASE SELECTION

The cases that are the subjects of the analysis include the Gulf War in 1990–1991 (chapter 4) because it appears to be an exemplar for full multilateralism: institutional authorization and a large, diverse coalition of states that had influence over decision making. It is the most multilateral intervention the United States conducted in the post–Cold War period, with UN Security Council blessing and the participation of almost every strategically and politically important state in the international system. Seawright and Gerring suggest that extreme cases "pose natural subjects of investigation" because the high value of a behavior in question (in this case, multilateralism) offers a way to explore the factors that contributed to that unusual outcome.[116] For a study of multilateralism, an intervention that was more multilateral than others is of significant interest for understanding why a high degree of cooperation was possible in that particular circumstance and, therefore, how it might be possible in others.

A second case, the 1994 Haiti intervention (chapter 5), offers a least likely case for multilateralism; the vast power disparities should have meant a low operational commitment for the United States and few incentives to assemble a multilateral response. It is also a most likely case for unilateralism, according to the regional power alternative explanation, which would expect a unilateral intervention in a region devoid of great powers other than the United States. The Haiti case fails a relatively easy test for the regional power argument.[117] Despite there being no major regional powers to block U.S. freedom of action, the United States nonetheless went through the UN and, at least in the postconflict phase, collected a reasonably broad multilateral coalition. Close study of the case shows that cooperation behavior in this intervention is, however, consistent with the multilateral logic advanced in this book, since U.S. concerns with the intervention centered not on whether it would succeed in taking over the island but on how to handle the open-ended commitment in the aftermath of intervention. This case also illustrates the possible merits of a hybrid strategy; in the Haiti intervention, the United States reduced cooperation costs by intervening with a predominantly U.S. force early in the intervention and then transitioning to a robust multinational force for the open-ended postconflict operations.

The Afghanistan case (chapter 6) is a useful case for two reasons. First, it defends against potential criticisms that this analysis focuses unduly on demand-side considerations and that supply-side factors better explain cooperation decisions. The intervention in Afghanistan presents a case in which supply was plentiful yet the United States nonetheless intervened alone. After 9/11, offers of allied assistance flowed from all corners of the globe, but the United States turned down multilateral support in the form of NATO's Article 5 collective security and intervened at most with selective bilateral support from the Northern Alliance and in the form of basing support from Central Asian republics. Only after the United States had completed major combat operations did it shift to a multilateral strategy, and only then in areas that had been stabilized. The United States continued to use a two-in-one strategy in which it layered unilateral offensive counterterrorism operations onto the multilateral reconstruction efforts of NATO. Second, the Afghanistan case is helpful because it introduces within-case variation—in which there is a significant change in cooperation strategy over the course of the intervention—and controls for factors such as regional power, geography, domestic politics, and norms that remain the same over time.[118] This case shows how the factors that did change—time horizon and operational commitment—account for decisions to shift from unilateralism for combat operations to multilateralism for postconflict reconstruction and stabilization.

Chapter 7 examines the case of the 2003 Iraq War. One of the most unilateral interventions in the post–Cold War period, this case challenges this book's argument. With long time horizons (absent a direct threat) and costly operational commitments, this theory would expect a highly multilateral intervention, the opposite of what obtained. This chapter shows the importance of *ex ante* assumptions about the nature of security challenges in influencing cooperation strategies. Inadequate assessments of both time horizon and operational commitment led to a flawed cooperation strategy in which the United States took on almost the entire burden. This chapter details these inputs and examines how each contributed to the unilateral strategy the United States pursued in the Iraq War. This chapter also sets up the policy implications outlined in the conclusion, both the importance of accurate assessments and the tendency to overestimate the ease of intervention.

As the following pages show, these four cases offer support for the effect of time horizons and operational commitment on decisions to sidestep allies and multilateral institutions. In some cases, multilateral norms, domestic politics, and regional powers offer additional insights into why the United States would be interested in going multilaterally or at least in being seen as acting multilaterally. Rarely are those alternative accounts determinate, but in some cases, they explain why the United States would be interested in eliciting a particular state's acquiescence, why it would frame its intervention in multilateral terms, and why it would go back to the UN for a resolution that it neither wanted nor felt it needed.

4

The Gulf War and the New World Order

The Gulf War coalition has been called "a monument to multilateralism."[1] The size and diversity of the coalition that intervened to expel Iraq from Kuwait was extraordinary. Among the participants were NATO countries, former members of the moribund Warsaw Pact, states from the Non-Aligned Movement, historically neutral countries such as Sweden, and states with enduring rivalries such as Greece and Turkey.[2] This constellation of former foes, large powers and small states, and democracies and autocracies seemed to be a refreshing reminder that perhaps the Cold War alignment was a thing of the past.

The degree to which Desert Storm was multilateral is surprising not only because it broke with 40 years of largely unilateral precedent during the Cold War but also because of the nature of the provocation. Secretary of State James Baker defended unilateralism as a legal option that the United States seriously considered: "Desert Storm could have been a unilateral American initiative. Legally, the President was within his prerogatives to act under Article 51 of the UN Charter, which allows member states the right of self-defense to protect their national interests."[3] As Secretary Baker implied, the most clear-cut, legal use of force in the Middle East would have been through Article 51, which provides for the "inherent right of *individual* or *collective* self-defense."[4]

British Prime Minister Margaret Thatcher, the most ardent supporter of U.S. responses in the Gulf, sided with the American view that the UN's condemnation of the invasion and Article 51 were adequate. Her experience in dealing with the UN during the Falklands crisis highlighted the complication of collective action and the degree to which multilateralism could "force unsatisfactory terms" of dispute settlement, particularly given the "anti-colonialist attitude of many nations at the UN" as she put it.[5] As a result, Thatcher was not bullish on going multilaterally in a crisis situation.[6] A multilateral strategy would especially backfire if the United States proposed a resolution that did not receive international support, an outcome that was worse than altogether forgoing the United Nations.[7]

Seeking authorization was certainly risky. Many states that eventually provided political or material support to the coalition, such as the Soviet Union and China, thought that sanctions would work and were committed to giving them more time. The Arab League was divided, and a third of its members would not condemn the invasion, nor would they request that Iraq leave Kuwait.[8] Convening and maintaining a coalition was yeoman's work. Even before combat operations began in January 1991, France was running as a renegade, supporting an approach that would give more authority to the UN and less to the coalition. By late fall 1990, the sanctions had seemed to reach a stalemate, Saddam Hussein had effectively increased his clout, and the fledgling coalition was "showing strains" from diverging views on how to proceed.[9]

That the multilateralism of the Gulf War worked and looks obvious in retrospect should not be used to rewrite the prevailing view at the time: unilateralism was legal and a multilateral coalition would be difficult to bring together and keep together. Resisting these legal and efficiency justifications for unilateralism, President George H. W. Bush declared the emergence of a "new world order" of great-power cooperation and collective security that would see "an historic period of cooperation."[10] The administration spent the ensuing months assembling a multilateral force that pushed Saddam Hussein out of Kuwait in 1991 and was subsequently seen as a success for both the UN Security Council specifically and multilateral cooperation in general.

Close inspection of the Gulf War case reveals that the initial phase of that intervention, until UN Resolution 678 was passed on 29 November 1990, was actually almost entirely unilateral—or at best bilateral with Saudi support—, as this chapter will show in more detail. Only after the UN resolution authorizing "all necessary means" to expel Iraq from Kuwait passed did coalition partners start to become more central in the overall effort.[11] Thirty-eight states ultimately contributed more than 200,000 troops, 600 warships, 750 aircraft, and 1,200 tanks.[12] States such as Kuwait, Saudi Arabia, Germany, and Japan financed $53 billion of the $61 billion cost of the war.[13] These states, particularly Saudi Arabia but also Kuwait, the United Kingdom, Syria,[14] and the United Nations, ultimately influenced strategy, decision making, and the overall objectives of the conflict.

What explains this within-case variation, in which the initial phase of the operation was far from multilateral, only to be matched in the latter phase with a large multilateral force virtually unprecedented in its magnitude? Why did the United States take the step of soliciting and producing multilateral support for what would have been a legal use of force? As this chapter shows, the reason is that the combination of Iraq's invasion of Kuwait and possible invasion of Saudi Arabia would mean possession of 90 to 95 percent of Gulf oil and considerable regional instability and international leverage.

The United States concluded that it could not "tolerate him [Saddam] succeeding"[15] in these goals and therefore would unilaterally send in a deterrent force capable of defending against the taking of additional territory. Once that deterrence force was in place, however, the United States looked toward an encounter with an Iraqi army that was expected to produce a large-scale ground confrontation and large numbers of casualties. The operational commitment required to defeat "the fourth largest army in the world, an army hardened in long years of combat against Iran," according to the Final Report to Congress on the Persian Gulf War, was impressive and would be virtually impossible as a unilateral operation.[16] This chapter develops this explanation more fully and addresses the alternative accounts, following a brief overview of the events leading up to the intervention.

BACKGROUND TO THE INTERVENTION

Saddam Hussein's invasion of Kuwait on 2 August 1990 initially appeared to come at an unusual time. Iraq had ended its eight-year war with Iran two years earlier and was heavily in debt to Kuwait and Saudi Arabia, both of whom had lent Iraq money to defeat Iran in the Iran-Iraq War.[17] A potentially costly intervention would seem to be an unwise strategy for a heavily indebted country such as Iraq. Saddam Hussein saw it differently; it was precisely because of his financial obligations that invading Kuwait made sense. Iraq had a series of grievances toward Kuwait, including that Kuwait was overproducing oil and keeping prices artificially low, that it was pumping oil that was rightfully Iraq's, and that the "assistance" Kuwait provided Iraq during the Iran-Iraq War was now being charged to Iraq as "debt." Invading Kuwait could redress those grievances.[18] And it appeared he could intervene with impunity, not expecting an international response.

The evolution in U.S. bilateral relations with Iraq had given some hint of its potential acquiescence in the face of an Iraqi invasion of Kuwait. During the Iran-Iraq War, the United States had indirectly supported Iraq by sharing intelligence, protecting its oil tankers, offering credit guarantees to Baghdad, and looking the other way when Iraq was charged with using chemical weapons.[19] At the end of the Iran-Iraq War, the prevailing policy of the United States toward Iraq was more actively conciliatory. National Security Directive 26 (NSD-26), signed 2 October 1989, suggested: "Normal relations between the United States and Iraq would serve our longer-term interests and promote stability in both the Gulf and the Middle East."[20] It was intended to offer Iraq a carrot in exchange for moderated behavior on human rights, weapons development, and terrorism. Along with the policy came attempts to engage Iraq in bilateral discussions. In spite of these diplomatic overtures,

Saddam Hussein's rhetoric became inflammatory, as he threatened to "incinerate" Israel and accused the United States of direct interference in Iraq.[21]

Iraq foreshadowed its bellicose actions in the summer of 1990, when Saddam criticized the United States for provoking the "poison dagger" of his enemies and cautioned that if his threats were ineffective, he would have to resort to something more powerful.[22] In response, the Department of State sent out a cable to its embassies in the Middle East in July 1990, offering the following guidance: "The United States takes no position on the substance of bilateral issues concerning Iraq and Kuwait. However, US policy is unchanged. We remain committed to ensure the free flow of oil from the Gulf and to support the sovereignty and integrity of the Gulf states . . . we will continue to defend our vital interests in the Gulf."[23]

On 15 July, the Foreign Ministry in Baghdad summoned U.S. Ambassador April Glaspie, who transmitted the government policy of the July cable, signaling a U.S. commitment to friendship rather than confrontation. In this meeting, she told Saddam Hussein that "I also welcome your statement that Iraq desires friendship. . . . Let me reassure you . . . that my Administration continues to desire better relations with Iraq . . . both our Governments must maintain open channels of communication to avoid misunderstanding and in order to build a more durable foundation for improving our relations."[24] Such a conciliatory note was evidently interpreted as a green light for invasion and as fodder for Saddam Hussein's assumption that the United States would not retaliate if he invaded Kuwait.[25] In a memo back to the State Department, Ambassador Glaspie recommended against antagonistic rhetoric toward Saddam, a recommendation that would later paint Glaspie as an "accommodationist" for tacitly permitting Saddam's invasion of Kuwait.[26]

On 2 August, Iraq crossed the border into Kuwait, surprising the Kuwaiti army and quickly assuming control over the small but oil-rich country.[27] International reaction on how to respond to the invasion was far from unanimous. The United States, which eventually galvanized an international response, was initially unclear and hesitant on how to respond. According to President Bush and his National Security Advisor, Brent Scowcroft, there was a sense that the outcome—Iraqi control over Kuwait—was a "fait accompli."[28] As Scowcroft wrote, "There was a huge gap between those who saw what was happening as the major crisis of our time and those who treated it as the crisis du jour."[29] In other words, there was a difference between those who saw the crisis as the challenge that would set the post–Cold War precedent and that therefore it required a strong response and those who thought it would pass quickly and that it did not necessitate as determined a response.

Economic sanctions seemed obvious, but U.S. military options all looked unpalatable.[30] Prime Minister Thatcher, who famously told President Bush not to "go wobbly,"[31] was more forceful in her initial response. Arab countries were cautious and slow to condemn the invasion. Internal divisions within the Saudi kingdom made it unclear whether Riyadh would request U.S. assistance. Jordan urged the United States to wait to respond until the Arab states could produce a diplomatic solution.[32] The former Soviet Union suggested that a military option would be "unacceptable" and continuously pushed for a political settlement to the Gulf crisis.[33] China was also deeply skeptical of using force, though assuaged by assurances that its support of U.S. efforts in the Security Council would go some way to restoring bilateral ties after Tiananmen.[34] Overall, there was far more international support for prolonged economic sanctions than for talk of military action.

Without an international consensus yet galvanized, the United States crafted and undertook its initial responses almost entirely alone. Within one hour of Saddam's 2 August invasion, the U.S. Department of Defense had ordered the USS *Independence* battle group to relocate from Diego Garcia to the Gulf of Oman. The *Dwight D. Eisenhower* was ordered from the eastern Mediterranean to the Red Sea and placed on alert for "sustained combat operations on arrival."[35]

Having repositioned these two carrier groups, the National Security Council (NSC) met on 3 August to discuss additional policy options. Treasury Secretary Nicholas Brady suggested cutting off Iraqi and Kuwaiti oil; Chairman of the Joint Chiefs of Staff Colin Powell raised the possibility of air strikes; President Bush suggested international sanctions. The principals agreed on the need for sanctions on military and economic assistance. They also agreed on the need for a U.S. military presence in the Gulf to deter Saddam from invading Saudi Arabia, the United Arab Emirates, or even Israel.[36] The United States therefore deployed naval forces, Delta forces that could undertake a hostage rescue effort, light airborne troops from the 82nd Airborne, and squadrons of fighter jets.[37] By 9 August, the United States was flying combat air patrols along the Iraq-Saudi border. These deployments amounted to within two weeks of the invasion, 50,000 troops that President Bush had deployed within days of the invasion were arriving in Saudi Arabia, and within three weeks, 100,000 troops—including seven brigades, three carrier battle groups, 14 tactical fighter squadrons, four tactical airlift C-130 squadrons, and a strategic bomber squadron—had arrived or were on their way.[38]

Compared with Iraqi forces that by the middle of August numbered about 200,000, the 100,000 U.S. forces looked meager. Therefore, the next, relatively immediate step was the invocation of Title 10, Section 673b of the US Code[39] on 22 August 1990, which authorized the mobilization of 200,000 National Guard troops to active duty. Specific units were notified to report and began undertaking deployment actions on 24 August 1990.[40] By the middle of October, U.S. troop deployments numbered more than 200,000;[41] the deployment of yet 200,000 additional troops in the middle of November shifted further the posture from one that was defensive to what the *New York Times* referred to as a "unilateral declaration of offense."[42]

In deed, in these early phases of the intervention, the response was at best bilateral. As President Bush indicated, "I approved the plan, although we couldn't implement it until the Saudis agreed to accept our troops."[43] Once the United States made the decision that airpower would be insufficient and ground forces would be required, a purely unilateral response would have been impossible, since the plan called for troops to deploy to Saudi Arabia. Deterring Iraq and defending Saudi Arabia would not be credible at standoff distances. The United States therefore needed Saudi acquiescence on deploying hundreds of thousands of its forces into the Arabian desert.[44] Beyond Saudi complicity and British moral support, additional coalition support was limited in autumn 1990. The disparity of contributions in the fall of 1990 prompted appraisals within the United States that allied forces were not close to on par with what one critic referred to as "Uncle Sucker's" contributions in the Gulf.[45] In the months preceding combat operations, however, the Bush administration embarked on its ambitious attempt to provide the resources that ultimately made combat operations genuinely multilateral.[46]

The Two-Dimensional Operation: Deterrence and War Fighting

The overall intervention in the Gulf, according to the Pentagon, had "two dimensions":[47] the deterrence operation and the subsequent war fighting.[48] Whether it is warranted to consider this first dimension as part of the intervention might seem dubious, except that they both required large deployments, both risked immediate confrontation and bloodshed, and both were deployments of combat-ready, regular military troops that were intended to coerce Iraq into leaving Kuwait. In short, both dimensions meet the criteria for intervention. Whether the deterrence part of the intervention actually led to bloodshed is immaterial in "counting" as part of the intervention. As Herbert Tillema has noted, intervention need not be associated with battle deaths.[49] The counterfactual question is what the deterrence deployment would be called if it had also compelled Iraq to leave Kuwait. Half a million troops parked in Saudi Arabia for five months would almost unequivocally be called an intervention.[50] Whether the deterrent force was successful and compelled Iraq to exit Kuwait also should not bear on whether that action, which risked but did not prompt immediate bloodshed, was considered part of the intervention.[51]

This two-dimension distinction is important because it corresponded with two different cooperation strategies. The early phase of the intervention proceeded without multilateral support. On 2 August 1990, the Security

Council had passed Resolution 660 condemning the invasion, and multilateral economic sanctions followed with Resolution 661 on 6 August, but multilateral authorization for military force did not come until 29 November with Resolution 678, long after the United States had completed its initial unilateral deployments. Uninterrupted diplomatic efforts continued for several months before the United States could assure the passage of Resolution 678, which authorized the use of force and produced the prodigious multilateral contributions. Having undertaken the early phase of the intervention bilaterally with Saudi support, why did the United States then shift to a multilateral strategy for the second dimension, combat operations themselves?

FROM BILATERALISM TO MULTILATERALISM

The reason for the shift in cooperation strategy—from the period of August to November 1990 and then November 1990 until the end of conflict—has to do with short time horizons in the early phases combined with the expectation of a daunting level of commitment in the combat phase itself. Declassified minutes from a NSC meeting on 3 August 1990 outlined both concerns. "He is 40 kilometers from Saudi Arabia, and its oil production is only a couple of hundred kilometers away...looking at the military possibilities and options, we should not underestimate the U.S. military forces we would need to be prepared for a major conflict," said a cautious Secretary of Defense Richard Cheney.[52]

After the initial hesitation about how to respond to developments in the Gulf, Iraq's possible invasion of Saudi Arabia became a near preoccupation for the administration. By the third of August, the Iraqi military presence in Kuwait had exceeded 100,000, a worrying sign since that was far more than were necessary to occupy Kuwait.[53] President Bush became convinced that "the Iraqis would indeed move across the border into Saudi Arabia. With so many tanks heading south, it seemed incontrovertible that Saddam had such plans."[54] On 5 August, CIA Director William Webster reported, "I was asked before what would be the earliest that Iraq could attack (Saudi Arabia)...the answer is now." President Bush declared that the "first objective is to keep Saddam out of Saudi Arabia...our second is to protect the Saudis against retaliation when we shut down Iraq's export capability."[55]

Prince Khaled bin Sultan, the Saudi commander who eventually co-led the coalition in the Gulf, shared the concern that Saudi Arabia might be Saddam's next target. He predicted that "no military strategist would expect him [Saddam] to stop at the Saudi border."[56] In retrospect, it is clear that an invasion of Saudi Arabia was logistically impossible, but as the *Final Report to Congress* makes clear, "The ominous presence of overwhelming military force at the Kingdom's northern border, coupled with the fresh evidence of his willingness to attack his neighbors, constituted a threat to the vital interests of both Saudi Arabia and the United States."[57] This concern dominated early thinking on how to respond to Iraq's aggression.[58]

Thus, the first-order effects of an invasion of Kuwait and possibly Saudi Arabia were direct: an immediate, military attack on a close ally and a possible near-term attack on a second close ally. The second-order effects were also consequential. Since Saudi Arabia held 20 percent of the world's proven oil reserves and was the largest net exporter, and Saddam already commanded the 20 percent of the world's oil reserves that resided in Iraq and Kuwait, the potential economic reverberations from an additional annexation would be far-reaching. Saddam would then control 70 percent of Gulf oil and 90 to 95 percent if he then moved into the United Arab Emirates, giving him vast control over the world's oil, "with potentially devastating consequences for the Western industrialized world."[59] Even the prospect gave Saddam Hussein considerable international leverage.[60]

The result, according to the principals in the 3 August 1990 NSC meeting, would be domination of the Organization of the Petroleum Exporting Countries (OPEC), Palestinian politics, and the Arab world. Deputy Secretary of State Lawrence Eagleburger went even further to suggest that success in invading Saudi Arabia could encourage Saddam Hussein to continue on to Israel: "As to his intentions, Saudi Arabia looks like the next target. Over time he would control OPEC and oil prices. If he succeeds, then he would target Israel. This is what we could face unless he leaves the scene. We need to think of this as a very, very critical time."[61] The principals deemed first- and second-order effects as related; success early would translate into more momentum, more resources, and better means to acquire even more power. General Scowcroft summarized the tenor of the meeting as follows: "The stakes in this for the United States are such that to accommodate Iraq should not be a policy option. There is too much at stake."[62]

Expectations of a chain reaction—in which invasion of Saudi Arabia would produce more wealth and greater ability to conquer other parts of the region—produced short time horizons. The effect was a "window of vulnerability"[63] mentality and a decision to deploy troops quickly. A congressional official closely involved with the U.S. response predicted that "the most dangerous time is right now...there will be more American troops there tomorrow and more still next week. If he's [Saddam] going to act militarily," it would have to be in that window before the United States arrived.[64] General Powell agreed that "to deter further Iraqi action with Saudi Arabia would require U.S. forces on the ground...Saddam looks south and sees a U.S. presence."[65] Brent Scowcroft concluded that "now is the time to get the Saudis everything we have."[66]

In principle, the United States was not opposed to multilateral action, but according to declassified Central Command (Centcom) documents, "It quickly became apparent that the JDOP [Joint Department of Operational Planning in Saudi Arabia] would not be sufficiently responsive to develop *combined* plans or resolve *multinational* issues in a crisis situation."[67] Collective decision making was thought to be too onerous to be effective in coordinating a timely response to Iraq's invasion of Kuwait and possible invasion of Saudi Arabia. "The reality of an imminent Iraqi attack against Saudi Arabia" required immediate action that could not be met through a collective security response.[68] President Bush made it clear that he was comfortable with these trade-offs: "Whatever resolve it takes, with or without friends, we will do it."[69]

Once that deterrent force was in place by early October, the commander of Centcom, General Schwarzkopf, believed that the United States had narrowed the window of vulnerability and that the U.S. military "had built a deterrent force capable of defending against any Iraqi offensive."[70] With the risk of an Iraqi intrusion into Saudi Arabia in check, the United States could then exercise some patience in what proved to be a time-consuming process of convincing allies and the UN to agree to the use of force.[71] Extinguishing the threat of an invasion into Saudi Arabia lengthened the U.S. time horizon and allowed the United States to pursue a multilateral strategy that would be important for the next phase of the operation.

It also gave the United States a chance to solidify its military plan, which was still under construction in October. As late as October, President Bush remarked that "we had a long way to go before the military was 'gung ho' and felt we had the means to accomplish our mission expeditiously, without impossible loss of life. I still had a lot of unanswered questions, especially how we might eventually initiate war."[72] Without clear answers to these questions of execution, the United States was itself unprepared militarily for an attack. While the U.S. continued to flesh out the military plans, it could work through diplomatic channels and assemble its multilateral coalition without costly delays beyond what the United States had needed for its own planning.

"Not Ten Feet Tall, but…"

Although the United States could mobilize a sufficient deterrent force on its own, the prospect of fighting a protracted battle of attrition with the fourth largest ground force in the world looked prohibitively costly. Freedman and Karsh, scholars of military strategy, characterized the prevailing view leading up to the 1991 conflict: "It was widely expected that Iraqi forces would only be expelled from Kuwait following a ferocious land battle."[73] As this section

shows, the United States virtually had no choice but to assemble a broad coalition of states, and going through the UN was the best way to lure states,
such as Egypt and Turkey, for whom a UN blessing was a prerequisite.

At the time Iraq invaded Kuwait, the consensus view of Iraq's armed
forces was that they were among the world's largest—certainly the region's
largest—and most advanced. General Schwarzkopf characterized the Iraqi
military as "not ten feet tall, but...formidable. They have an army of nine
hundred thousand men, sixty-three divisions, over fifty-seven hundred
tanks."[74] General Powell's predecessor, Admiral William Crowe, cautioned
that Iraq was "a long ways away and it's a harsh climate...the question of
ground troops in that vast desert, that's another matter altogether."[75]
Chairman of the Joint Chiefs of Staff Colin Powell predicted that war "would
be the NFL, not a scrimmage....Most US forces would have to be committed
to sustain, not just for one or two days....They [Iraqi forces] are also experienced from eight years of war."[76] What concerned military leaders is that
Iraq was thought to have highly capable, even state-of-the-art tanks, fighter
planes, and artillery. The Iran-Iraq War had shown that the Iraqi forces and
equipment were both "formidable and battle-tested."[77]

In addition to its capabilities, the sheer size of the military was also cause
for concern. During the period of the Iran-Iraq War, Iraq had increased the
size of its military through conscription, putting 1.6 million soldiers under
arms, with a total of 1.3 million men between the ages of 23 and 32 and 2.7
million men between the ages of 18 and 45 who could be expected to serve
as reinforcements, according to 1990 statistics. The quality and morale of
the non-Republican Guard forces was questionable, but Iraq's ability to
mobilize vast numbers of men—which they had demonstrated in the battle
attrition during the Iran-Iraq War, from which they had not demobilized by
1990—was not.[78]

By October, the Defense Intelligence Agency estimated that 540,000 of
Iraq's troops (43 divisions) were in the Kuwaiti theater.[79] Not only did Iraq
initially have the numerical advantage, but senior commanders expectated
that these forces might engage in the kind of warfare Iraq had employed in
the 1980s. Saddam Hussein had used poison gas against both the Iranians
and the Kurds; he clearly had both the capability and the willingness to use
these weapons.[80] If he did use them, the conflict would be lengthy and costly.
One British commander speculated that "it is going to be the sort of warfare
people never realized....Modern equipment and the effect it has are much
more powerful than in any previous war. The results are going to be fairly
terrific."[81]

General Norman Schwarzkopf shared this cautious view, writing in his memoirs: "Even assuming things went well, casualties would be substantial....
I sat there imagining a half-dozen scenarios in which the attack might bog

down....Iraq could throw its huge army north of Kuwait against us in a counterattack. A battle of attrition would follow, in which Iraq's numerical superiority would give it a decided advantage."[82] Expected casualty numbers ran high. British sources predicted 15 percent wounded, or 120,000 assuming an 800,000 force. Estimates on the U.S. side were about 65,000 total deaths (on both the allied and Iraqi sides) and as many as 230,000 wounded.[83] Still other estimates predicted about 45,000 U.S. casualties, of which 10,000 would be fatalities.[84] The concern about high casualties did not subside in the run-up to conflict. Just days before the conflict's start, when the coalition had three-quarters of a million troops in the Gulf, Iraq's troop movements indicated that Saddam was ready for conflict and in a position to inflict high casualties.[85]

In short, the Iraqi military appeared to be combat-wise and highly effective after its long slog through the Iran-Iraq war.[86] The operational commitment would be enormous, and the motivation to share it with allies considerable. As Scowcroft and Bush concluded in their memoirs, the operation in the Gulf War was expected to be "difficult but doable. It will be expensive to project and sustain a force of this size. I had no doubt we needed a coalition of partners. There was no percentage in deciding at the outset to go it alone. I thought that to do so would significantly lessen our chances of overall success."[87] General Schwarzkopf agreed that "even though the United States was supplying two thirds of Desert Storm's ground force, for the plan to work, I needed the combat power of the entire coalition."[88]

Thus, the United States welcomed all the coalition forces it could muster. Syria provided backfill for the Egyptians in Kuwait, French units protected the far western flank, and Czechoslovakia contributed its expert chemical warfare units. The United States accepted Egypt's offer for an additional division, since the menacing predictions about Iraq's military capability made it clear that the coalition could use more "combat power" in the northern area of Kuwait.[89] The United States simply did not have the capacity to respond to the large-scale, force-on-force conflict it expected with Iraq. As its initial deployments show, it was equipped to mobilize tens of thousands of soldiers but was unable to deploy comfortably the number of forces that would eventually be necessary.

Despite some of the cataclysmic projections, the actual confrontation proved to be anticlimactic. Saddam Hussein did not unleash any chemical or biological weapons, the allies did not have to fight door-to-door, and the coalition largely remained intact; the air war lasted just over a month and the ground war 100 hours. Despite the potential for problems on the coalition side and the expected strength of the Iraqi military, the combat phase itself passed quite quickly and with few casualties. One early critic of the conflict who was later forced to praise its execution noted that "the odds of achieving this kind of rout against the world's fourth-largest army were infinitesimal."[90] The military itself, which had stocked months' worth of supplies at logistics bases, found itself surprised by the "easy fight."[91] The Bush administration built the vast coalition not with the expectation of those infinitesimal odds, however, but the likelier odds that the conflict would be long enduring and high intensity and therefore benefit from allied participation.

ALTERNATIVE EXPLANATIONS

"A New World Order"?

This section makes several arguments about the effect of norms in the Gulf War. First, concerning rhetoric, if a "sign of an international norm's domestic impact is its appearance in the domestic political discourse,"[92] then the assertion that the multilateral norm emerged with the Gulf War is inappropriately scoped, since leaders during the Cold War also sought to rationalize interventions under the banner of multilateralism. Second, if rhetoric was similar both after and before the end of the Cold War, and the onset of the norm is thought to have been the end of the Cold War, then maybe rhetoric is not a valid indicator of normative salience. I cite further examples of why rhetoric is shallow evidence of normative salience, including the signals that Bush was willing to intervene unilaterally as necessary and that the norm was not a constraint on his behavior. Third, to the extent that President Bush invoked multilateral rhetoric and sought multilateral participation, he did so not out of "oughtness," as the multilateral norm argument would suggest, but out of instrumental, means-end calculations. This finding lends further support to the argument that leaders would rather act legitimately not because it is appropriate but because it pays. Fourth, to the extent that a pattern of multilateralism followed the Gulf War, it did so not out of a sense of appropriateness but because the Gulf War had appeared to validate multilateralism as an effective vehicle of intervention.

A brief survey of Cold War interventions indicates that attempts to frame interventions in multilateral terms were not new in 1990-1991. When leaders made such claims during the Cold War, the intention was to make the intervention appear less imperialistic than in fact it was. At the inception of the 1965 Dominican Republic intervention intended to oust "communists" from the island, President Johnson argued that "this will be the common action and the common purpose of the democratic forces of the hemisphere...the danger is also a common danger, and the principles are common principles. So we have acted to summon the resources of this entire hemisphere to this task."[93]

Johnson employed such rhetoric in the hope that collective action would legitimate the intervention. It intentionally shrouded, however, the overwhelmingly unilateral nature of the intervention and, as one news paper noted, sought to assuage the "damage done to Latin-American sensibilities by the unilateral United States intervention." Latin American governments detected such language as an "international figleaf" for unilateral U.S. actions.[94] In this case, Johnson's rhetoric of principled multilateralism was clearly incongruous with the actions, but the effort nonetheless showed an effort to appeal to such principles while not at all being constrained by them.

As a similar example, on the day that the United States invaded Grenada in 1983, President Reagan justified the intervention based on an "urgent, formal request from the five member nations from the Organization of Eastern Caribbean States to assist in a joint effort to restore order and democracy on the island of Grenada. We acceded to the request to become part of the multinational effort." He spoke of the "collective action" to restore "conditions of law and order" in Grenada, asserting that the action was "forced on us by events that have no precedent in the eastern Caribbean and no place in any civilized society."[95] In the case of Grenada, the American president was conscious about reassuring other states by citing its broad sanction, but in fact the actions themselves were quite unilateral, what one legal scholar maligned as a "resurrection of the Johnson Doctrine."[96]

The multilateral rhetoric behind these two very unilateral actions in the Cold War differs little from that used by the Bush administration in 1990–1991. In a joint session of Congress on 11 September 1990, President Bush reported that "we stand today at a unique and extraordinary moment. The crisis in the Persian Gulf, as grave as it is, also offers a rare opportunity to move toward an historic period of cooperation. Out of these troubled times, our fifth objective—a new world order—can emerge.... An era in which the nations of the world, East and West, North and South, can prosper and live in harmony."[97] Secretary Baker took a similarly quixotic perspective in a speech to the Security Council itself. Despite the East-West tensions that followed World War II, he urged the council to appreciate that "history now has given us another chance. With the Cold War behind us, we now have the chance to build the world envisioned by the founders of the United Nations. We have the chance to make this Security Council and this UN true instruments for peace and justice across the globe."[98] As with its Cold War predecessors, the Bush administration sought to frame its response in collective terms.

Even Margaret Thatcher, reluctant to go through the United Nations at all, echoed these statements and spoke in collective security terms about the legitimacy of the allied cause: "Iraq's invasion of Kuwait defies every principle for which the United Nations stands. If we let it succeed, no small country can ever feel safe again. The law of the jungle would take over from the rule of law."[99]

These statements on the legitimate basis of the Gulf War may have been justified by Iraq's egregious invasion of Kuwait. A comparison with rhetoric associated with Cold War interventions suggests that if rhetoric is seen as an indication of normative strength,[100] then the multilateral norm was not new with the end of the Cold War.[101] The problem may be with rhetoric itself as an indicator of normative salience. Many interventions in the Cold War were neither multilateral nor particularly a choice between right and wrong, yet leaders nonetheless cast them in this light. The divergence between actions and rhetoric is in indictment of rhetoric as cheap talk from leaders who want credit for a legitimate intervention while not accepting any of the collective constraints.

That criticism is not limited to Cold War interventions. While President Bush has been cast as a hearty multilateralist interested in a new world order, evidence suggests that such a perspective is in fact revisionist. A closer look suggests that the "new world order" rhetoric is justification for realpolitik and power politics as usual. In the initial days and weeks after Iraq's invasion of Kuwait, according to declassified White House documents, Bush was primarily interested in U.S. assets in the region, which amounted to "access to oil," since the U.S. economic engine ran on oil and half of U.S. oil was imported.[102] In those early weeks, however, it became abundantly clear that the U.S. domestic public was not interested in wars fought for oil, and "No Blood for Oil" placards began following President Bush on the 1990 midterm election trail. Secretary of State Baker's assertion that "if you want to sum it up in one word, it's jobs"[103] was not popular among the public either.

Gradually, President Bush's public relations campaign shifted. At one campaign stop in Vermont, Bush told his crowd that he had noticed "No War for Oil" signs, and that while "I can understand the sentiment, I would simply say that the rape and the dismantling, the systematic dismantling, of Kuwait defies description. These are crimes against humanity. There can never be compromise—with this kind of aggression. So it isn't oil that we're concerned about, it's aggression."[104] President Bush adopted an evocative rhetoric about the need to establish a new world order to forestall a character whom he deemed "Hitler revisited."[105]

Several other factors suggest that rhetoric may not be a salient measure of the multilateral norm's robustness. One is that the administration made it clear in its words and actions that it was willing to act unilaterally and would therefore have been unconstrained by the prospect of not generating multilateral backing for its intervention. As one senior White House official said, "Our strategy was that we were going to do whatever we had to do on our own, and if we could bring along the UN, then fine."[106] In keeping with that approach, the United States did undertake an impressive amount of diplomacy, but meanwhile it deployed half a million American troops without more than Saudi acquiescence. It unilaterally interdicted Iraqi commerce at sea, which a Canadian-led group at the UN called a unilateral blockade, "using a questionable legal formula to justify it and doing it without telling anybody."[107] In case it was not yet clear, the United States signaled its willingness to act alone days before the passage of Resolution 678, when President Bush again cited his authority and willingness to act without a UN resolution.[108]

Against the backdrop of President Bush's other foreign policy actions, it seems even less likely that multilateralism in the Gulf War stemmed from some pursuit of elevated collective security principles. If it had we would have expected to see some consistency toward that end throughout his administration, and yet year after year, he expended no political capital to convince Congress to pay UN dues—in arrears during his administration—despite having encouraged Secretary General Boutros Boutros-Ghali to expand the UN's peacekeeping role. In addition, the administration altogether avoided multilateral organizations and coalitions in the 1989 unilateral intervention of Panama. Rather, President Bush instructed aides to inform allies by phone after the United States had already invaded Panama.[109] In the specific case of the Gulf War, senior administration officials confessed that what looked like principle by design was an accident at best and self-serving at worst: "the effort to enlist the United Nations was largely improvised, and did not flow from lofty principles of international unity."[110]

Rather, it appeared to be purely instrumental. For reasons offered earlier, the United States sought a large coalition to share what was expected to be an onerous operational commitment. For some states, UN authorization was a prerequisite for participation in the coalition. French President François Mitterrand famously asserted that while Article 51 of the UN Charter might technically make intervention legal, "Fifty-five million French people are not international lawyers."[111] Mitterrand argued that his support for the intervention was contingent on his public's support, which he indicated would be swayed only by a UN authorization. Turkey and Egypt also made their support contingent on UN authorization to "protect themselves against domestic political opposition" to intervening without UN sanction.[112] A UN authorization became the way by which the United States could bring along the substantive contributions of these allies, but this instrumental motivation is altogether distinct from a motivation of "appropriateness."

In the end, U.S. behavior—which combined multilateral rhetoric with a genuine effort to collect allies and UN authorization—nonetheless appeared to revivify faith in the United Nations.[113] Whether the multilateral nature of the coalition and the favorable outcome of the war were related by correlation or causation did little to subdue the enthusiasm that flowed on behalf of the UN after the Gulf War. As the British ambassador to the UN said, "There is no question that the successful bringing to an end of the state of hostilities in the Gulf war is a feather in the cap of the Security Council."[114]

If increased multilateralism did follow from the Gulf War, it did so because multilateral cooperation had been a success rather than a failure, not because it was now seen as appropriate. Writing before the Gulf War began, Stanley Hoffmann predicted that collective security would fail, and when it did, it would only prejudice the international community against multilateralism. "Collective security," he wrote, "will be the casualty, not the winner, if we lose a sense of proportion, if we launch a war that will divide the coalition and the public far more than a protracted reliance on sanctions."[115]

But because collective security *did* work as the drafters of the UN Charter had hoped, it became an obvious institutional strategy after the Gulf War experience. That conclusion derived less from the philosophical advocacy of collective security as an end in itself than from the experience of collective security as having been effective in the Gulf War. Regardless of the motivations, however, an unintended consequence of UN success in the Gulf War was the creation of an expectation that future interventions might also go through the UN. United Nations observer David Malone has written that "in the heady new post–Cold War era, the success of Council-mandated Operation Desert Storm made international police action seem both obvious and easy."[116] The result was an unprecedented level of UN Security Council activity in the following years, which set the stage for the approach taken in Haiti several years later.

THE ROLE OF DOMESTIC POLITICS: MUST THE PRESIDENT "SEEK A DECLARATION OF WAR"?

Addressing the U.S. domestic environment throughout the Iraq crisis appears to have been almost an afterthought for the Bush administration. At least in terms of public opinion, the administration's combination of neglect and flailing about for a justification for war came at little cost. Early on, and with little prompting, the U.S. public was favorable toward intervention. As veteran public opinion analyst Everett Carll Ladd noted, "In the 45 years since World War II, I can find no other instance when so large a segment of the public has endorsed committing U.S. troops prior to their actual engagement."[117] In the week following Iraq's invasion of Kuwait, 64 percent of Americans reported that they approved "using U.S. troops to force the Iraqis to leave Kuwait."[118] In the following week, an ABC News survey found that 79 percent of Americans supported taking "all action necessary, including...military force, to make sure that Iraq withdraws its forces."[119]

Support for two different approaches to the intervention—multilateral and unilateral—varied little. In November 1990, Americans were asked two sets of questions. First, "do you agree or disagree that the U.S. should take all action necessary, including the use of military force, to make sure that Iraq withdraws its forces from Kuwait?"[120] In response to this question, 65 percent agreed, 26 percent disagreed, and 8 percent didn't know. Second, Americans were asked the following: "Recently the UNSC passed a resolution that allows one final opportunity to pull out of Kuwait by Jan 15th or else face possible military action. If Iraq lets this deadline pass, would you favor the U.S. and its allies going to war with Iraq in order to drive the Iraqis out of Kuwait?" This question, which makes explicit reference to the UN and allies, elicited a comparable response: 64 percent favored going to war, 31 percent were against, and 5 percent did not know.[121] Reference to multilateral institutions or assistance made little difference in the responses, and in fact, the negative responses increased when the UN and allies were specifically cited in the question.

The absence of staunch support for multilateralism is matched by the presence of fairly consistent trend lines over time. In his systematic study of Gulf War public opinion, John Mueller has suggested that "the most remarkable aspect of public opinion on such matters was that it changed very little, particularly during the interval between November 8, 1990, when Bush announced he was increasing troop levels in the Middle East, and January 16, 1991, when the war began."[122] Consistency throughout therefore cannot explain the change in cooperation strategy that took place in late November. Only increases in the support for multilateralism during this period or perhaps strong preferences for multilateralism from the outset and a delayed response from the Bush administration could explain variations in the cooperation behavior manifested across the Gulf War, and neither pattern is in evidence here.

That the public was generally supportive of intervention is surprising, given that the Bush administration itself seemed to equivocate on the reasons for war. In the initial phases of the war, President Bush had suggested several reasons for the potential need of force: protecting U.S. access to Middle East oil, maintaining the American way of life, and preventing a "contemporary Hitler" from achieving his goals. None of these seemed to resonate particularly well with the public, which as of late 1990 remained unclear as to the exact nature of the threat that Saddam Hussein posed[123] and "restive" with Bush's seemingly incoherent management of the conflict until that point.[124] In spite of these mixed and sometimes unconvincing

messages that the president conveyed, the public was nonetheless supportive of all policy options considered and all approaches to those options
(whether multilateral or unilateral). Even though only 41 percent of
Americans thought that the president had adequately explained the
situation and the potential need for force—compared with 51 percent who
thought the explanation had been murky—more than a two-to-one majority
still supported the use of force.[125] In this particular case, the public presented a low hurdle on the path to war.

By comparison, Congress and other public figures were far less convinced
by the need for force and pushed for sanctions as an alternative approach.
James Webb, the navy secretary during the latter part of the Reagan
administration, testified that the mistake in deploying troops in August 1990
should not be compounded by using those troops offensively.[126] House
Majority Leader Richard Gephardt suggested that a majority of Democratic
congressmen would vote for an extension of economic sanctions against
Iraq, citing 18 months as the amount of time needed before resorting to
force. He then went even further, threatening the termination of financing
for Operation Desert Shield if the president ordered an attack prior to obtaining congressional approval.[127]

Several members of Congress expressed a willingness to support a use of
force conditional on multilateral assistance. Senator Ernest Hollings argued
that "while I am supportive of the President's approach in general to this
crisis, I remain deeply dissatisfied with our allies' response to our appeals to
share the burden. I hope the administration will press even harder on this
front. The current allied response is simply unacceptable."[128] Another vocif-
erous supporter of a more multilateral response was U.S. Representative and
future Defense Secretary Les Aspin, who was concerned about the disparity
between the hundreds of thousands of American troops and the relative
dearth of others. Without deeper multilateral support, he said, a UN vote
"will look like a United Nations resolution that says: 'Yes, the United States
should fight Iraq.'"[129]

One reason for the congressional reluctance to lead unilaterally is that the
Gulf crisis coincided with what one journalist characterized as a "budget
mess, plunging stock market, soaring oil prices, and stagnant real-estate
market."[130] While the United States emerged from the Cold War as the lone
superpower, the domestic environment leading up to the conflict was less
auspicious, creating incentives for multilateralism as a way to reduce the
burden of the war. Secretary Baker noted his awareness of these domestic
constraints: "At a time of economic uncertainty at home, it would be politically
impossible to sustain domestic support for the operation unless we demonstrated that Uncle Sam wasn't footing the bill while others with pockets as
deep as ours sat on the sidelines."[131]

On his trips to generate international support, Secretary of State Baker used domestic reluctance to his advantage. When soliciting funds from Germany, he argued that "if it looks like you're being skimpy on the money, you're getting all the benefits of this and you're not contributing....You have to put me in the position where I can argue when I appear before the congress that Germany is doing its fair share. I know how important the U.S.-German relationship is to you, and you know how important it is to me. But you can't leave me hanging out there."[132] Baker petitioned on behalf of a congressional audience that had voiced a need for proportional burden-sharing, making the case to Germany that he would be unable to gain domestic support for the intervention without Germany assuming a larger share of the burden. Using this two-level strategy, Baker was able to collect $15 billion from the Saudis, the same from Kuwait, and $2 billion from Germany.[133]

While Secretary Baker cited the domestic political and economic environment as a basis for seeking multilateral support, it was as much an excuse for him as a requirement. Certainly, Congress was threatening that it would oppose force, but several related factors indicate that congressional opinion was not the driving factor behind multilateral-seeking behavior. First, all of the Bush administration's actions and rhetoric reflect an executive who did not see Congress as an obstacle to the use of force. Secretary of Defense Cheney testified on 3 December 1990 that Bush did not need "additional authorization from the Congress."[134] By "additional," he referred to UN Resolution 678, which had been passed days earlier. According to Cheney, congressional approval was superfluous, given that the UN had already authorized the international mission. Though the administration might prefer congressional support, it would carry out the mission whether or not it had congressional *authorization*.

Despite Speaker of the House Tom Foley's warning that the president "must seek a declaration of war from the Congress,"[135] President Bush defended what he said was his authority to wage war without approval from Congress. A week before bombs started dropping, and with no congressional approval in hand, Bush said, "I don't think I need it...there are different opinions on either side of this question, but Saddam Hussein should be under no question on this: I feel that I have the authority to fully implement the United Nations resolutions....I still feel that I have the constitutional authority—many attorneys having so advised me."[136]

Such apathy toward congressional authorization was not inconsistent with President Bush's predecessors. Since the War Powers Act was passed in 1973, presidents have brushed it off as though it had few constraining effects on their ability to deploy troops and wage war.[137] As one expert on constitutional law observed, "President Bush, like so many presidents before him, is acting as though the Congress doesn't have any authority to exercise" over the armed forces.[138] Constitutional law scholar Laurence Tribe went further to call the War Powers Act "largely a dead letter."[139]

That the White House viewed it in this way was patently obvious and went beyond rhetorical polemics. From the unilateral deployment of U.S. forces in early August, to the follow-on deployment in November, to the diplomatic passage of various UN resolutions, President Bush acted as though he were unconstrained by his domestic audience generally and Congress in particular. Not only did he not consult with Congress during these stages but he did not ask its approval until after he had deployed half a million troops, assembled the coalition, and obtained UN authorization, making it virtually impossible for Congress to then oppose the intervention.[140] At this point, Desert Storm was already a "fait accompli."[141] And indeed, this was part of the Bush administration's hand-tying strategy with respect to Congress. Having worked diplomatically to pass the UN resolution authorizing "all necessary means," the president essentially cornered Congress. If Congress did not pass an analogous resolution, it would look like it was sabotaging both U.S. and international efforts to right a wrong. As David Gergen, who has worked with four U.S. presidents, noted, "In effect the White House was boxing in Congress, leaving it only two options: go along with a huge international coalition against Iraq or pull the plug and let the United States suffer a devastating defeat."[142] President Bush may not have needed Congress, but his administration was deftly able to use international reluctance to push desirable domestic outcomes, as well as domestic reluctance to push desirable international outcomes.

In his memoirs, President Bush tellingly admits that "the timing of the decision to reinforce the troops was determined by practical military considerations, but the timing of the announcements of the increase was driven by political ones."[143] President Bush had waited until November 8—after the midterm elections—to *announce* the massive troop augmentation. The actual decision to increase troops was divorced from domestic political factors, however, particularly those dealing with Congress.

In the end, the political gamesmanship worked. The Senate voted 52–47 to authorize the use of force, while the House voted 250–179. In its vote, Congress cited that its own authorization was "in accordance with United Nations Security Council Resolution 678, which called for the implementation of eleven previous Security Council Resolutions."[144] Through its wording, the U.S. Congress made it clear that its intention was to carry out actions that an IO had already authorized, using the international actions to justify its domestic agenda. With international backing, Congress could engage in the "politics of blame avoidance," sharing the political blame with the international community if the intervention went awry.[145]

REGIONAL POWER DYNAMICS AND "THE RELAXED BIPOLAR SYSTEM"

At the time of the Gulf War, the international system was in a state of flux and the subject of much debate. Charles Krauthammer wrote in the winter 1990-1991 issue of *Foreign Affairs* that "there is but one first-rate power and no prospect in the immediate future of any power to rival it."[146] John Mearsheimer disputed claims that the system was unipolar; he insisted on a regional structure of bipolarity in Europe (the United States and Russia), balanced multipolarity in Asia, and multiple great powers (China and Russia) at the international level.[147] William Pfaff had an apolar view of the world in which superpower status ceased to exist, and accordingly, the leadership role appropriated to a superpower would also recede, leaving the United States with a dramatically different and diffident foreign policy.[148]

Despite these competing claims of international structure, key U.S. decision makers believed they were in what Secretary of State Baker called a "relaxed bipolar system,"[149] a designation that emerged in the 3 August 1990 NSC meeting. Deputy Secretary Eagleburger said that "this is the first test of the post war system...the bipolar contest is relaxed."[150] The bipolar system was relaxed but not defunct. Although Soviet power had declined, the United States was wary about possible Soviet involvement because of its historical regional influence. In the 40 years preceding the Gulf War, Iraq had been a client state of the Soviet Union. The relationship provided the Soviets with its only access to the Gulf and a market for Soviet-produced arms; it had served both countries' interests by providing a balance to Western economic and political influence in the region.[151] Soviet power was on the wane in 1990-1991, but political and economic connections between the Soviets and Iraqis were still strong in 1990, and the United States had an interest in minimizing any counterproductive involvement on the part of the Soviets.[152] As a result, the "real starting point for producing a coalition" was not necessarily with the UN but with the Soviets.[153]

The Soviet regional influence could affect the intervention in a couple of ways. Since the Soviet Union had been the primary arms supplier for Iraq, any effective arms embargo against Iraq would require Soviet participation to be effective. Without their cooperation, the Soviets could continue supplying Iraq and essentially counterbalance the coalition's efforts to remove him from Kuwait. In addition, the historically close political relationship between the Soviet Union and Iraq conferred greater bargaining leverage on the Soviet Union than the United States and its allies had in convincing Saddam Hussein to withdraw from Kuwait. Because of their historical channels of cooperation and communication, Gorbachev had avenues of diplomacy that

were less open to the United States and that he exercised (albeit unsuccess-
fully) in the months leading up to Desert Storm.[154]

Whether the Soviet Union did have influence with Iraq is immaterial,
since the United States proceeded toward the intervention as though it did.
In his memoirs, Secretary of State Baker notes: "In every strategy calculation, I considered their [the Soviets'] support a prerequisite to a credible
coalition.... Their endorsement was so critical...that I was willing to go
many an extra mile to keep them on board."[155]

Keeping them on board by reconciling the two powers' policy differences
was far from trivial. The Soviets preferred economic sanctions to the use of
force; they wanted to extend the sanctions deadline and delay the intervention; they also sought more limited goals within the intervention. That the
United States engaged in a flurry of high-level diplomatic meetings with the
Soviets, compromised on the intervention's inception date, and negotiated
financial transfers from Saudi Arabia is testimony to how much the United
States feared Soviet interference and valued its cooperation in the intervention.[156] Any costs associated with diplomatic bargaining, either in terms of
delay or financial costs, would be offset by the expectation of political and
military advantages.[157]

Other than the Soviet Union, the regional power explanation would also
expect the United States to incorporate powerful regional actors such as
Saudi Arabia and Turkey. Their participation would be helpful in providing
local resources such as bases and troops that would offset the costs of intervention. As David Lake has pointed out in his study of the 1991 Gulf War, "In
large-scale uses of force...technological limitations demand that the United
States have available to it forward land bases."[158] Saudi Arabia was geograph-
ically the most proximate both to Kuwait and to Iraq, a regional economic
powerhouse, and the most obvious location for a forward operating base.
Turkey was host to a major U.S. Air Force installation, as well as an active oil
pipeline that ran from Iraq through Turkey to the Mediterranean. Given the
positioning of the pipeline, the United States needed Turkey's cooperation to
make sanctions more effective, since allowing Iraq to pump oil through
Turkey meant economic benefit to Iraq, which could give it additional
strength in fighting the United States.

The U.S. efforts to recruit Saudi Arabia and Turkey are consistent with
the expectations of these regional power arguments. Saudi Arabia was the
one country without which a U.S. intervention would have been nearly
impossible. U.S. decision-making concessions were consequential and reflect
what little bargaining power the United States had vis-à-vis Saudi Arabia. In
return, the United States was obliged to grant Saudi Arabia a parallel
command to the American chain of command under Schwarzkopf. According
to General Khaled, who led the parallel command, "it was to be 50–50.... The

Americans were unhappy with my title. Clearly, there was some resistance in a part of the American bureaucracy to the notion of a parallel command."[159] Dual chains of command—in which Saudi Arabia commanded all Arab forces—risked undermining a fundamental principle of battle: unity of command.[160]

In return for Turkey's support, the United States facilitated World Bank loan increases from $400 million to between $1 and $1.5 billion over the following two years. As important, however, was the U.S. commitment to support Turkey's request to be treated as a full NATO partner and its bid to join what was then the European Commission.[161]

Despite these concessions, emergent unipolarity and its attendant material power proved to be a strong force of persuasion. Once the United States had decided that multilateralism would be the most expedient means to achieve political and military objectives in the Middle East, Secretary Baker admits that the United States took full advantage of its standing to convince important states in the region to fall into line: "We were also able to exploit another reality: As communism collapsed, America's status as the preeminent superpower was magnified. As a result, everyone wanted to get closer to the United States. This gave us formidable leverage, which we didn't hesitate to wield throughout the crisis."[162] That extended to shamelessly luring regional states with economic sweeteners, for example. Recognizing that Egypt was experiencing a particularly acute recession that would be exacerbated by conflict in the region, for example, President Bush made promises to President Hosni Mubarak that he would "recommend to the Congress that it forgive Egypt's entire debt to the United States."[163] The leverage translated into tools for co-opting middle-size Arab states by "cajoling, extracting, threatening, and occasionally buying" their support.[164]

CONCLUSION

In evaluating cooperation behavior in the Gulf War, the time horizon–operational commitment hypothesis is most consistent with the U.S. decision to act bilaterally at the outset and then multilaterally for combat operations. The direct attack on a U.S. ally (Kuwait) as well as the possibility of a near-term attack on another ally and critical economic interest (Saudi Arabia) provided incentives to act quickly and therefore to sidestep multilateral channels. In the months after Iraq's invasion, the United States acted by deploying hundreds of thousands of troops to the Gulf, establishing an offensive, bilateral posture prior to UN authorization or substantial support from allies other than Saudi Arabia, which hosted those troops. But the expectation of a large, force-on-force conflict with the fourth-largest army was almost a model contested zone for the United States, replete not just with a sizable army but one that was seasoned and had a history of using chemical weapons. The prospect for an enormous commitment and casualties prompted strong U.S. interest in collecting allies and generating a UN solution that would produce a more robust multilateral coalition.

The other hypotheses find less support in the Gulf War case. First, while there are useful post hoc accounts of multilateral norms in the wake of the Gulf War, nothing in those accounts would have helped predict the normative change leading into the Gulf War or explained why the norm operated differently in this context than it did in the Cold War, when leaders also sought to cloak their unilateral, realpolitik missions in the banner of multilateralism. Rhetoric, since it was similar across a period in which the norm was thought to change, may not be the best indicator of normative salience. Gauging behavior, however, also casts doubt on the normative assertions, since the Bush administration was certainly willing to intervene unilaterally in the Gulf and pursued multilateral channels not out of a sense of oughtness but because of instrumental calculations on why it would be more helpful to have more rather than fewer allies.

Second, domestic politics was neither an enabler nor an obstacle for U.S. intervention in general, or for multilateralism specifically. If anything, public preferences were ambivalent toward multilateralism and highly supportive of intervention, which might have led a public-conscious executive to circumvent multilateralism and intervene unilaterally. Moreover, the domestic audience's level of support changed little from August 1990 to January 1991 and therefore cannot explain the change in cooperation approach over time. Secretary Baker did use congressional reluctance as bargaining leverage abroad, but evidence suggests that the administration was willing and prepared to use force without congressional approval. Ultimately, it expended more capital obtaining international authorization and then backed Congress into a corner in which it effectively had to authorize the intervention.

Third, the regional power explanation does help explain the prodigious effort to recruit the Soviet Union, a state that contributed nothing materially and in fact asked for a $4 billion transfer of funds, which the United States negotiated from Saudi Arabia. Only for the Soviet Union was the United States willing to postpone its start date under UN Resolution 678 from 1 January to 15 January 1991.[165] The historical Soviet influence in the region made it an important player both for the active political support it could provide and as a hedge against the potentially destabilizing influence it could incite if it were not acquiescent. It also explains the concessions toward Saudi Arabia and Turkey, which the United States needed for its forward operating bases.

Whether the Gulf War heralded a new norm of multilateralism or the interest in appearing to intervene multilaterally was consistent with previous interventions, it is incontrovertible that the number of interventions *with* UN authorization increased after the Gulf War. The absence of great-power paralysis in the Security Council is a crucial reason that authorizations could henceforth be obtained. Another reason is that the success of this multilateral outcome breathed new life into collective security. Had multilateralism failed in the Gulf War, as Stanley Hoffmann suggested, collective security would have been the casualty, not the winner. Instead, however, "the successful cooperation between states in the first Persian Gulf War abruptly turned the SC into the natural first stop for coalition building."[166] The United States followed a similar model of intervention and multilateralism as President Bush handed off unrest in Haiti to his successor, President Clinton.

5

Haiti: Quid Pro Quo Multilateralism

At the time the United States intervened in Haiti in 1994, the U.S. defense budget of $288 billion was 20 times the entire gross domestic product of Haiti.[1] Along with that spending came highly advanced equipment, training, and manpower that the Haitians lacked. The well-trained American military consisted of about 2 million people, compared with the military in Haiti, which was denigrated as an army of "60,000 invisible zombies."[2] Hardly a "contested zone" for the United States, the intervention in Haiti should have been easily handled by the United States without the need for a multilateral force. Moreover, the United States had historically "exercised sufficient military power to enforce its own absolute hegemony" in the region.[3] Reaching out to the international community to police its own hemisphere was unprecedented for a state that had thought nothing of intervening unilaterally in Haiti in 1915, the Dominican Republic in 1965, Grenada in 1983, and Panama in 1989. The United States acted as though it had a "free hand in its own sphere of influence" and had even fewer checks on its power with the end of the Cold War.[4]

Yet in July 1994, the United States sought UN authorization and a coalition of 19 states to intervene in Haiti. On 31 July 1994, the UN passed Resolution 940 that authorized "all means necessary" for the restoration of democracy in Haiti. The United States led a multinational force of 20,000 six weeks later. The intervention force, however, was multinational in name only. United Nations authorization came as a quid pro quo for the U.S. authorization of a Russian peacekeeping force in Georgia. And until the spring of 1995, the peacekeeping force operated with UN authorization but scant participation from allies. As with the Gulf War, the Haiti intervention proceeded as a hybrid operation, with two forms of cooperation behavior across the intervention. Formal multilateralism characterized the early phases—from the intervention's inception in September 1994 until the handoff to the UN in spring 1995—giving way to a full multilateral peacekeeping force for the postconflict phases.

As this chapter shows, the shift in cooperation strategy finds strong support from the underlying security context of the intervention. Unrest

in Haiti started during the Bush administration and continued to degen-
erate until the mid-1990s. Even at its peak, unrest meant political instability in Haiti but few effects in the United States other than the spillover
of refugees. Time horizons were long, and the Bush and Clinton administrations exhausted diplomatic and economic avenues before recourse to
military action, taking three years to produce UN authorization. Seeing
that the United States could conduct the so-called combat phase relatively
cheaply, it undertook this phase without allies. The problem was not how
to win the war but how to keep the peace, however. Realizing the long-term
commitment required to keep the peace, the United States co-opted the
support of allies, who agreed to support the intervention, assumed responsibility for the open-ended aftermath, and assuaged an American public
concerned about footing the entire cost of an intervention of little percep-
tible value. Before discussing the 1994 intervention itself and the reasons
for the type and timing of multilateralism more fully, this chapter briefly
traces U.S. involvement in the region, a history marked far more by
American unilateralism than the engagement with allies and international
organizations that characterized the 1994 operation.

BACKGROUND AND COOPERATION IN THE 1994 HAITI
INTERVENTION

The 1823 Monroe Doctrine provided the seeds of what has since been a very
assertive set of policies in the Western Hemisphere, largely manifested as
"closed door diplomacy" in which the United States has tried to proscribe
outsiders' intervention in Latin America by asserting its own hegemony in
the region. President Theodore Roosevelt expanded the scope by designating
the United States as the hemisphere's policeman. The policy paved the way
for a series of twentieth-century unilateral interventions in the hemisphere,
including an almost 20-year occupation of Haiti in the early part of the
century undertaken with the justification that it would help make the region
"safe for democracy" and indeed safe for American investment.[5]

President Franklin D. Roosevelt's Good Neighbor Policy moderated U.S.
interventions in the Western Hemisphere,[6] but this benign policy came to a
quick halt during the Cold War, when the United States again unilaterally
patrolled its hemisphere to guard against communist incursions, whether in
Cuba, the Dominican Republic, or Grenada, while in Haiti, the United States
limited its Cold War pressure to economic and political attempts to institute
reforms. To some extent, political reform emerged in 1990, with the largely
free and fair election of Jean-Bertrand Aristide, who was overthrown by
Colonel Raoul Cédras in a coup the following year and replaced with a

military regime, or junta, that was undemocratic and produced considerable instability in Haiti.

The United States responded to reports of human rights repression soon after the junta assumed power, thus beginning the long slog toward intervention. Secretary of State James Baker worked with both the Organization of American States (OAS) and the United Nations Security Council (UNSC) to address the political and human rights infractions in Haiti. The OAS authorized UNSC-supported sanctions in October 1992. Though the sanctions initially cut fuel supplies to Haiti, they were generally ineffective. They particularly lost their bite after the United States unilaterally withdrew from the sanctions, under the pretext of humanitarian considerations but with the more plausible motivation of protecting U.S. industries in Haiti.[7] In June 1993, the UN followed up on the OAS voluntary sanctions by passing UNSC Resolution 841 demanding the restoration of rights in Haiti and authorizing an arms and fuel embargo against Haiti.[8]

President Clinton continued escalating the responses to unrest in Haiti, issuing Executive Order No. 12853, essentially the domestic legislation of UN Resolution 841. The executive order froze assets of Haitian nationals who were providing financial or material contributions to the regime.[9] Following a number of additional steps designed to calm the unrest in Haiti, the UN responded in September 1993 by passing Resolution 867, which authorized the United Nations Mission in Haiti (UNMIH). Though intended to establish the "commitment of the international community to the solution of the Haiti crisis,"[10] the first deployment of UNMIH forces, about 200 American and 25 Canadian troops aboard the USS *Harlan County*, did just the opposite, turning into something of a debacle. Greeted in Port-au-Prince by armed civilians, the troops returned unilaterally and unceremoniously to the U.S. mainland.[11] The retreat decision, while it seemed reasonable given the limited security stakes, signaled to both the local Haitian community and the international community in general that the United States was indecisive rather than committed to resolving the Haiti crisis.[12] It also signaled to potential contributing states, particularly France, that the United States might not be serious about intervening in Haiti, which later made it more difficult to garner multilateral support in the form of troop contributions. French Foreign Minister Alain Juppé mocked the *Harlan County* incident, remarking that the French were close to joining the peacekeeping force months earlier, "only to have someone make a sharp U-turn at the last minute because people were shouting on the docks."[13]

Despite the derision, the United States continued to pursue diplomatic channels as it planned for military intervention, "sound[ing] out other countries" for what was advertised as a "peacekeeping mission," in contrast to the forceful intervention that had characterized U.S. military planning to date.

For example, Secretary of State Warren Christopher's rhetoric judiciously employed language such as "peacekeeping" and "smoothing a transition to democracy" to woo potential allies.[14] Even with these semantic efforts to allay the concerns of potential allies, most other states continued to prefer political or diplomatic solutions to the Haiti unrest. Of the major players, Russia favored diplomacy, Germany expressed complete reluctance to use force, and Canada was unwilling to provide its own troops for an intervention. As late as March 1994, Secretary General Boutros Boutros-Ghali sought several weeks of continued sanctions before considering tougher measures against Haiti's military leaders. This was far less time than the several months Alain Juppé had said France would need to buy into tougher Security Council action.[15]

In the end, U.S. diplomats were willing to wait several months and continue with sanctions while working to convince key states of the need for harsher Security Council action. Resolution 940 ultimately passed on 31 July 1994 with 12 votes in favor and 2 abstentions. It authorized member states to convene a multilateral force and "use all necessary means to facilitate the departure from Haiti of the military leadership" and "establish and maintain a secure and stable environment."[16] Brazil and China had opposed the resolution during debate but ultimately abstained from the vote, despite expressing reservations about intrusions on sovereignty.[17] Through UNSCR 940, the UN finally authorized U.S. plans for intervention, which were already all but complete.

GOING IT ALONE IN HAITI: U.S. PLANNING AND OPERATIONS

Although Haiti is sometimes lauded as an example of the post–Cold War "new world order" of cooperation, largely because of the UNSC authorization it received,[18] it had few of the attributes of collective decision making. Indeed, the United States operated multilaterally at the diplomatic level, working with allies and international organizations over a period of three years to pass resolutions in favor of its Haiti agenda. And while the UN authorized the intervention, it produced few boundaries around the intervention. A few Caribbean states scattered some troops at the periphery, but none had influence over decision making. The plans and execution of the intervention itself were almost exclusively the product of U.S. decision making. As an astute observer of the Haiti intervention suggests, "Until the UN took over in April 1995, U.S. troops formed the bulk of, determined the policy of, and were virtually synonymous with, the MNF [multinational force]."[19] United States planning and troop numbers over the course of the intervention support this characterization.

Almost immediately following the 1991 coup, the U.S. military began planning for possible action in Haiti. The 82nd Airborne unshelved a 1980s intervention plan called Contingency Plan 2367 that called for a noncombatant evacuation order (NEO) and the U.S. Atlantic Command (USACOM) in Norfolk developed a plan in which marines would seize an airfield in Guantánamo Bay and, from there, proceed to conduct an NEO in Haiti.[20] The need for such contingency planning appeared to dissipate, particularly after the signing of the Governor's Island Agreement in July 1993, in which Cédras, who had taken control of the government, agreed to cede control to the exiled Aristide.[21] Conditions deteriorated soon thereafter, however, leading to a continuation of domestically controversial repatriation policies for Haitian refugees and prompting the formation of the Joint Task Force Haiti Assistance Group, based at USACOM and comprised of special forces officers, planners from all services, and Haiti experts.[22]

With increasing pressure from congressional groups such as the Black Caucus and pro-Aristide lobbyists in the United States, as well as increasing indications that neither sanctions nor the Governor's Island agreement were effectively stemming the unrest, the U.S. military continued its planning for an NEO.[23] Based on the continuing unrest and guidance from Chairman of the Joint Chiefs of Staff (JCS) General John Shalikashvili, USACOM shifted from planning a peaceful-entry NEO to a forceful entry. The result, code-named "Jade Green," called for the invasion of Haiti by the 82nd Airborne Division, followed by peacemakers from the 10th Mountain Division, and ultimately a transition to UN forces.[24] Of the five phases, the United States would conduct all except the last, postconflict phase, which instead would be undertaken by the United MNF. An alternative plan, peaceful entry rather than combat entry, developed at the request of General Shalikashvili, had similar phases but assumed a permissive entry, relying on the light but combat-ready infantry from the 10th Mountain Division.

Only in July 1994, a month from the operation's inception and almost as an afterthought, did commanders begin to consider multilateral involvement. General Shalikashvili ordered senior military planners to seek "as many flags as possible" from the Caribbean countries.[25] The pursuit of "flags" stands in contrast to active participation, input, or contributions. The extent to which the United States engaged international actors and specifically those in the Caribbean was not unlike the way the United States had involved eastern Caribbean states in the 1983 Grenada intervention.[26] In Grenada, the United States sought nominal contributions from Antigua and Barbuda, Dominica, St. Vincent and the Grenadines, and St. Lucia to invade Grenada, but the United States had clearly been in charge and the eastern Caribbean presence merely gave cover for U.S. unilateralism.[27] Similarly, in the 1994 Haiti intervention, the Caribbean Community (CARICOM) said that it would "coordinate their efforts" with the United States,[28] but little real coordination actually took place. Belize, Jamaica, Barbados, Antigua and Barbuda, Guyana,

Trinidad and Tobago, and the Bahamas provided just one platoon each, amounting to 266 troops that did not have a say in decision making, were relegated to the role of a noncombatant police force, and received logistics support and training not from their respective capitals but from the United States.[29] The Jamaican foreign minister admitted that the troops would not participate in the invasion and would join only after the United States had secured Haiti.[30]

The U.S. engagement with states outside the Caribbean was only somewhat more vigorous. In July 1994, the U.S. State Department enlisted support from Argentina, France, and Canada—the so-called Friends of Haiti group—to participate in a multinational observer group that would control the border of the Dominican Republic and Haiti, which the United States suspected to be a smuggling route for the Cédras regime. France, however, reiterated the position that it would not join an intervention force; Minister Juppé registered his qualms with the intervention, stating that "we aren't going to play the conquerors all over the world."[31] France did agree, however, to support a stabilization force after Aristide returned to power.

Having obtained nominal support from small island states in combat operations and support from larger states for postconflict operations, the United States continued its independent planning for two possible contingencies: permissive and forced entry into Haiti. With the hope of reaching an eleventh-hour settlement, however, President Clinton sent a negotiating team to Haiti in September 1994. The team, which included Jimmy Carter and Colin Powell, met with the junta's leader, Cédras; the meeting yielded unexpected acquiescence when Cédras agreed to transition power to Aristide. Because of the diplomatic successes, the United States had to change its intervention plans, since the military no longer needed to undertake a forced entry but did not necessarily have the conditions for a peaceful one.[32]

Rather than intervene with either the nonpermissive or the peaceful entry plan, General Shalikashvili ordered a combination of the two. He called for a semipeaceful landing in the spirit of the Carter negotiations instead of the forced entry. On 19 September, a combination of a special operations task force, members from the 10th Mountain Division, marines with specialized air-ground expertise, and members of the XVIII Corps headquarters landed in Haiti for Operation Uphold Democracy. The 10th Mountain Division and marines secured urban centers, and special forces secured the countryside.[33] Of the 20,000 troops who participated in the initial intervention, almost all were American except for the couple of hundred Caribbean police forces that operated at the periphery of the island. Almost a month later, on 15 October 1994, 97 percent of the troops in the area were still American.[34]

The high proportion of U.S. troops is consistent with the fact that none of the combat plans included foreign troops at any of the intervention points. Coalition troops that were later added to those plans operated under U.S. military command and were instructed to guard the airport, conduct security operations in peripheral Haitian cities, and more generally operate in peacekeeping capacities rather than combat operations. Only after the United States had undertaken the initial phases of the intervention did the proportion of U.S. to multinational troops shift. By 13 January 1995, many of the initial U.S. troops had already evacuated Haiti and instead of making up 96 percent of the coalition were only 74 percent as they began to transition authority. The United States officially transferred peacekeeping responsibilities to UNMIH on 31 March 1995[35] to do what one observer called the "nation-building equivalent of mopping up."[36]

WHY THE CHOICE OF MULTILATERALISM IN NAME ONLY?

The Sense of Diminished Urgency

The story of U.S. decision making on the Haiti issue is one of deliberation, ambivalence, and vacillation. Torn between vocal congressional and public opposition to intervention, on the one hand, and the "demands of a small, but dedicated minority, whose votes he [Clinton] needed to advance his legislative agenda,"[37] on the other, the Bush and Clinton administrations took a muddled approach to Haiti after the 1991 coup that overthrew Aristide. The main reason the United States could afford to be ambivalent on the issue is that time horizons were long. Events on the ground did not pose a significant perturbation to U.S. security interests. Nothing catalyzed decisiveness, which meant that the United States could plod along, drafting plans for intervention and considering allies and international organization (IO) authorization, without being concerned about direct threats to U.S. security.

Although Haiti's stability had ebbed and flowed since the 1991 coup, the only threat emanating from Haiti was the flow of refugees. A flood of refugees may have been troubling from a U.S. domestic politics standpoint, particularly in those states with high Haitian populations, but not a high security threat to the nation as a whole. Nor did the political objective require urgency. The situation in Haiti was not one of mass killing, genocide, or starvation. It was about democracy restoration, perhaps an important matter of principle, but as critics pointed out, "the instability in Haiti did not dent U.S. security,"[38] nor did it qualify as a "vital interest" worthy of U.S. intervention and potential loss of life.[39]

The long time horizons are evident in how the United States approached resolution of the Haiti issue, specifically in terms of the instruments the United States employed and when. It expended three years on diplomacy, working to obtain support from the OAS, CARICOM, and the UN. As Clinton himself asserted on the eve of the intervention, "The United Nations labored for months to reach an agreement acceptable to all parties…the nations of the world continued to seek a peaceful solution while strengthening the embargo we had imposed."[40] In reality, the UN worked for several *years*, not *months*, to arrive at the eventual resolution on the use of force.

Consistent with these long time horizons and low security stakes, the United States was willing to make a number of concessions on the timing and conditions of intervention. Despite three years of escalation from diplomacy to economic sanctions, a number of key states remained reluctant to intervene even in 1994, requiring flexibility on the part of the United States. For example, in exchange for Russia's decision not to block the U.S. authorization to intervene in Haiti, the United States agreed not to block Russia's request for peacekeepers in Georgia.[41] France sought to extend economic sanctions on Haiti, requiring that the United States negotiate some compromise on when force would be authorized in Haiti. President Clinton's preference was a one-month extension of sanctions, whereas France preferred four months; the United States ended up granting all four months, not necessarily as a concession to France but because the lack of urgency meant that four months came at little cost to the United States. The issue had been simmering in Haiti for three years, so why not wait another few months to let the sanctions work? There was no plausible way that further degeneration of the situation in Haiti could have an appreciable impact on U.S. interests.[42]

As one *New York Times* journalist correctly summarized, "The decision [to seek UN authorization] reflects a sense of diminished urgency within the Administration now that the flood of refugees has dwindled to a trickle."[43] The newspaper went further to editorialize that "except for refugees, what is going on in Haiti affects only Haiti. Fear of the political consequences of admitting legally qualified but politically unpopular refugees is not a very good reason for invading a country."[44] Even the administration was unable to cite a threat to U.S. national security interests from Haiti, but rather proffered an interest in "protecting democracy in our hemisphere…and stopping this migration of potentially thousands or tens of thousands of Haitian refugees."[45] That Haiti was not an immediate military threat to U.S. interests meant that the United States could take a long view of the situation, considering the potential longer term advantages of expending few resources and generating multilateral support for the postconflict stability operations that would certainly follow.

THE OPERATIONAL COMMITMENT: HOW TO LEAVE HAITI?

Having made the decision against unilateralism, the United States then had a second choice, whether to incorporate allies (full multilateralism) or intervene operationally alone (formal multilateralism). As the previous discussion outlines, the United States assembled a combination of both: it had formal multilateralism—and few allies—in the early phase and transitioned to a sizable multinational force in the postconflict phase.

The reason for the shift is that in the early phases, the operational commitment was expected to be low. The Haitians were thought to have about 12 police companies (about 1,200 individuals) and 4,100 members of the Armed Forces of Haiti (FAd'H) in cities around the island. Military planners expected that they would need just one morning to eliminate the FAd'H and take over Haitian police stations. The forcible entry itself would last no more than a few hours. Neutralizing the opposing force and creating the conditions under which the Aristide government could be reinstalled would last less than 45 days, according to the 82nd Airborne Division commander, Major General William Steele.[46] In short, military planners predicted that a "U.S. invasion would overwhelm Haiti's poorly trained and lightly armed military quickly and easily."[47]

Calculations of a quick operational victory translated into cost assessments that were moderately low for the U.S. military. Pentagon cost analysts had given congressional appropriators a $55 million estimate for the first three weeks of the Haiti operation and $372 million more for the first seven months. In addition, the Department of Defense (DoD) had estimated training costs of $2.6 million for the Caribbean troops participating in the intervention.[48] To put these costs in perspective, the DoD budget in that year was 670 times the budgeted amount for the first seven months of the operation, which was expected to be the most intensive phase of the intervention, particularly since other states had committed to assist in the postconflict phase and the U.S. force totals were expected to drop. These costs were far from burdensome for a U.S. military that had few defense commitments in the mid-1990s and was in a position economically to front such minimal costs.

The postconflict phase, however, was uncertain and had the potential to be burdensome, less in financial terms than in time (opportunity costs). Colin Powell assessed: "We can take over the place in an afternoon with a company or two of Marines." The problem, he said, was how to leave once they had invaded. He noted that the last American intervention in Haiti had lasted 19 years, pointing to the possibility of an open-ended commitment this time around.[49] The chairman of the Senate Foreign Relations Committee, Claiborne Pell, similarly warned, "As we learned the last time U.S. forces were in Haiti, it is easy to go in but could be harder to get out."[50] Indeed, the easy part would be confrontation with the Haitian military and regime change. The hard and costly part was addressing what would likely be an open-ended commitment in postconflict operations. Decision makers were concerned with getting bogged down in the "deep, costly engagements in their tangled internal politics."[51]

The obvious recourse was to design a way to leave Haiti quickly. As Michael Mandelbaum wrote in his critique of interventions of the 1990s, "As in Haiti, the chief purpose of an American expeditionary force in Bosnia will be to leave as soon as possible, with as few casualties as possible, rather than to do whatever is necessary, for as long as necessary, to keep (or make) peace."[52] One way to minimize the degree to which the United States would be involved in the those deep, costly engagements would be to turn operations over to a multinational force once the United States had restored Aristide to power. That force could serve as the U.S. exit strategy in Haiti, since the multinational force would then be responsible for the indefinite period of stability operations that the United States had little interest in pursuing. The best way to enlist a multilateral force was to obtain UN blessing, since other states conditioned their support on the operation being UN authorized. Canada and Venezuela, for example, were willing to participate in the peacekeeping force, but only if it had UN blessing.[53]

In the end, the United States was able to collect token Caribbean forces for the initial phases of the intervention and give the appearances of multilateralism without compromising the effectiveness of the mission[54] since these countries operated at the periphery and were not incorporated into combat plans. Once the United States had achieved some stability, it brought in the more robust multilateral peacekeeping force to assume responsibility in what was expected to be a long-enduring postconflict phase.

ALTERNATIVE EXPLANATIONS

The Strength of Norms: Haiti as a "Truly Multinational Effort"?

To the extent that rhetoric is an indicator of normative salience, then U.S. behavior in the 1994 Haiti intervention does offer some evidence that the multilateral norm had an effect on the *mode* of intervention. For example, Deputy Secretary of State Strobe Talbott touted the multilateral, legitimate nature of the intervention in congressional testimony: "Operation Uphold Democracy is a truly multinational effort, with participation from 30 other nations...Haiti's CARICOM neighbors...has matched its words with deeds, by contributing soldiers or police, or both, to the multinational force."[55] The

United States was clearly interested in being seen as multilateral and went to some lengths to frame its intervention in these terms. Contrary to normative accounts, however, the United States did *not* go to great lengths to orient its actions around multilateral strategy, and nor did it go multilaterally because it was "appropriate." It co-opted the participation of small Caribbean states, referred to by one military planner as "window dressing"[56] since these states did not influence combat plans, contributed few of the initial troops, and did not have a leadership role in the intervention. Claims of a "truly multinational effort" look dubious when compared with the peripheral role these states played in the intervention.

That the United States did go through the UN at all was something of a disjuncture for a state with a history of unilateralism in the region, however. The reason it did so is that U.S. power and leadership after the Cold War made UN authorization achievable and therefore obvious. The Israeli ambassador to the UN attributed the difference in opportunities for cooperation in the post–Cold War period with the one preceding it as follows: "In the past there were two drivers, the American and the Soviet. Now, the Soviet driver is more in the back seat of the car [with their political influence] less overwhelming."[57] The effect on the Security Council was that it was no longer deadlocked as it had been in the past but rather was now controlled by the interests of the United States.

In the specific case of Haiti, the effect of power manifested itself in several ways. It allowed the United States to buy the participation of small states such as Jamaica, Antigua and Barbuda, Belize, Trinidad and Tobago, and Barbados by paying their way.[58] The United States also "defray[ed] certain types of expenses" of the 24 other countries that would send postconflict stabilization troops into Haiti after the U.S.-led invasion, making it more attractive for them to participate. Those countries that did provide stabilization troops expected to keep the equipment that the United States issued to them during the operation.[59]

For Security Council states such as Russia, the cost was a quid pro quo. Russian Federation officials threatened a veto on a proposed Security Council resolution, arguing that the United States had not supported a Confederation of Independent States–sponsored peacekeeping mission in Georgia. Russia also protested that it would not support a mission that would impose a large bill on the organization. Ultimately, the United States accommodated Russian criticisms first by paying for almost the entirety of the Haiti mission and then by agreeing to authorize a Russian peacekeeping mission in Georgia,[60] both of which were relatively low-cost ways to avoid a Russian veto on the UNSC's Haiti resolution.

The process of logrolling in the UN, in which the United States pressured states to approve what was largely a unilateral intervention, did not go unnoticed by other states. As Cuba's ambassador to Mexico complained, "What is most disconcerting about all this is that the United States essentially made a unilateral decision which it railroaded through the United Nations without considering Latin American sentiments." Another Latin American diplomat agreed: "The U.S. didn't consult; it arm-twisted."[61]

The ease with which the United States was able to translate its preponderant power into a resolution on Haiti was not lost on outside observers either. As one critic of the possibility that U.S. power was being used to manipulate UN actions warned: "For the first time, the world's supreme international institution, in total disregard of its own Charter, gave legitimacy to the *realpolitik* tradition practiced by the United States…known as the Monroe Doctrine."[62] Draping the blue flag of the United Nations over a U.S. intervention demonstrated the possibility that the "hegemonic tactics and aspirations"[63] of a superpower could translate into a "planetary Leviathan"[64] in which the United States would enact its geopolitical objectives through the vehicle of the UN. Another critic of this outcome argued that the Security Council's "action in Haiti offers a lesson that has more to do with the power of the United States in the Council and the willingness of the P-5 to trade political support on issues of particular interest than it does on the notion that the Council members were moving into a new era" of principled collective justice.[65]

In short, the multilateral outcome of Haiti was less about the righteous pursuit of collective security and more about the ease with which it could obtain UN authorization and coax allies, albeit just for the convenient post-conflict phase of intervention. This combination made multilateralism an obvious, instrumental vehicle for the Haiti intervention. Had the United States recruited reluctant allies, compromised on the goals of the intervention, or ceded decision-making authority, the argument that the United States adhered to a multilateral norm would be stronger. Instead, U.S. cooperation was shallow. Its actions in a multilateral setting were little different from what they would have been had it intervened entirely alone.

To leave material power out of the analysis of why there was more cooperation at the end of the Cold War ignores the structural changes and the effect those changes had on cooperation. Because of the preponderance of U.S. power and the absence of a check on U.S. power in the Security Council, generating multilateral outcomes became almost pro forma. Multilateralism, both through the UNSC and with allies, was accessible at little cost, making it imprudent *not* to consider going through these channels.

THE SKEPTICAL DOMESTIC AUDIENCE

The 1994 Haiti intervention was the least popular use of force since the low points of the Vietnam War.[66] The prevailing view leading up to the intervention—both within Congress and among the skeptical American public—was that American troops "should only be asked to die when vital national interests are involved"[67]—and Haiti did not meet that criterion.

Few in Congress could identify strategic interests that warranted becoming mired in an open-ended conflict in Haiti. Fiercest opposition came from Republicans, with the likes of Senators McCain, Dole, and Thurmond suggesting that the Clinton administration had "backed into this mess" and that "risking American lives to keep Aristide in power is not an option."[68] More surprisingly, the president faced strong opposition from his own party. "I believe this is a formula for disaster," Democratic Senator Tom Harkin argued.[69] Another Democratic Senator, John Breaux, argued, "The situation in Haiti does not threaten national security...to a degree that would justify invasion."[70] In a letter to President Clinton, Oklahoma Democratic Senator David Boren cautioned: "An invasion could lead to a long period of unrest in Haiti which could require a continued American military presence for months or even years."[71]

The American public was no more disposed to support the intervention. Just one month before the intervention, less than 1 percent of Americans viewed Haiti as the most important problem facing the United States, well behind crime, health care, and the economy. When asked during the month of the intervention—a time that might normally see some "rally round the flag" bounce—whether Americans thought the national interests were at stake in Haiti, only 24 percent of Americans said yes, compared with 68 percent who did not.[72] More inauspiciously, a separate poll indicated that only 13 percent of Americans thought that national interest was at the source of a possible U.S. intervention in Haiti.[73] When asked whether sending troops to Haiti would be worth the potential cost, 61 percent responded negatively.[74] Asked a week ahead of the intervention whether the United States should lead a military invasion of Haiti, still only 23 percent said yes, and 73 percent responded no.[75]

With domestic levels of support being what they were, any intervention would seem to undermine a domestic politics argument. Casting further doubt on the influence of domestic politics, then National Security Advisor Anthony Lake admitted in a personal interview that decisions about consequential matters of national security such as the use of force were indeed not made on the basis of U.S. domestic preferences. The Haiti intervention was no exception to that.[76] Defending this view just days before the intervention, Secretary of State Warren Christopher asserted that "sometimes a president has a responsibility...to do what is in the nation's interest."[77] The administration had little choice but to take this perspective. Domestic opposition, particularly that in congress, had reached such a high pitch that intervening without domestic sanction was likely. Consulting Congress and not receiving its endorsement would be worse than bypassing it altogether.[78]

Despite arguments to the contrary, it is hard to dismiss altogether the influence of domestic politics. Though Congress as a whole was not supportive of intervention, support came from a vocal minority. Narrow blocs in Congress—particularly the Congressional Black Caucus and representatives from New York, New Jersey, and Florida, which all had large Haitian constituencies—advocated efforts to restore Aristide to power. Haitian immigrants in Manhattan had protested in support of action in Haiti; the "New York–Florida" lobby in Congress, which was important in supporting Clinton's domestic agenda, supported action; and African American leaders in the United States pushed for action in Haiti. Representative Maxine Waters supported Clinton's efforts "1,000 percent," and John Conyers concluded that "all other alternatives have failed, while the repression, torture and anti-democratic activities have continued."[79] The lobbying efforts of the Congressional Black Caucus—which included high-visibility hunger strikes and framing Clinton's existing Haiti policy as "racist"—elevated the issue of Haiti on the political agenda.[80] This constituency's efforts go some way toward explaining *why* the United States intervened, but cannot explain *how* the United States intervened.

A plausible account emerges with more nuanced data on public opinion. Despite the Haiti intervention being generally unpopular, support rose when Americans were asked about sharing the commitment with other states. When asked whether they supported unilateral intervention, only about 10 to 17 percent of Americans responded affirmatively, far lower than when asked about whether the United States should participate in a multilateral intervention. For example, when asked whether they would support U.S. intervention "along with troops from other countries," support rose to as high as 64 percent. While the "with allies" clause brought support up to only 39 percent in some polls, that number was considerably higher than the abysmally low numbers for "unilateral" or "leading an intervention" polls.[81] Polls consistently showed a gap between the level of support for the United States fighting unilaterally and for an operation in which the United States shared the burden with other states. The only polls that showed a plurality of support were those in which the question explicitly noted participation by other countries.[82]

Thus, with support for unilateral intervention in Haiti in the teens and multilateral intervention in the 50s to 60s, unilateralism implied some political costs and multilateralism afforded political, and therefore military, advantages. By claiming that the intervention was multilateral, the administration could thereby defuse any political or military missteps, asserting that the United States was merely acting as part of a broader multilateral, UN-authorized intervention. As Kenneth Schultz has suggested in his own case study of the intervention, "though public support for the intervention was never impressive, it mattered a great deal to the administration to have an international blessing."[83]

The perception of a multilateral intervention had the added benefit of playing to the political sensitivities of the local Haitian audience. Military planners had identified that the "enemy" center of gravity was as much about politics as force. The strategic center of gravity was the politico-military leadership structure, and the operational center of gravity was the army itself. Haiti was considered a military operation other than war, as with other humanitarian missions, peacekeeping, and stabilization operations. As the doctrine on operations other than war points out, "All military operations are driven by political considerations. However, in military operations other than war, political considerations permeate *all* levels and the military may not be the primary player.[84]

Against this operational backdrop, political sensitivities became as important as relative military size and technological capability. Putting an international face on the intervention was more likely to gain acceptance from the local domestic audience than a U.S.-only intervention.[85] Thus, generating even a "patina of UN legitimacy" and coalition support for a largely U.S. operation was useful for justifying the intervention to the local community.[86] It would demonstrate the international consensus against Cédras's rule and for regime change and be less likely to appear as an extension of U.S. imperialism.

Thus, while the operational imperatives created incentives to intervene through formal multilateral channels before incorporating full participation, the domestic audience's reluctance to use force in principle and the resulting preference for burden-sharing reinforced those incentives. The Clinton administration therefore gave the external appearance of multilateralism throughout, flaunting UN authorization and the coalition in a way that belied the less multilateral approach of the early phases.

ABSENCE OF REGIONAL POWERS AS A GREEN LIGHT FOR UNILATERALISM?

Since the regional power thesis would predict a unilateral intervention in the Western Hemisphere, given the absence of great powers, it is difficult to see how the Haiti case offers anything but disconfirming evidence for this thesis. Though the intervention shifted its cooperation strategy from formal to full multilateralism, at no time was it entirely unilateral as this thesis would predict. On the contrary, regional structure dynamics in the Western Hemisphere acted as an enabler for *multi*lateralism.

Several of the states with regional influence, including Mexico and Brazil, opposed the intervention, but their international influence was insufficient to block UN authorization. Mexico issued a statement proclaiming that authorizing the intervention "sets an extremely dangerous precedent in the field of international relations" because the situation in Haiti was not a disruption to peace and security. This position was in line with that of Uruguay, which indicated that it would not support an interrention, unilateral or multilateral. Brazil was a rotating member on the Security Council and said that "the Security Council's special powers should not be invoked in an indiscriminate manner in the name of a 'search for more rapid means' to respond to attacks on democracy, because it violates the basic principles of peaceful co-existence between nations and normal UN legal principles."[87] Brazil abstained from the vote, and Mexico had no institutional means by which to block the vote since it was not a rotating member on the Security Council. In short, some states in the region did oppose the intervention and multilateral authorization for the intervention but lacked the institutional power to block passage of the vote or the influence to convince veto players to block authorization.

The main international impediment to multilateralism in the Cold War—power politics between the United States and the USSR—had ceased to exist by 1994 and made cooperation possible in the case of Haiti. Whereas the Soviet Union had had geopolitical interests in the Western Hemisphere during the Cold War, such as with Grenada and Cuba, it had neither the resources nor the political commitment to pursue those interests in earnest after the Cold War, which opened up the possibility for broader cooperation since the USSR and the states allied to it would no longer have directly opposing interests in the region.

Thus, no states had reason or power to oppose multilateral authorization for a U.S. intervention in the region. The absence of regional interest or power translated not into a green light for *uni*lateralism but as an open avenue for *multi*lateralism. Regional power dynamics gave the United States license to intervene unilaterally, but contrary to these predictions, U.S. behavior varied between two types of multilateralism. The regional power argument is therefore an unsatisfactory guide to U.S. cooperation behavior in the 1994 Haiti intervention.

CONCLUSION

Despite the Clinton administration's rhetoric heralding multilateral involvement in Haiti, the degree of multilateralism looks less impressive when closely scrutinized. The United States intervened with UN authorization but paltry contributions from allies, especially in the initial phases. Nonetheless, the multilateral efforts it did make broke with a long history of unilateralism in the region. The basis of those efforts finds strong support from the time horizon–operational commitment thesis. Because Haiti was relatively inconsequential as a U.S. security interest, decision makers' time horizons were long, which allowed the United States to muddle through a three-year negotiation that culminated in UN authorization. But out of concerns for an open-ended intervention, the United States was careful to generate support for a multinational force that could act as a U.S. exit strategy for leaving Haiti, lest the United States become entrenched in a protracted nation-building exercise. In short, what drove the United States was not a principled pursuit of collective security but the knowledge that multilateralism was possible on its terms.

The case of Haiti offers less support for the multilateral norm argument, despite its being a most likely case for normative arguments. Why else would the United States bother with multilateralism against a mismatched adversary if not because of norms? The problem with this account is that it conflates the multilateral outcome with normative pressures to act multilaterally, without tracing how and why the United States arrived at a multilateral outcome. As this chapter shows, U.S. power in the post–Cold War period allowed it to dominate its allies, as well as UN decision-making outcomes. In exchange for underwriting the participation by Caribbean states and for voting to authorize Russian peacekeepers in Georgia, the United States co-opted states into participating and forestalled a veto in the UN Security Council. Indeed, U.S. influence in the UN Security Council reached such a point that the United States earned the moniker of the "Permanent One" in that it drove the agenda and essentially operated as the only veto player.[88] And contrary to the normative claim that states are willing to intervene multilaterally even when it compromises operational effectiveness, the analysis here shows that the United States was entirely *unwilling* to compromise the effectiveness of its operations and therefore only included allies once it had conducted the potentially more complex combat operations. The United States therefore did not act multilaterally out of a sense of "oughtness" but on the basis of means-end calculations.

In the case of Haiti, the domestic audience hypothesis does offer some useful insights. One the one hand, it may seem surprising that the Clinton administration intervened at all, given the unpopularity of the intervention both in Congress and among the public. On the other, the remarkable difference in public opinion on the question of unilateral intervention versus multilateral intervention—about a 40 to 50 percent difference in support— made multilateralism an obvious choice. Once the United States had decided to intervene on an issue that ranked low as a security issue for most Americans, multilateralism provided a way to defuse any political costs of an unpopular intervention. Not only did UN authorization garner greater public support but also it enabled the United States to leave Haiti more quickly because it had recruited states to which it could later transfer the peacekeeping responsibility, since states such as Canada and Venezuela had offered to participate under a UN-authorized intervention. Domestic support for multilateralism, however, would not explain why the United States pursued one multilateral strategy in the early phases of the operation and a fully multilateral strategy in the postconflict phase.

Last, the regional power dynamics argument found little support from a case in which unilateralism should have been the outcome but instead gave way to multilateralism. In fact, the Haiti case turned this explanation on its head. Whereas the absence of regional powers was hypothesized to give a green light to unilateral intervention, it instead gave a green light to multilateral authorization. The states in the region that opposed the intervention were simply not powerful enough to block the UN authorization for the use of force. States such as Brazil had to be content with an abstention and Mexico with words signaling that it hoped that the multilateral authorization would not set a precedent.

6

Afghanistan: The Mission Determines the Coalition

Q: "Is the coalition unraveling?"
A: "Well, let me make it clear. No single coalition has raveled. Therefore it's unlikely to unravel."

Press conference with Secretary of Defense
Donald Rumsfeld, October 2001

In the wake of 9/11, the United States saw an outpouring of international support on its behalf. From the now-famous "nous sommes tous americains" headline in *Le Monde* to the unprecedented Article V invocation by NATO to the unanimous condemnation of the attacks within the Security Council, the United States enjoyed a rare respite in anti-Americanism and resistance to U.S. policies abroad.[1] In principle, that support extended to U.S. retaliation through the use of force, supported by United Nations Resolution 1368 that affirmed "the right of individual or collective self-defense."[2] Yet in practice, the United States exercised its self-defense almost entirely individually, intervening in Afghanistan with minor participation from the United Kingdom but otherwise with its own financial and personnel resources. With overwhelming levels of support and numerous offers for operational assistance, why did the United States undertake the Afghanistan intervention unilaterally? What explains the willingness to engage the international community at later phases of the operation and the degree to which it did so along the way?

The question of American unilateralism is even more puzzling when one considers that the strategic goal of a full elimination of the Taliban, combined with a destruction of al Qaeda's infrastructure in Afghanistan,[3] was highly ambitious, particularly given the historical cases of war in Afghanistan. Britain had expended untold resources in the course of three wars with Afghanistan, none of which produced favorable strategic outcomes for Britain.[4] The Soviet Union had also attempted to conquer Afghanistan and committed national treasure to do so, only to evacuate a decade later, having failed in its objectives and suffered economic despair as a result.[5] Afghanistan had come to be known as a "graveyard of empire." Its history of bringing advanced militaries to their knees made it reasonable to assume that the United States might see a reprise of those challenges and therefore want to assemble a formidable offense.[6]

Indeed, the list of states that contributed to the broader U.S. "war on terror"—assisting with intelligence, freezing financial assets, and providing basing support and overflight rights—was impressive. Willing contributors were readily available: "The uniquely appalling character and magnitude of the September 11 attacks, coupled with the determined yet measured character of the administration's gathering response, naturally helped to bring together many coalition players who otherwise would have been more hesitant."[7] Most of the contributions the United States accepted, however, initially fell under the heading of "support." In terms of direct contributions to the early phases of military intervention and later combat operations, state participation was limited. France, Canada, and Australia promised forthcoming support, but with the exception of Britain, which was involved mostly in launching standoff Tomahawk missiles, supplying refueling, and contributing some commandos,[8] the United States operated largely on its own.[9] Three weeks into operations, Thomas Friedman observed, "My fellow Americans, I hate to say this, but except for the good old Brits, we're all alone. And at the end of the day, it's U.S. and British troops who will have to go in, on the ground, and eliminate bin Laden."[10]

Over time, however, the United States did seek a UN mandate and allied participation for its postconflict reconstruction operations. Thus, careful consideration of cooperation behavior across the Afghanistan case suggests that this single longitudinal case is actually better treated as two cases because of an important change in multilateral cooperation over time. This paired comparison controls for several alternative explanations—international norms, domestic politics, and regional power, all of which remained constant across time—and isolates the operational factors that I suggest account for differences in cooperation outcomes over time: time horizon and operational commitment.

This chapter begins by discussing the U.S. military response to 9/11, tracing how the United States largely eschewed offers of allied assistance and intervened in Afghanistan with limited support from the British and the Northern Alliance. It then suggests that the short time horizon after 9/11 and faith in what became known as the Afghan Model—reliance on small numbers of special operations forces (SOF) instead of large numbers of conventional forces—made allied support seem both unnecessary and potentially counterproductive. Longer time horizons that followed the fall of the Taliban coupled with the realization that postconflict operations would be lengthy and costly produced the multilateral strategy that later incorporated

international institutions and a number of allies that had offered to contribute at the outset. As the chapter then shows, norms and domestic politics
had little effect on the cooperation strategy, the former because norms were
relegated to a distant second priority behind effectiveness after 9/11 and the
latter because both the public and Congress wrote the president a blank
check for the post-9/11 response. The Afghanistan case study finally turns to
the regional power argument, which finds support from U.S. actions to obtain
logistics support from states in the region whose assistance was imperative
and whose interference would have created prohibitive obstacles.

THE POST-9/11 REACTION

After each of the smaller scale terrorist attacks prior to 9/11, the United States
had responded largely through law enforcement actions and limited air
strikes.[11] As individuals in the CIA and executive branch quickly and asser-
tively concluded, the magnitude of the 9/11 attacks called for a considerably
stronger response: "The classical European model—it has no application here"
according to Cofer Black, the former Director of the CIA's Counterterrorism
Center.[12] Law enforcement, in other words, would not be the answer. Cultivation
of intelligence assets over time would not work either. Rather, the so-called war
on terror would begin as a military response. In this spirit, President Bush
promised the public that while "this conflict was begun on the timing and
terms of others, it will end in a way and at an hour of our choosing."[13]

Within days of 9/11, CIA teams moved into Afghanistan, followed by
12-man Operational Detachment Alpha teams operating as part of Task
Force Dagger. Working with some indigenous forces on the ground, these
SOF teams proceeded to degrade Taliban positions in the north, take Mazar-
e-Sharif and Kabul, and ultimately provoke the Taliban's surrender in
Kandahar, almost exclusively with U.S. special forces, close air support,
command and control, logistics, and decision-making authority.[14] The early
phases of the air campaign were also relatively light, designed to eliminate
air defenses (which it did within two weeks), damage al Qaeda training sites,
and target the major Taliban stronghold cities, including Kabul, Jalalabad,
and Kandahar. In November 2001, the air campaign escalated, and the United
States targeted Taliban front lines with 15,000-pound daisy cutter bombs,
paving the way for the Northern Alliance to take Mazar-e-Sharif, on the route
of a major Taliban supply line. The Northern Alliance took Mazar-e-Sharif
on 9 November, seizing the main military base, and Herat, Kabul, and
Jalalabad followed soon thereafter.[15]

By November, the United States had made significant progress against a
state that as of 7 October 2001 had had 80 percent of its territory controlled

by the Taliban. By the end of November, Kandahar remained as the last Taliban stronghold; a thousand marines arrived at the desert south of Kandahar and ultimately prompted its surrender, which allowed the marines to capture the Kandahar air base as its own. The marines secured Kandahar by mid-December, and the inauguration of the Afghan interim government took place on 22 December 2001, just 78 days after the launch of operations.[16]

In this initial intervention, the United States kept allied participation limited. Though specific data on troop numbers remain guarded, it is clear that while the United States had sought a global coalition for coordinating the law enforcement, intelligence sharing, and financial network aspects of the war on terror, it imposed serious restrictions on international participation in the military aspects of the campaign and resisted offers of assistance. Early evidence of this preference for unilateral control is clear in the principals' meetings that took place soon after the 9/11 attacks. In their discussions on the potential role of allies, then National Security Advisor Condoleezza Rice mentioned the number of allies—specifically, the Australians, French, Canadians, and Germans—who were offering their assistance to the operation. To this, Secretary Rumsfeld responded that "we want to include them if we can," but he voiced his concern that allied military forces could interfere with the effectiveness of U.S. forces. Instead of molding the operational plan to the availability of allies, the coalition had to be hand-selected to accommodate the operational needs of the conflict.[17] The military commanders and the administration had an interest in minimizing allied forces' integration into operational plans until the United States had secured regions of Afghanistan. From the get-go, "the Pentagon did not want to open up its operational military plan against the Taliban to a lot of other players."[18]

Further, the United States was reluctant to intervene in Afghanistan with a formal multilateral institution. Instead of accepting material offers and integrating NATO into its campaign plans, the United States chose to position NATO assets domestically as part of Operation Noble Eagle, the homeland security mission. None of NATO's collective assets deployed to Afghanistan. As evidence of the fact that Europe would not be any center or periphery of gravity, one U.S. senior official said, "I think it's safe to say that we won't be asking SACEUR [the Supreme Allied Commander, Europe] to put together a battle plan for Afghanistan."[19] There was a clear interest in avoiding the "cumbersome military command and planning structure" of a multilateral military organization such as NATO.[20] As Deputy Defense Secretary Paul Wolfowitz made clear in September 2001: "We think we had a collective affirmation of support with what they said with Article Five, and if we need collective action we'll ask for it. We don't anticipate that at the moment.... We need cooperation from many countries but we need to take it in appropriately flexible ways."[21] A spokesman for Central Command (CENTCOM), Rear Admiral Craig Quigley, defended this approach, saying, "You take them [allies] up on their offers at the location and time and manner that fits into the overall fabric of Enduring Freedom...the best intentions in the world, if provided in an uncoordinated way, makes things worse instead of better."[22] American military and civilian commanders made it abundantly clear that the United States was unwilling to engage in what it saw as the unreliability of multilateralism while still in the midst of combat operations.

With regard to the allies it did incorporate, it did so bilaterally, cautiously, and largely after or outside combat operations rather than multilaterally and during the early phases of combat. While the British military supplied the Nimrod reconnaissance platform and tanker support, contributed logistics support, and launched some Tomahawk cruise missiles from submarines in early October 2001, it did not have any aircraft in a shooting role or ground forces in Afghanistan as of late October 2001, several weeks into combat operations.[23] At that time, British Defence Secretary Geoff Hoon predicted that it would be "some time" before the British actually became involved in direct military action in Afghanistan.[24]

Not until mid-November did Britain dispatch its first 100 commandos to Bagram and put an additional 6,400 regular forces on 48-hour alert for action, allocations that would have constituted the first major foreign contribution in Afghanistan. In what amounted to an awkward diplomatic incident between the United States and Britain, CENTCOM instructed forces to stand by because Afghan leaders had not cleared the British deployment. Afghan Foreign Minister Abdullah Abdullah reportedly said that the British forces had not been invited, asserting to one of the U.S. CIA officers: "This is a violation of our sovereignty. If we are not to be a sovereign nation I should resign. We would prefer that they [the British] leave."[25] The British deployment was subsequently put on hold, prompting Britain's top minister for international assistance to accuse the United States of snubbing its British partner.[26] One of Britain's conservative newspapers, typically supportive of operations in Afghanistan, scored the incident as "the British Government's first real embarrassment since Mr. Blair gave his full backing to America after the September 11 terrorist attacks."[27]

Part of the confusion on the part of eager allied participants resulted from the disorder coming from the United States, which was not necessarily making decisions as a unitary actor but separately as the State Department and the Pentagon, which had different views on whether and when allied peacekeepers should be integrated. State Department officials tended to be more receptive to the European and allied position, agreeing to accept their deployment earlier rather than later, but the Defense Department was highly skeptical, resisting their participation at all, and certainly not until the military finished the combat phase of the campaign.[28]

Other states such as Australia, Canada, Denmark, France, Poland, and Germany did contribute some SOF, but most of these were deployed several months after the fall of the Taliban and were not integrated into U.S. campaign plans. Jordanian and French forces had deployed to Uzbekistan as part of a plan to set up a field hospital. However, CENTCOM postponed all of these offers until they had established better security, which was in most cases after the fall of the Taliban at the end of 2001.[29] Canadian special forces numbered about 250 to 300 but were deployed as part of a small security detail operating mostly outside Afghanistan.[30]

Though not a state ally, the Northern Alliance produced one of the more notable contributions to early operations in Afghanistan. Reliance on their loose coalition of forces was central to the Afghan Model of warfare, which called for involvement of local opposition armies. Working closely with U.S. SOF teams, the Northern Alliance helped capture areas such as Mazar-i-Sharif and Kabul, in part through its experience fighting a 20-year civil war with the Taliban.[31] Though the Afghan Model hinged on an alignment with the Northern Alliance, this group's role was limited to the following tasks: "Screen U.S. SOF from hostile patrols...mop up surviving remnants, to occupy abandoned territory (often politically important that local forces be the ones to take control of the ground that the Precision Guided Munitions effectively clear)."[32] The Northern Alliance may have been an important condition for intervention, but it was generally limited in its role, capability, and influence on U.S. campaign plans. But other than this nonstate and to some extent the British, the United States conducted the combat phase of operations largely alone, using a combination of Army Green Berets and CIA teams to achieve its early goals.[33]

When the Taliban fell, the vanquisher's identity was relatively clear. As the British *Independent* concluded, "In military terms the capitulation of the Taliban was a U.S. victory. British troops played only a peripheral part."[34] Given that the British were the most central of any ally, this observation is a telling reflection of the degree to which U.S. operations during these early phases fell well short of being multilateral.

The Transition to Multilateralism for Stabilization and Reconstruction

The operation in Afghanistan ultimately transitioned into a genuine multilateral coalition in which the United States assumed about half the personnel burden alongside dozens of other troop-contributing nations.[35] That Afghanistan eventually became multilateral may prompt some criticism about the characterization that the operation was not multilateral. In fact, however, the Afghanistan intervention can be considered as two separate campaigns, and the varying degrees of cooperation between the two shed important light on motivations and willingness to engage in multilateral military cooperation under varying conditions.[36]

The primary campaign was the removal of the Taliban regime and the destruction of Al Qaeda's safe haven and disruption of its organization. Activities in this first campaign were characterized by high-intensity combat operations. This campaign saw its greatest intensity in the early months— from October 2001 to Operation Anaconda in March 2002—but continued with offensive counterterrorism operations in the years following. Initially operating under Combined Forces Command-Alpha until its disbandment in early 2007, and since generically as Operation Enduring Freedom (OEF) counterterrorism operations, the participants in this mission were mostly American, along with a few Canadian and British forces that were mostly unconstrained in the rules of engagement by which they operated.[37]

The follow-on set of operations began after the fall of Kabul and with the December 2001 Bonn Conference for Afghanistan reconstruction that created the grounds for the International Security Assistance Force (ISAF), created to help the Afghan Transitional Government create security in the country. While this campaign overlapped temporally with the ongoing combat operations in parts of Afghanistan, it was responsible for what would normally be considered stabilization and reconstruction operations. It involved lower intensity operations mandated by explicit UN authorization. Originally operating only in Kabul, the subsequent mandate of 13 October 2003 expanded ISAF's mission to areas beyond the capital as different quadrants of the country stabilized.[38] That same year, ISAF—which became NATO-led in 2006—expanded its area of responsibility to all of Afghanistan.[39] Its portfolio was largely restricted to stability operations rather than active, offensive counterterrorism operations. Rules of engagement generally allowed NATO ISAF to confront spoilers, but the NATO secretary general made it clear that "that does not mean that there is no difference between the counterinsurgency, counterterrorism mandate of Operation Enduring Freedom and ISAF."[40] The former had a mandate for offensive operations, while the latter primarily for defensive stabilization operations.

In most cases of conflict, the progression from combat operations (the OEF mission) to postconflict reconstruction and stability (the ISAF mission) is linear; the latter follows once combat operations are complete. In the case of Afghanistan, those phases overlapped, varying more by geography and by whom the operations are conducted rather than distinguished chronologically.[41] The United States conducted its counterterrorism areas in the hostile regions of the country, including the eastern Waziristan area bordering Pakistan, and other troop-contributing states, particularly those such as Germany that are bound by national caveats[42] restricting their ability to conduct combat operations, operated in less restive parts of the country, such as the north.[43]

WITH FRIENDS LIKE THESE, WHY GO IT ALONE?

Two factors combined to make multilateralism less attractive than undertaking combat operations alone in Afghanistan. First, the attacks of 9/11 had the effect of making short-term interests a higher priority than longer term considerations. In his testimony to the National Commission on Terrorist Attacks Upon the United States, Cofer Black testified that in terms of how the government viewed and acted on threats, "All I want to say is that there was 'before' 9/11 and 'after' 9/11."[44] Before 9/11, the United States had had an ad hoc approach to counterterrorism. Most of "the government only glimpsed the problem" of terrorism and assumed that episodes such as embassy bombings were isolated events that did not warrant a systematic strategy. Anything beyond limited airstrikes was off-limits, and even airstrikes were undertaken only with high levels of fidelity that the United States would hit the target and cause little to no collateral damage.[45] Richard Clarke, then the counterterrorism advisor on the National Security Council, described the approach in the following way: "You are left with a modest effort to swat flies, to try to prevent specific al Qaeda attacks by using [intelligence] to detect them and friendly governments' police and intelligence officers to stop them. You are left waiting for the big attack, with lots of casualties, after which some major U.S. retaliation will be in order."[46] The big attack was 9/11, and it dislodged what had been a firmly planted notion that a terrorist attack on U.S. soil was a "remote" possibility. It ended the "risk averse" approach to counterterrorism that had characterized the government throughout the 1990s.[47]

With this post-9/11 mentality came a momentum toward quick retaliation, the concern being that "the longer UBL [Usama bin Laden] is free, the greater risk of a hit here at home" according to Vice President Cheney.[48] Director of the CIA George Tenet generally shared this view. Still weeks after 9/11, he continued to think "we're behind the eight ball here…UBL either has a bomb now or won't rest until he has one…my gut instinct is we're in big trouble."[49] A sense of panic about "second wave" attacks dominated after 9/11.[50] Uncertainty about when and where the next attack would come had the effect of making longer term priorities subordinate to short-term security requirements. Multilateral burden-sharing might pay in the longer term, but several other shorter term factors complicated the incorporation of allies.

The first was the campaign planning process. What was typically a 12-month process was severely compressed; military planners had to scramble to expedite planning and to coordinate, mobilize, and deploy joint U.S. assets in the less than one-month window between 9/11 and 7 October 2001, when operations began.[51] Generating intelligence analysis of Afghanistan, developing military plans, identifying contingency plans, and mobilizing military forces had proven to be a considerable interagency challenge in that short window. Multinational contributions would be prohibitively challenging since as Secretary Rumsfeld pointed out, "we're not able to define a special operations role for our own forces…until we do that, how can we talk about including others?"[52]

Second, the problem of incorporating other states' interests and assets was compounded because few institutional structures were in place for sharing classified information. In the weeks after 9/11, representatives from a multitude of countries descended on CENTCOM headquarters. Though these would-be contributors were well intentioned, military planners indicated in interviews that genuine coordination of national policies was next to impossible because of the number of countries and interests represented, the lack of existing information-sharing agreements with many of these countries, and the fact that their arrival coincided so closely with frenzied American campaign planning. "National policy coordination" took the form of each country taking sanitized—unclassified or lower levels of classification—U.S. planning documents back to their state capitals as a document on which they had no veto rights.[53] If planning quickly for a major war was already a challenge, turning to outside sources for support was even more questionable, especially given the inability to share critical planning documents.

Third, the short time line created constraints on the degree of multilateralism from a mobilization and logistics standpoint. Many states appeared willing to help materially, but few if any had assets that could deploy to Afghanistan within the short window from 9/11 to the inception of operations.[54] For example, Europeans lacked strategic airlift that would have been required to deploy assets to landlocked Afghanistan. Without U.S. airlift, which was focused on deploying U.S. rather than foreign assets to theater within this short window, allied assets were unavailable to be incorporated, which added to concerns about reliability.[55]

In sum, where short-term security challenges were at unprecedented levels, the travails of interagency planning, the sharing of sensitive operational intelligence, and the deployment of a number of coalition partners without their own airlift became prohibitively onerous, making a go-it-alone strategy seem far more expedient. Remarking on the potential consequences of incorporating allies, one RAND study sympathized that "American commanders, for good reason, were concerned that the integration of allied forces might retard or degrade combat."[56] As the next section details, campaign plans that called for small numbers of special operations forces gave further incentive to sidestep multilateral channels.

The Afghan Model and Low Payoffs for Multilateralism

Soon after 9/11, CENTCOM and the CIA began drafting potential plans for an invasion of Afghanistan, since the U.S. government had never anticipated or planned for an intervention in Afghanistan. The two sets of plans diverged dramatically. In one plan, CENTCOM had created 150 PowerPoint slides whose force flow changed daily but revolved around three main options: "bombs, more bombs, and even more bombs," as one army officer referred to the plans. This plan involved sending large numbers of ground forces—about five divisions—into Afghanistan.[57]

The CIA created an alternative plan, which focused on a lighter force reliant on U.S. SOF units working with CIA pilot teams that would enter Afghanistan in October 2001. They viewed the next six months as a Valley Forge in which they would link up with the Northern Alliance units and build up their military capability, setting the stage for the arrival of the first of four U.S. Army divisions in the spring of 2002. Early deployments of SOF units and CIA partners were intended to be part of a 180-day preparation that would do classic SOF missions: training plans, working with resistance forces and guerrillas, and fighting until the heavier divisions could arrive six to nine months later, whether from Pakistan and above Kabul, or through Uzbekistan.[58]

In a presentation to the Bush administration at Camp David on 15-16 September 2001, Director of Central Intelligence George Tenet presented the lighter, more agile CIA plan. The approach resonated with the Bush administration, which believed that "you don't fight terrorists with conventional capabilities. You do it with unconventional capabilities."[59] What came to be known as the Afghan Model had an emphasis on small numbers of SOF units working with indigenous allies and with the aid of precision-guided munitions.[60] It became the working plan of CENTCOM.[61]

In addition to Rumsfeld's bias toward transformational, agile special operations forces, several factors pointed in the direction of using SOF troops. One was geography; Afghanistan was extraordinarily mountainous compared with the desert flats of the Middle East, so hauling in five divisions of ground forces would be challenging at best. Moreover, it had no access to the sea; as one military planner said, "Due to the land-locked nature of Afghanistan, traditional ground forces were a non-starter. Therefore, heavy reliance on SOF became standard."[62] The mountainous terrain of Afghanistan was more likely to require forces riding on horses, a practice in which U.S. and British forces had some experience, than large divisions of ground forces.[63]

Planners also concluded that the Soviet experience with large conventional forces in Afghanistan had led to their ultimate demise and should not be replicated; the United States knew that if its military forces "repeated the mistakes of the Soviets by invading with a large land force, they would be doomed."[64] Smaller numbers of special operations troops seemed to offer the most favorable prospects for victory.

Moreover, military leaders intended to rely on SOF because of the lack of high-value targets; as Rumsfeld noted two days into the bombing: "That country has been at war for a very long time. The Soviet Union pounded it year after year after year. Much of the country is rubble. They have been fighting among themselves. They do not have high-value targets or assets that are the kinds of things that would lend themselves to substantial damage."[65] Without high-value targets, military planners concluded that a combination of special operations forces, precision munitions, and an indigenous ally would be the most successful way to wage the campaign.[66] Operational success using this model of warfare looked overdetermined.

The Afghan Model, however, which theoretically employed 50 U.S. special forces to achieve the conventional military equivalent of 50,000 ground troops, had little slack in it for additional coalition forces.[67] While the United States also had fewer SOF forces, slightly less than 50,000 in late 2001,[68] far fewer troops were needed than would be required for a conventional attack. In the days after 9/11, U.S. special forces and intelligence officers landed in Afghanistan and began setting up contacts with the Northern Alliance's leadership and intelligence entities; these forces kept an extremely low profile and were few in number.[69] At least two weeks into the campaign, there were still just a handful of U.S. personnel on the ground,[70] and as late as November 2001, only several hundred American forces—largely special operations forces—were on the ground in Afghanistan,[71] generally operating under the organizational unit of the 12-man Operational Detachment Alpha groups, or A-teams.[72] By March 2002, the United States had just 5,200 combat troops in Afghanistan,[73] fewer troops than the United States had sent to safeguard the Salt Lake City Olympics. Operations in Afghanistan imposed challenges to U.S. forces, but in no way overtaxed the military or threatened draining the Pentagon's financial or personnel coffers.[74]

As CENTCOM Commander Tommy Franks said in reference to the few resources deployed in Afghanistan, progress in Afghanistan would need to be measured by different yardsticks than those used for past operations. "Those who expect another Desert Storm (and the huge number of ground troops) will wonder every day what this war is all about. This is a different war."[75] In Desert Storm, military planners had expected a large conventional war with a large, well-trained Iraqi military. Planners for the Afghanistan war expected an altogether different style of warfare, one that was lighter and less onerous. The Afghan Model's emphasis on the efficiency of SOF meant fewer operational burdens and fewer incentives to incorporate allies.

Not only were more troops not needed, but more might actually have been unhelpful. The U.S. goal was to eliminate the Taliban and al Qaeda while leaving infrastructure such as roads and electrical power in place for humanitarian relief and reconstruction.[76] With these goals in mind, a massive campaign, such as the air and land campaign of the Gulf War, would vastly outsize what was thought to be the appropriate amount of force in Afghanistan. Rather, they intended to have "the smallest possible military presence on the ground in Afghanistan, a concern that ruled out any heavy US conventional ground force involvement."[77] It also essentially ruled out assistance from other states that would add to the footprint and thereby be counterproductive to setting the stage for postwar reconstruction. A smaller, lower impact force that disrupted the terrorist networks but left infrastructure largely in place would be more suitable and effective.

Though there was some notional idea that the Afghanistan operation would necessarily require "regime change," the focus going into Afghanistan was on military objectives rather than on institution building after combat. As Conrad Crane, a leading author of the Army's Counter insurgency Field Manual, observed "a campaign plan was not completed until late November," and the combination of the unexpected Taliban collapse and the planning focus on combat rather than on postconflict plans meant that no serious consideration had been given to the political objectives,[78] including who would govern Afghanistan, how the United States would go about constructing a democratic government, and how the military objectives related to any political objectives.[79] The United States was focused on its immediate military objectives of hitting specific targets, ridding Afghanistan of the Taliban and al Qaeda, and finding foes such as bin Laden and Mullah Omar. Rebuilding the country was a distant goal, one that the United States confronted sequentially, after it had achieved its more immediate security objectives.[80]

The result was that "in Afghanistan, there was no phase IV [postconflict planning] ... there was then a scramble to create a Phase IV plan. It was done initially from a top down approach and modified to employ provisional reconstruction teams."[81] In a memo dated 11 October 2001, four days after the invasion, the under secretary of defense for policy outlined that "creating a stable, post-Taliban Afghanistan is desirable but not necessarily within the power of the US."[82] The main goals were shorter term in nature: the elimination of al Qaeda and the Taliban's leadership and forces.

In prioritizing these goals, however, planners neglected the longer term goals of postconflict stability. As an internal Army War College memo observed, "The Afghanistan situation had been marred by the excessively short-term approach of the top defense leaders...who maintained a 'tactical focus that ignores long-term objectives.'"[83] As late as November, 2001, U.S. senior leaders were asserting that the United States would not maintain a long-term military presence in Afghanistan.[84] Emphasis on shorter term military objectives rather than longer term reconstruction plans meant that the advantages of having allies in the postconflict phase were obscured by the potential challenges they might introduce in the combat phases. Only in early 2002 did the administration have its "first chance to look beyond its initial retaliation in Afghanistan."[85]

In short, what became known as the Afghan Model put an emphasis on small numbers of special forces, which meant that there was little burden to share in the combat phase and few incentives to incorporate allies. Campaign planning in Afghanistan was short-term and ignored the longer term consideration of reconstruction and stability operations, which further minimized the potential benefit of allies.

WHY SHIFT COOPERATION STRATEGIES MIDSTREAM?

Afghanistan's within-case variation—largely unilateral in combat operations and multilateral in postconflict reconstruction—offers a way to control for several possible explanations, such as norms, domestic politics, and regional power dynamics. As later sections show, none of these changed over time. What did change was the U.S. time horizon and its expectation about operational commitment; only once it addressed the short-term security challenges was it willing to incorporate allies. Having confronted some of the short-term issues, the United States recognized the high operational commitment associated with stability operations and sought multilateral assistance for the open-ended commitment in Afghanistan. This section traces in more detail how changes in cooperation strategies over time corresponded with changes in time horizon and operational commitment.

One of the clearest indications for why the United States cooperated as it did is the timing with which it moved from unilateral to multilateral strategies. It is no coincidence that the transition to ISAF occurred counterclockwise in Afghanistan, from the north to the west, the south, and then finally to the east, as this is the direction in which stability took root in Afghanistan. Not until it had established a robust degree of security and addressed the short-term threats in a given quadrant did ISAF take over. Commanders in Afghanistan kept a color-coded chart that cited the number of daily attacks across Afghanistan. Only once those areas attained a certain level of stability—with levels of stability being a proxy for the level of Taliban and al Qaeda presence and therefore for possible short-term security concerns—was the United States willing to transition responsibility to ISAF. In areas where security remained tenuous, such as the border with Pakistan, the United States retained control with a large counterterrorism force that operates outside NATO-ISAF. That counterterrorism force remained unencumbered by rules of engagement or coordination costs associated with collective decision making by acting largely alone.[86]

After the fall of the Taliban, it became clear that the stabilization and reconstruction phases would be lengthy and costly; the recognition that postconflict operations would be a multibillion-dollar, multiyear process and that the United States could not win this phase "cheaply" made allies more attractive. As Richard Haass testified to the Senate Foreign Relations Committee in December 2001, the United States had conducted the "lion's share of the work" in the combat phase and successfully defeated the Taliban. He called on the international community to share the burden of the "the reconstruction effort, which should not be a mostly U.S. effort."[87] Pentagon spokesperson Torie Clarke affirmed that "the United States doesn't plan to have a large presence in a peacekeeping operation,"[88] and indeed, the United States transferred much of the peacekeeping burden to allies.

It also helped that in this longer and costlier second phase, the coordination exercise represented a different and significantly more manageable set of issues than those of the combat phase. Interoperability problems and prohibitive rules of engagement among coalition members remained as frustrating challenges throughout peacekeeping operations. A former commander of U.S. and Allied Naval Forces, Admiral Johnson, referred to the problem of prohibitive national caveats, a set of restrictions on where and how a state can conduct operations, as "a cancer that eats away at the effective usability of troops."[89] But that cancer is much less damaging in postconflict than in combat operations. One reason is that a principal task of the peacekeeping mission is the conduct of patrols and reconstruction and development efforts, activities that are much more about demonstrating a physical presence than about wielding a weapon. Former Combined Forces Command-Alpha commander and later Ambassador to Afghanistan, Lt. Gen. Karl Eikenberry, pointed out that in this phase of operations "establishing presence is as important as clever military equipment."[90] This is in large part because, as the former Supreme Allied Commander General Jones indicated, "the solution in Afghanistan is not a military one."[91] And in these nonmilitary endeavors, in which the coalition is playing a strong role, national caveats are much less likely to come into play than in combat operations.[92] Moreover, the consequences of divergent approaches to economic development and patrols are likely to be less lethal than, for example, divergences in active, offensive counterterrorism operations.

Multilateral postconflict operations have not been without challenges, of course. The typically diplomatic Secretary of Defense Robert Gates criticized coalition forces in Afghanistan who "don't know how to do counterinsurgency operations."[93] It is clear that despite these challenges, the benefits of multilateral operations, in which the U.S. has been able to share the costly burden of intervention, have far exceeded these cooperation challenges.

ALTERNATIVE EXPLANATIONS

In addition to the operational motivations behind unilateral and later multilateral behavior, the United States had few domestic and international constraints on the way it approached the intervention. The international multilateral norm seemed to be superseded by the dramatic nature of the 9/11 attacks and was limited in its effect. The domestic audience was overwhelmingly supportive of military force and granted the administration considerable autonomy with respect to its desired cooperation strategy. Finally, the United States had sufficient power and ample goodwill, including from Russia, to minimize its investment in regional allies for the operation in Afghanistan.

The Subordination of Norms after 9/11

After the end of the Cold War, the degree to which states intervened multilaterally increased, in large part because the power politics that had paralyzed cooperation efforts during the Cold War had yielded to a new sense of international cooperation, further reinforced by the positive example of the 1990–1991 Gulf War. According to some scholars, these events heralded the post–Cold War internalization of a multilateral norm, in which states would intervene multilaterally not based on the logic of consequences—in which states consider their material interests and make decisions through a means-ends calculation of what is in their interests—but rather on the logic of appropriateness,[94] which considers "identities more than interests" and is based on the "selection of rules more than with individual rational expectations."[95]

Although those two logics are not mutually exclusive and can coexist under certain conditions, one of the two tends to dominate. "When preferences and consequences are precise and identities or their rules are ambiguous, a logic of consequences tends to be more important."[96] The post-9/11 environment matches these conditions closely. Under a direct attack, prefer-ences for state survival became the clearest, highest priority. Moreover, rules for how to retaliate against this new type of threat and adversary were decid-edly unclear. An attack of this scale had not hit the United States since Pearl Harbor, leading, as the 9/11 Commission wrote, to a "nation transformed" as of 8:45 on the morning of 9/11. That nation was unequipped with precedents on how to handle the terrorist threat.[97] In the absence of clear retaliatory rules and in the presence of clear threat to security, the logic of consequences dominated U.S. decision making.

International norms in general, and the multilateral norm specifically, became less salient to decision makers than considering what actions would most likely contribute to security. Coalition-building strategies may have been the norm during the 1990s, when state security appeared to be dominated by economic considerations and the United States became more involved in a post–Cold War affinity for humanitarian interventions and needed a host of other states to share the burden.[98] The new approach, or at least that in Afghanistan, could not afford to be quite as inclusive in bringing in the panoply of states that had tended to dominate the peacekeeping missions of the 1990s. Common in these UN-led operations was the participation of less advanced militaries in multilateral peacekeeping coalitions; as of 2007, 8 of the top 10 troop-contributing states were developing countries.[99] Though at times criti-cized for their military capabilities, commitment, and performance in some peacekeeping missions,[100] their participation was a hallmark of UN missions after the Cold War.[101]

Unlike many of the previous post–Cold War interventions, the Afghanistan intervention lacked almost all pretense of multilateralism. As General Franks said regarding allied involvement, "When the timing is appropriate, we will put them in as required."[102] In spite of the many coali-tion offers, the highly selective use of allies reflects no normative pressure to conduct its intervention multilaterally; rather, the United States was more inclined to intervene in a way that it deemed would maximize effec-tiveness rather than a perception of legitimacy. Secretary Rumsfeld infa-mously derided allied contributions to the Afghanistan mission in the following way:

> We did a couple of other things I think that were helpful. One was we said there's not a single coalition. Had there been, that coalition, the first person that peeled off on something they wanted to do, we would have said it's crum-bling, it's all over, we've lost the coalition. So we from the get-go said look, there are floating coalitions, and the mission's going to determine the coalition. The coalition is not going to determine the mission because it will dumb down everything to the lowest common denominator.[103]

Between such flippant references to coalitions and General Franks's utilitarian argument about allied involvement, the United States made it clear that this was an operation predicated entirely on effectiveness and consequences rather than on normative appropriateness. In spite of the largely unilateral combat operation in Afghanistan, with some notable exceptions, the United States did take some care to generate multilateral assistance for its broader "war on terror" and rhetorically cast the operation as widely sanctioned by the international community. Even Secretary of Defense Rumsfeld, who often showed contempt for coalition operations,[104] at other times expressed appreciation for "the representatives of the many nations in our coalition, [who] are helping to defeat an adversary that has declared war on our people and indeed on our way of life."[105]

Such rhetoric may indicate normative pull but does not meet the benchmarks that proponents of normative arguments have outlined: Was the United States willing to adhere to multilateralism even when doing so compromised the mission's effectiveness? Did it expend significant resources to build a coalition even in a clear case of aggression that would legitimately provoke a unilateral response? Did the United States work through the UN even though the source of provocation was uncontested, as it had been during the Gulf War?[106] The U.S. military response in Afghanistan exhibited none of these indicators of appropriateness. Rhetoric may be an indicator of normative salience, but U.S. rhetoric largely failed this test; moreover, it is a dramatically lower bar than a test of action, which the U.S. propensity for unilateralism certainly did not meet.

The Permissiveness of Domestic Politics after 9/11

In the case of Afghanistan, international and domestic public opinion supported U.S. reactions to terrorism to such an extent that the United States had as much latitude as it desired in carrying out the operation. Immediately after 9/11, as many as 94 percent of Americans supported taking military action against the perpetrators, and 80 percent of Americans maintained their support for military action even if that response led to war.[107] A separate poll a week later indicated that 82 percent supported military action, even with the use of ground forces, 77 percent still supported military force even if the use of force resulted in thousands of casualties,[108] and 65 percent were prepared to support military force even if it meant resorting to conscription and a high economic toll.[109] With 84 percent of Americans supporting the president and 86 percent of Americans seeing the 9/11 attacks as acts of war against the United States, American leaders were receiving signals from the domestic audience that indicated full and unconstrained support for military force.[110]

None of these polls or questions distinguished between collective and individual self-defense, implicitly making the assumption that the United States would undertake retaliation unilaterally as necessary. Though general levels of support declined somewhat over time, a large majority of the public continued to believe that the United States should continue its counterterrorism operations in Afghanistan.[111] Thus, the broad support the public granted soon after 9/11 generally continued in the years since—being seen as the "good war" compared with Iraq[112]—and posed few constraints on American leaders conducting the war.

The U.S. Congress imposed even fewer constraints on how the United States undertook its response in Afghanistan. On 14 September 2001, the 107th Congress authorized the president to "use all necessary and appropriate force against those nations, organizations, or persons he determines planned, authorized, committed, or aided the terrorist attacks that occurred on September 11, 2001, or harbored such organizations or persons, in order to prevent any future acts of international terrorism against the United States by such nations, organizations or persons."[113] The authorization was unprecedented and sweeping. It effectively emasculated the oversight powers of Congress and gave the president wide berth to enhance the power of the executive, from preventive detention to enhanced interrogation measures to the way he carried out the Afghanistan War. Only with violence reaching unprecedented levels in 2008 did Congress step up and take a renewed interest in Afghanistan. Even then, however, it remained relatively silent on the increase in unilateral drone attacks in the region and continued to fund the Afghanistan operations largely unquestioned. Lack of oversight had persisted so long that in 2009, the General Accountability Office reported "Afghanistan as an urgent oversight issue facing this Congress."[114]

Overall, the domestic effect on strategy in Afghanistan, including the form of cooperation, was negligible. With unwavering support from the public and Congress, the administration had a blank check in terms of how it undertook the post-9/11 military response. High levels of support turned into near apathy among pollsters, the public, and Congress, who all turned their attention to Iraq after 2002.

REGIONAL POWERS: THE RING AROUND AFGHANISTAN

That the United States put forth an effort to collect key states in the region offers some support for the regional power constraints thesis. The United States was concerned with having enablers in the form of overflight rights and basing support in the central Asian republics. It was also concerned with possible counterbalancing behavior from states such as Russia, Pakistan, and

Iran. Before it intervened in Afghanistan, the United States made an effort to recruit both categories of states.

In large part because of the Soviet history in Afghanistan and the region more generally, the United States appeared to regard the region almost as a Russian sphere of influence in its preparations for the Afghanistan intervention. Russia did have valuable experience in what had been their own "bleeding wound," as Gorbachev referred to Afghanistan,[115] and was important logistically because the United States needed Russia's combat search and rescue support for U.S. operations in the north of Afghanistan. But Russia was most important for its political influence on other actors in the region that were more proximate and crucial to operations in Afghanistan.

Despite the fact that the Cold War had ended more than a decade earlier, Russia had maintained a close hold on its near abroad, including Uzbekistan, Tajikistan, and Turkmenistan, all of which were crucial for their close access to Afghanistan and their Soviet-era air bases. The United States needed these central Asian republics for basing support, but the Russian government made it abundantly clear that this area was Russian territory, not territory of the West. Putin's defense minister, Igor Ivanov, argued that he did not "see absolutely [any] basis for even hypothetical suppositions about the possibility of NATO military operations on the territory of Central Asian nations."[116]

Without Russia's acquiescence, the United States might have run the risk that Russia could counterbalance U.S. efforts in Afghanistan, indeed, much as the United States had done to the Soviets in the 1980s.[117] Given its influence in central Asia, it may also have meant not having those states' basing and overflight support, which were crucial for landlocked Afghanistan. The United States therefore courted Russia for its influence. Russia and its central Asian client states became targets of U.S. "coalition-building and military spadework" efforts, as several high-level U.S. officials made a number of visits to secure basing and overflight rights[118] from the areas surrounding Afghanistan in the run-up to the October 2001 military attacks.[119] Countries in the "ring around Afghanistan"[120] consequently granted such access through an agreement that included rights for the U.S. SOF troops to launch strikes and relief efforts from bases on their territory.[121] Without these states agreeing to such access, there would have been a "total mismatch"[122] in what the United States needed versus what it had, according to Secretary of State Colin Powell. The cajoling amounted to sums of money that were small by U.S. standards but persuasive for the central Asian republics.[123] Russia's price of admission was that the United States temper its criticism of Russia's aggressive handling of Chechnya and give the Russians support along their southern border of central Asia.[124]

Iran and Pakistan were cause for concern for somewhat different reasons. They both had enough regional power and geographic proximity to impose friction and perhaps even failure on an operation, and they had both historically supported insurgent or hostile groups in Afghanistan, so their political buy-in was an important condition for intervention. Pakistan, for its part, had been the last state to recognize the Taliban as the legitimate government of Afghanistan, and the United States had evidence that Pakistan had actively supported the Taliban with direct aid, arms, and "buses full of adolescent mujahid" during the 1990s. If it continued to support the Taliban throughout the U.S. intervention to overthrow that same regime, the operation would be considerably costlier and could have resulted in the kind of bleeding that the mujahideen inflicted on the Soviets during the 1980s.[125]

To ensure Pakistani support, the United States granted hefty concessions.[126] Congress lifted economic sanctions imposed against Islamabad after they tested nuclear weapons in 1998 and allowed Pakistan to buy U.S. weapon systems, which had not been possible previously. Moreover, Secretary of State Powell agreed to finagle relief for Pakistan's $37 billion debt.[127] In return, Pakistan granted access to airspace and intelligence, allowed limited ground presence, and asserted that they would not actively oppose U.S. efforts.[128]

Out of concerns that Iran could play a similarly counterproductive role, the United States and the United Kingdom sought Iran's acquiescence for the intervention. Intelligence estimates suggested that Afghanistan had 2 million people in Iran and that despite ethnic, cultural, and linguistic similarities, Iran and Afghanistan were quite hostile toward each other. Iran had supported Shiite resistance movements in Afghanistan, largely through Iran Revolutionary Guard Corps volunteers who aided Afghan Shiites.[129] Seeking at least their tacit approval not to counterbalance coalition efforts in Afghanistan, British Foreign Secretary Jack Straw visited Tehran, the highest ranking British official to visit Iran since the 1979 revolution. Straw argued that "the most important consideration for any kind of action is to forge international consensus, particularly the public opinion of people of the region. Only then can we put our seal of approval on such actions."[130] Iran did not actively support the intervention but did so tacitly, looking the other way when the United States crossed through its airspace, for example.

CONCLUSION

Afghanistan's within-case variation—largely unilateral in the combat operations and highly multilateral in the peacekeeping phases—lends strong support to the logic of consequences argument as specified according to time horizon and operational commitment. Short time horizons after the 9/11 attacks compressed the planning phase and proved challenging for U.S. interagency planning and coordination of the air, sea, and ground assets that would be involved in the Afghanistan campaign. Trying to craft a multinational coalition or NATO-based campaign plan presented an insurmountable challenge for a state with short-term security challenges. The decision to intervene with small numbers of special forces—in what became known as the Afghan Model—meant that the United States had even fewer incentives to collect allies.

Following the collapse of the Taliban, many of the short-term security challenges seemed to have been addressed, which opened the possibility of multilateral participation from states that had clamored to provide support after 9/11. Realization that the postconflict operations would be a costly enterprise in terms of time, financial resources, and personnel added to the incentives for alliance-seeking behavior in the postconflict phase.

Cooperation behavior in the Afghanistan intervention, particularly considered as two discrete campaigns with varying strategies, also sheds light on the degree to which the U.S. cooperation strategy was guided by a logic of appropriateness. If a logic of appropriateness had guided U.S. cooperation, we would have expected to see multilateral participation across the intervention, not just when it was more convenient in the latter phase of the intervention. The latter half—stabilization and reconstruction operations—was a most likely scenario for multilateralism because the risks and consequences of coordination failure were far less grave than for combat operations.

Assessing whether the multilateral norm guides intervention behavior therefore requires not just seeking easy tests of the proposition, such as stabilization and reconstruction operations in which the stakes are low. It requires less likely cases, where multilateralism is difficult and not expedient. Combat operations, where dependence on an unreliable partner can have more severe consequences, are a harder test case for a state's commitment to multilateral principles.[131] The high-stakes combat operations of Afghanistan offer such a test. As this case shows, however, the United States was entirely unwilling to compromise effectiveness by undertaking what would be more time-consuming planning of a multilateral operation and instead opted for unilateral action. It was unwilling to integrate less capable allies in a phase of operations where the stakes were high. The United States asserted its Article 51 right of individual self-defense rather than ask for specific UN authorization to use force in Afghanistan and risk hamstringing operational flexibility or compromising strategic goals.[132]

Such aversion to the constraints of cooperation is consistent with concern about consequences and inconsistent with the predictions of appropriateness, which would expect a principled multilateralism, independent of the stakes. An honest reading of the case does show that even under heightened security conditions, the United States did not eschew appropriateness altogether. In the weeks after 9/11, the United States touted the breadth of its international support for the campaign against terrorism, acting as if there were some value to generating international consensus and sanction for its efforts. When it came to the largely unilateral substance of the military operation, however, claims of broad multilateral efforts look disingenuous, suggesting at least some more serious limitations to normative pull than constructivist proponents have previously identified.

To the extent that domestic politics mattered in the context of Afghanistan, it did so by acting as an enabler. The U.S. domestic audience was overwhelmingly supportive of the use of force and offered enormous degrees of latitude in how the United States undertook its intervention. Domestic politics was indeterminate with regard to the choice between unilateralism and multilateralism, since it did not weigh on one side or the other, and it is therefore not helpful in explaining the choice and variation between the two cooperation strategies in Afghanistan.

Regional power politics had some bearing on the choice of allies in Afghanistan. Aware of historical influences in Afghanistan, the United States was careful in minimizing the counterproductive influence of states such as Russia, Pakistan, and Iran and secured at least their acquiescence to intervene in the region. The U.S. effort to secure approval from these states, in an intervention that was otherwise apathetic toward multilateral cooperation, lends some strength to the regional power thesis.

7

Iraq, the United States, and the "Coalition of the Willing"

INTRODUCTION

In reporting on an investigation into Britain's role in the Iraq War, the *Economist* realistically observed that many questions about Iraq "will never be answered definitively and to universal satisfaction."[1] Each subsequent investigation, declassified document, or memoir makes these questions somewhat more soluble, but some of the documents about threats and challenges that might inform the clearest analysis remain classified. Even those will not produce the last word on a controversial and costly conflict.

What is largely indisputable is that, in retrospect, we know that Iraq did not have weapons of mass destruction when the United States invaded in 2003. In the lead-up to the war, much of the world thought otherwise. The United States, the United Kingdom, and Australia believed that Saddam Hussein had weapons of mass destruction (WMD). Even opponents of intervention, such as France, Germany, and the UN, believed that Saddam had WMD. The divergence between the two camps came not in whether Saddam had WMD but in how long they believed inspections should run before disarming Iraq by force.[2] As a number of postinvasion investigations showed, the pre-Iraq intelligence was wildly off the mark.

The prewar intelligence is what decision makers had, however, and it is what they used to decide whether and how to use force in Iraq. This analysis therefore takes into account the *ex ante* assessments under which decision makers made choices in 2002–2003 rather than the *ex post* assessments, which we now know are different from the original assessments. Diplomat Dennis Ross concluded in his study of Iraq that "The greatest single failure in Iraq is related to the assessments."[3]

As this chapter shows, those *ex ante* assessments made two fatal errors: they overestimated the threat and underestimated the operational commitment. As military observer Thomas Ricks summarized the consequences, "By overstating the threat of Iraq, the former made war seem necessary. By understating the difficulty of remaking Iraq, the latter made it seem easier and less expensive than it would prove to be."[4] The assessment combined to produce a decision to intervene with too few U.S. troops and a perfunctory effort to pursue multilateral strategies. As it became clear in the years after the initial invasion, this flawed intervention strategy reflected the flawed assessments. Former Under Secretary of State for Political Affairs Marc Grossman admitted in an a personal interview in 2007 that "knowing what we know now about the Iraq war, we would have waited until we had more allies to go in so we could be sharing the burden now."[5] In hindsight, going multilaterally—or, rather, not at all—looks obvious. With the assessments leaders had at the time, however, that choice does not look as clear-cut.

As this chapter shows, there were two sets of reasons for the failed assessments. Assessments of the threat itself were overestimated because of the mind-set about threats that followed 9/11. After the attacks, threats that had previously been addressed over time took on more urgency. Formal assessments—intelligence estimates—were based on relatively "poor tradecraft"[6] and arrived at conclusions that only reinforced the sense of urgency about Iraq. In contrast, assessments of the operational commitment were underestimated largely because of the dramatic operational success in Iraq (1991), degradation in the Iraqi military in the intervening years, and trust in the transformational model that seemed to be working in Afghanistan. Taken together, the short time horizon that followed 9/11 and expectations of low operational commitment produced a hasty approach to multilateralism. The United States had little patience for additional inspections—a requirement to break the UN deadlock—and its expectation of a low-cost victory made substantive contributions from allies seem unwarranted.

This chapter lays out that argument in more detail and considers the effect of norms and regional powers, found to be nominal, and the somewhat more influential impact of U.S. and allied domestic politics. Before evaluating these arguments, the chapter addresses a set of challenges to the officially declared premise of invading Iraq. Views that the Bush administration's motivations for going to war were disingenuous have gained currency in the years since 2003 and warrant close attention. If these charges are correct, they cast doubt on all arguments that assume prewar assessments that determined the U.S. cooperation strategy—whether of time horizon, operational commitment, or the domestic environment—were made in good faith. As this chapter shows in some detail, however, there is little evidence to support those charges. Before turning to those claims, however, the chapter presents a brief overview of events—including two other Gulf wars and many years of inspections—that set the stage for the 2003 intervention.

THREE GULF WARS

Over a period of two decades, there were three Gulf wars. The first was the Iran-Iraq War between 1980 and 1988. In this war, Saddam Hussein, concerned about spillover from the Iranian Revolution, invaded Iran, leading to a costly, eight-year battle of attrition in the Middle East. The second—what the West calls the Persian Gulf War—followed from the first: In debt from the first Gulf War, Iraq invaded Kuwait in 1990, hoping to appropriate Kuwait's oil revenues.[7]

The third—the 2003 Iraq War—was connected with the second Gulf war in that when the coalition exited Iraq in 1991, it left Saddam Hussein in power. Ricks describes this event as the coalition terminating "the fighting prematurely and sloppily, without due consideration by the first president Bush and his advisers of what end state they wished to achieve."[8] The end state they left was one of unfinished business. Saddam Hussein still had weapons of mass destruction. He still had a lock on power. He still had a way of harassing members of the international community, whether UN inspectors just months after the 1991 Gulf War or American and British pilots enforcing the no-fly zones in the 1990s. Rather than go back in and finish the business of removing Saddam Hussein, the United States and its allies adopted a strategy of containment: the United States and the United Kingdom enforced no-fly zones through Operations Northern and Southern Watch, the international community imposed a set of tough sanctions against the regime, and the UN tried to verify Iraq's compliance with disarmament.[9]

While the policy of containment "served the United States well after 1991, much better than most ever thought it could,"[10] according to Kenneth Pollack, who served on the National Security Council in the 1990s, the policy of the late 1990s took a more hawkish turn. Saddam Hussein's repeated defiance of inspectors, violation of no-fly zones, and apparent development of weapons programs provoked the 1998 Iraq Liberation Act (P.L. 105–338), which stated, "It should be the policy of the United States to support efforts to remove the regime headed by Saddam Hussein from power and to promote the emergence of a democratic government to replace that regime."[11]

The U.S. Senate unanimously approved the policy (the vote was 360–38 in the House) and, with the approval of President Clinton, it became the official Iraq policy after its passage on 31 October 1998. The legislation seemed to signal a growing impatience with Saddam's antics. It involved funding for opposition groups and provided the domestic legal backing for Operation Desert Fox, in which the United States bombed Iraqi WMD facilities over a three-day period. President Clinton defended the action to the nation, saying that "Saddam [Hussein] must not be allowed to threaten his neighbors or the world with nuclear arms, poison gas or biological weapons."[12] As Secretary of

State Madeline Albright admitted, "The weapons of mass destruction are the threat of the future...we know we can't get everything, but degrading is the right word."[13] In other words, the hope in undertaking Desert Fox was not to eliminate but rather degrade the WMD facilities, implying that many would remain.

With Iraq's WMD programs seemingly still in place, the United States pursued other means of disarmament. The U.S. Congress supported earmarks for the Iraqi National Congress, an Iraqi opposition group that promised to work with anti-Saddam groups to orchestrate an overthrow of the regime. Advocates of a more aggressive policy, including direct U.S. military action, were few.[14] Neither the Clinton administration nor the George W. Bush administration—at at least pre-9/11—gave any indication of launching a large-scale military operation to impose regime change.

The international community was even more hesitant during this period. At the end of the first Gulf war, it had supported and passed UN Resolution 687, which called for "under international supervision, the destruction, removal or rendering harmless of its weapons of mass destruction, ballistic missiles with a range of over 150 kilometers, and related production facilities and equipment."[15] Resolution 687 established a system that would monitor and verify Iraq's compliance with the UN-imposed ban on these weapons. The result was the United Nations Special Commission (UNSCOM), which began carrying out on-site inspections of Iraq's WMD facilities in June 1991. It continued carrying out verification of Iraq's compliance with Resolution 687 throughout most of the 1990s, until Iraq began prohibiting U.S. and UN weapons inspectors from operating within Iraq. Saddam Hussein blocked inspection teams in both 1997 and 1998 and finally declared a cessation of UNSCOM cooperation in October 1998, though he allowed the UN to resume inspections just one month later. The UN itself ordered inspectors to leave the country again in December 1998, after the chief of UNSCOM declared Iraq unwilling to cooperate. The United States and the United Kingdom undertook a massive bombing operation—Operation Desert Fox—soon thereafter.[16]

With the recognition that UNSCOM had lacked Iraqi cooperation and general effectiveness, two events followed. First, with Resolution 1284, the UN replaced UNSCOM with the UN Monitoring, Verification, and Inspection Commission (UNMOVIC), which was charged with monitoring and inspecting Iraq's WMD programs.[17] Although UNMOVIC was intended to be a "reinforced" system compared with UNSCOM, Iraq rejected Resolution 1284, immediately undermining the institution's credibility. Second, the Security Council split during the 1990s.[18] Britain and the United States favored a harder line toward Iraq. Russia, France, and China began siding more with Iraq, lured in part by generous oil contracts associated with the oil-for-food program.

They proposed less stringent sanctions and a return to "oil business as usual" that drove a wedge between their position and that of the United States and the United Kingdom.[19]

Despite growing differences on the Security Council, the permanent members generally agreed on their endorsement of UNMOVIC. As its executive chairman said, one reason for its more universal support is that contrary to UNSCOM, which was funded and staffed by Western countries, UNMOVIC had material backing from a broader set of countries. Its history and successes, however, were no more impressive. The main problem was access. From the beginning of its mandate in 1999 until the autumn of 2002, UNMOVIC lacked inspectors in Iraq. It therefore had to rely on media reports and information from UN member states. None of these sources were as effective as human inspectors, who as of 1998 had been prohibited from inspecting Iraq's weapons sites. The ability to "solve unanswered disarmament issues" was very limited in the absence of on-site inspectors.[20]

Only as the likelihood of an Iraq invasion increased did Saddam Hussein send a letter to Secretary General Kofi Annan on 16 September 2002 allowing the return of weapons inspections. As Blix admitted, "Without a military buildup by the U.S. in the summer of 2002, Iraq would probably not have accepted a resumption of inspections."[21] Military pressure helped move inspections and diplomacy forward, but the prospect of military force also moved forward, assisted in part by U.S. domestic developments. At the same time inspections were resuming, the U.S. Congress voted in October 2002 to authorize war against Iraq, pointing to Iraq's continued support for international terrorist groups, pursuit of weapons of mass destruction, and harboring of al Qaeda members on its soil.[22]

Despite having the domestic authorization, the United States pushed for an international resolution on Iraqi disarmament—Resolution 1441—that the UN Security Council (UNSC) ultimately passed unanimously on 8 November 2002. The resolution acknowledged "the threat Iraq's non-compliance with Council resolutions and proliferation of weapons of mass destruction and long-range missiles poses to international peace and security." It declared Iraq to be in "material breach of its obligations" to disarm and warned of "serious consequences" if Iraq continued to violate disarmament obligations under previous UN resolutions.[23] While the Iraqi parliament rejected the UN resolution, the government itself accepted it, allowing UN inspectors back into Iraq by the end of 2002.[24]

After the international consensus that coalesced around Resolution 1441, UNSC members' policy preferences began to diverge more dramatically. France, Russia, and China advocated allowing more time for inspections; since UNMOVIC had returned only in late 2002, these states argued for at least letting the inspections run their course and allowing the inspectors until July 2003 before making a decision on the use of force.[25] These states also argued that the United States and the United Kingdom would need a second UN resolution explicitly authorizing the use of force before intervening. The United States and the United Kingdom maintained that inspections had been fruitless. UNMOVIC's claims that no WMD had been found did little to diminish American concern about Iraq's WMD. As Rumsfeld had said in February 2002, "The absence of evidence is not evidence of absence."[26] In other words, if weapons had been moved, were hidden, or obstructed, then it would be impossible to find evidence that they existed. The strong presumption that Iraq had WMD made it seem plausible that Iraq must be manipulating the evidence. Inspectors themselves documented the number of experiences in which "Iraqis had cleansed each building" prior to an inspection.[27] Absence of evidence could simply mean that the evidence had been cleansed, according to the U.S. perspective.

The two sides were unable to bridge the gap. Russia, China, and France insisted on letting inspections run their course. The United States and the United Kingdom had lost faith in the inspections process and were unwilling to wait another several months or longer before intervening. Armed with what they thought was a credible case for intervention and unable to find the votes for a second UN resolution authorizing force, the United States and the United Kingdom cobbled together a "coalition of the willing" to intervene in Iraq. That coalition was a multilateral coalition in name only, however. It did not receive authorization from the UNSC or from any regional organization. Moreover, it consisted of about 95 percent British and American troops and financial backing. Some states such as Poland and Australia contributed a couple of thousand troops. Others, such as Palau, Micronesia, and the Solomon Islands, had small or no militaries themselves and were enlisted for their political backing. Arab states that had participated in the 1991 Gulf War remained on the sidelines in the 2003 Iraq War.[28] Tellingly, U.S. combat plans make reference only to American battle groups, air wings, and intelligence assets units; they did not incorporate allies such as the United Kingdom and only in passing optimistically mentioned that "co-opted Iraqi units will...not fight either U.S. forces or other Iraqi units."[29]

Intervening without more help from allies against a state that did not pose a direct threat now looks decidedly unwise. The mounting costs made that decision look less wise with every year that passed. One source for this error in judgment is that the 9/11 attacks cast new light on old threats. Threats that could previously have waited for certainty and international consensus seemed more perilous.[30] In addition, estimates of the war's costs emphasized the ease of combat and discounted what would turn out to be the more onerous stabilization phase. The combined effect was to minimize the value of allies.

Before turning to that argument, the next section looks at prominent challenges to the premise of intervening in Iraq, mostly about the role of individuals and ideology and the effect both are thought to have had on the decision to intervene. Such challenges are typically lodged more against the decision to go to war than the way in which the United States went to war, but they also bear on why the United States chose the cooperation strategy it did. They are important to take seriously, since if validated, they would undermine the argument about time horizons and operational commitment. The next section, however, casts doubt on those challenges.

CHALLENGES TO THE PREMISE OF INVADING IRAQ

One view of the decision to intervene is that the Bush administration was populated with crusaders hell-bent on invading Iraq. This narrative emphasizes the role of individuals including Vice President Richard Cheney, Secretary of Defense Donald Rumsfeld, Deputy Secretary of Defense Paul Wolfowitz, Under Secretary of Defense for Policy Douglas Feith, and defense advisor Richard Perle. According to this line of argument, these individuals were part of a "neoconservative cabal."[31] They were inherently promilitary and believed in Pax Americana, the idea that "American power and ideals are, on the whole, a force for good in the world."[32] Many of these individuals had "pined in exile" during the 1990s, hoping to push their preferred, prointervention policy toward Iraq upon their return to government. In the interim, they had signed the letter to President Clinton in 1998 arguing that containment was not working and advocated regime change as an alternative.[33]

According to this perspective, decision making on the way to Iraq was driven by the ideology of these few well-placed individuals. "Without the experience of military service, no less of warfare," this group of "chicken hawks"—individuals without military experience who were nonetheless bullish on war—relied on several misplaced beliefs: that the best defense is a good offense, that it is possible to do more with less (the supposed virtues of military transformation), and that multilateral cooperation served only to shackle rather than enhance American military operations.[34]

The domination of this ideology is associated with two related charges on the Iraq invasion. First, critics argue that the Bush administration entered office determined to undertake regime change in Iraq. They were unlikely to be dissuaded by arguments that Iraq could be contained and deterred. The implication is that the post-9/11 security environment became a convenient way to implement a predetermined policy.[35] Second, critics suggest that the Bush administration then pressured American intelligence agencies to produce estimates that were congruent with their obsession with Iraq or downplayed caveats from intelligence reports that the threat might not be as grave as the administration asserted.[36]

Retrospectively, this set of arguments seems to track closely with the Iraq case. Taking each line of the reason in turn, however, it is clear that each suffers either from omissions or commissions. First, though the pre-9/11 record from the Bush administration is short, there is little to suggest that the Bush administration had any intention of invading Iraq before 9/11 or had there been no 9/11. Condoleezza Rice, later the national security advisor, argued in a 2000 *Foreign Affairs* article that Iraq was deterrable. Even the hawkish members of the administration, such as Paul Wolfowitz, claimed that he had not seen a tenable plan for regime change in Iraq. Rather, the State Department, which ran Iraq policy before 9/11, was focused on keeping Saddam "in the box" through "smart sanctions."[37] It was also preoccupied with traditional threats such as the rise of China—particularly surrounding the Navy EP-3 collision with a Chinese F-8 over the South China Sea earlier in 2001[38]—than with the intersection of rogue regimes and nonstate actors. Before 9/11, there was little reason to think that Saddam could not be contained. As a result, "the Saddam Must Go School," according to Thomas Ricks, was a dissident minority voice, generally disdained by those holding power in the US Government."[39]

This is not to suggest that the United States had ignored the issue of Iraq altogether. Early in his administration, President Bush had wanted to take a firm stance on Iraq, even, as with his predecessor, undertaking limited strikes to enforce the no-fly zone in Iraq. There is no evidence, however, that before 9/11, the administration intended to act in a way that diverged considerably from its predecessor; it talked of enacting additional sanctions against Iraq, increasing support to the opposition Iraqi National Congress, and undertaking sporadic, targeted airstrikes to enforce no-fly zones, but not regime change.

A declassified memo from Secretary Rumsfeld to Condoleezza Rice on 27 July 2001 lays out this thinking on Iraq. Sanctions did not appear to be working, and enforcement of the no-fly zones was having a limited effect while threatening U.S. pilots, Rumsfeld wrote. With this reality in mind, the United States could stay the course, carry out airstrikes against Iraqi military assets, or reduce the enforcement sorties. In terms of the "broader context," Rumsfeld suggested perhaps cutting and running on the no-fly zone enforcements or putting pressure on Iraq through moderate Arab intermediaries. Another option was "opening a dialogue with Saddam," which he acknowledged "would be an astonishing departure for the USG [U.S. Government], although I did it for President Reagan the [sic] mid-1980s." Channeling realist logic, Rumsfeld concluded that "there ought to be a way for the U.S. to not be at loggerheads with both of the two most powerful nations in the Gulf—Iran and Iraq—when the two of them do not like each other, are firing at each other and have groups in their respective countries that are hostile to the other side." He advocated a strategy in which "my enemy's enemy is my friend."[40] The memo acknowledged that the strategy in place during the summer of 2001 was not working but did not even hint at invasion or regime change. In his memoirs, weapons inspector Hans Blix confirmed a similar story. Documenting his April 2001 meeting with Condoleezza Rice, he noted that he detected no hardening of the U.S. stance on Iraq in early 2001.[41]

The relatively ambivalent position of the United States toward Iraq did not pass unnoticed by advocates of a harder line. The *Washington Post*, for example, lamented that the Bush administration, like the Clinton administration, seemed to be "quietly abandoning the struggle against Saddam Hussein."[42] To be sure, the Bush administration was populated with hawks. This, however, is a different claim from one that says they were hawks with the ability or intention of invading Iraq.

The second part of the argument previously outlined implies that with the inexorable push toward war, the Bush administration manipulated intelligence to co-opt the public into going to war. Knowing that Saddam Hussein did not have weapons of mass destruction, the administration reverse-engineered the case. According to this part of the argument, President Bush and his subordinates lied to the public or at least disingenuously favored evidence that justified war over evidence that favored caution. The administration played up disturbing aspects of the 2002 National Intelligence Estimate (NIE), such as that Saddam could decide to team up with a transnational terrorist group such as al Qaeda. It minimized the NIE's caution that Saddam did not appear to be going down that road.[43]

If the argument about manipulation of intelligence is right, then U.S. assessments of Iraqi weapons programs should have been different from those of other agencies or governments. However, the U.S. government was far from the only actor whose assessment of Iraq was suspicious. As U.S. weapons inspector David Kay testified after not finding WMD in Iraq, "We were almost all wrong, and I certainly include myself here...many governments that chose not to support this war—certainly, the French president...referred to Iraq's possession of WMD."[44] In a February 2003 interview with *Time* magazine, President Chirac said, "Are there other weapons of mass destruction [in Iraq]? That's probable. We have to find and destroy them....I repeat: Iraq must be disarmed."[45] The UN inspector Hans Blix told the UN Security Council that "Iraq appears not to have come to a genuine acceptance—not even today—of the disarmament which was demanded of it."[46] Up until the invasion, Blix remained unconvinced that Iraq had resolved the UN and member states' concerns about Iraq's WMD.[47]

Fellow weapons inspector Richard Butler shared a similar view: "The main point to be made about Saddam's evident addiction to weapons of mass destruction is not that it exists, but rather that its existence has been widely known for a very long time."[48] One of Iraq's own nuclear scientists, Khidhir Hamza, agreed: "I have no doubt that Iraq is pursuing the nuclear option.... Saddam must be kept in a box or, better still, removed."[49]

If this argument about dogmatic members of the administration selling the war is right, then we would also expect to see heterogeneity and resistance from corners of the U.S. government, particularly from the opposition. On the contrary, there was a notable bipartisan consensus that Iraq had weapons of mass destruction. The uncertainty was not about whether Iraq was developing and might use the weapons, but whether it was deterrable and, if not, how the United States should respond. Belief that Saddam had WMD was not reserved for Republicans, who might be expected to fall in line behind the president. A number of Democrats voiced their concerns about Iraq's weapons program:

President Bill Clinton

Other countries possess weapons of mass destruction and ballistic missiles. With Saddam, there is one big difference: He has used them, not once, but repeatedly. Unleashing chemical weapons against Iranian troops during a decade-long war. Not only against soldiers, but against civilians, firing Scud missiles at the citizens of Israel, Saudi Arabia, Bahrain and Iran. And not only against a foreign enemy, but even against his own people, gassing Kurdish civilians in Northern Iraq. The international community had little doubt then, and I have no doubt today, that left unchecked, Saddam Hussein will use these terrible weapons again.[50]

Senator Edward Kennedy

We have known for many years that Saddam Hussein is using and developing weapons of mass destruction.[51]

Senator John Kerry

I will be voting to give the President of the United States the authority to use force—if necessary—to disarm Saddam Hussein because I believe that a deadly arsenal of weapons of mass destruction in his hands is a real and grave threat to our security.[52]

Senator Jay Rockefeller

There is unmistakable evidence that Saddam Hussein is working aggressively to develop nuclear weapons and will likely have nuclear weapons within the next five years. And that may happen sooner if he can obtain access to enriched uranium from foreign sources.... We also should remember we have always underestimated the progress Saddam has made in development of weapons of mass destruction.[53]

Representative Nancy Pelosi

Saddam Hussein certainly has chemical and biological weapons. There's no question about that.[54]

Senator Carl Levin

We begin with the common belief that Saddam Hussein is a tyrant and a threat to the peace and stability of the region. He has ignored the mandates of the United Nations and is building weapons of mass destruction and the means of delivering them.[55]

As these policy positions show, the belief that Iraq had WMD was not reserved for rogue elements within the Bush administration. Rather, the view was held systematically within the U.S. political system. So convinced were they that Saddam Hussein had WMD that few members of Congress actually made the effort to read the 2002 NIE. According to the congressional aides whose responsibility it was to guard the NIE vaulted on Capitol Hill, only six senators and a few House members read anything other than the executive summary. Their views had been formed by Saddam Hussein's history of using and concealing WMD and reinforced by the post-9/11 concerns about the vulnerability of U.S. security.[56] The vote was far more lopsided than the Gulf War vote in 1991 and a far bigger endorsement than for the 1994 Haiti intervention, in which the House passed a nonbinding resolution opposing force, or for the Bosnia intervention, in which the Congress passed a resolution expressing support for troops but reservations about their deployment.[57]

As late as 2004, long after revisionism had become fashionable, former President Bill Clinton defended his position on Iraq and President Bush's decision to use force. As he told *Time* magazine in an interview:

I have repeatedly defended President Bush...even though I think he should have waited until the UN inspections were over. After 9/11, let's be fair here, if you had been President, you'd think, Well, this fellow bin Laden just turned these three airplanes full of fuel into weapons of mass destruction, right?...So you're sitting there as President, you're reeling in the aftermath of all this....My first responsibility now is to try everything possible to make sure that this terrorist network and other terrorist networks cannot reach chemical and biological weapons....That's why I supported the Iraq thing. There was a lot of stuff [weapons] unaccounted for....You couldn't responsibly ignore [the possibility that] a tyrant had these stocks...when you're the president and your country has just been through what we had, you want everything to be accounted for.[58]

President Clinton's forceful defense implies that the invasion was a natural response to the 9/11 attacks. Though he differed on the timing of the invasion,

Clinton was nonetheless empathetic to the pressures his successor faced in preventing another attack. This view fundamentally undermines claims that the decision to invade Iraq was ideological and that the administration came into office with those designs. That Clinton—who essentially had access to the same intelligence that the Bush administration had leading up to the Iraq War—took Iraq's stockpiles as a given is also a challenge to critics who suggest that the latter sold the war on manipulated intelligence.

In retrospect, it is not all that surprising that intelligence assessments got it wrong on Iraq's WMD programs. Iraq had developed and used WMD since the 1980s, and it was almost inconceivable that it would have broken that pattern of behavior. When inspectors left in 1998, it was natural to assume continuity rather than a break in Iraq's behavior. Director of Central Intelligence George Tenet laid out the logic behind the systematic error: "In 2002, to conclude that Saddam Hussein was not pursuing WMD, our analysts would have had to ignore years and years of intelligence that pointed in the direction of active programs and continuing evidence of aggressive attempts on Iraq's part to conceal its activities."[59] He adds that "in retrospect, we got it wrong partly because the truth was so implausible... intelligence reports and analysis used over the years on the WMD issue, and repeated in the NIE, were flawed, but the intelligence process was not disingenuous."[60]

Saddam Hussein did not help his cause; he "strutted about" as though he had WMD[61] and made his case worse by blocking or misleading inspectors.[62] As Fouad Ajami correctly observes, "A more cunning man would have ducked for cover. But this had never been Saddam Hussein's way."[63] This posturing, coupled with Iraq's history, produced the overwhelmingly prevailing view that Iraq maintained active WMD programs.

Following the Iraq War, the British, Australian, and American governments all conducted investigations into the intelligence failures and the possibility of politicized intelligence. None found evidence of politicization. Rather, the problem was that analyses had neglected political and cultural contexts, succumbed to group think, overreacted to earlier errors on Iraq's Gulf War capabilities, and favored a systematic prioritization of short-term products over long-term analysis.[64] The absence of politicization and the investigations' conclusions that intelligence failures were to blame do not settle the debate, but they are consistent with an environment of incomplete information and cast doubt on the more conspiratorial counterarguments about neoconservatives hijacking U.S. foreign policy and misleading the American public into Iraq.

The explanation that is more consistent with the evidence is that the 9/11 attacks created an environment of uncertainty and few clues on the next attack. They produced short time horizons that made the risk of not acting quickly seem worse than acting now and finding out later that the intelligence was faulty.[65] Waiting for allies and giving multilateral inspections more time therefore seemed costly. The view that the United States could win on the cheap reinforced the belief that the United States could win with little support from allies. The next section develops that argument.

THE ROAD TO IRAQ LEADS THROUGH 9/11

Discussing the invasion of Iraq is almost impossible without explicit reference to the 9/11 attacks. As Ajami has written, "The road to Iraq led through the terror attacks of September 11."[66] Prior to 9/11, a sense of complacency dominated. Enjoying the post–Cold War "peace dividend," the United States downsized its military and intelligence services and assumed a less assertive international posture. Commenting on the reactive nature of American strategy in this period, Jeremi Suri, a historian of American grand strategy, wondered whether the White House or CNN was determining how events unfolded. The translation: The years after the Cold War and before 9/11 were "lost years" for U.S. strategy.[67] Instead, American strategy drifted along, lacking a coherent replacement for the strategy of containment that had endured across administrations during the Cold War. When it came to terrorism, the U.S. response—despite growing evidence from a series of attacks that the threat was not isolated—was woefully ad hoc. Actions were limited to conservative covert action, freezing financial assets, and labeling the Taliban as a state sponsor of terrorism.[68]

The 9/11 attacks made the notion of a peace dividend look naïve. They shattered the American sense of complacency and created a "sense of peril" about American security.[69] Samuel Johnson's aphorism proved all too apt after 9/11: "When a man knows he is to be hanged in a fortnight, it concentrates his mind wonderfully." If critics of the administration's counterterrorism had criticized it for being too passive prior to 9/11, there would be no ammunition for that criticism after 9/11. On the contrary, the attacks had "terrorize[d] the imagination,"[70] made any subsequent attack seem possible, and shook the United States out of its strategic torpor. They had certainly concentrated the mind on the need to address threats before they could strike again.

Where and how the next attack would strike was anyone's guess. Daniel Benjamin and Steven Simon, counterterrorism advisors to President Clinton, note that "it is the nature of terrorism for attacks to be unpredictable." After 9/11, they write, "America's warning dilemmas have now multiplied."[71] Attacks could seemingly come from anywhere at any time. Fear of the next attack became the guiding principle behind every action taken after 9/11. In describing the source of the mind-set that permeated the government after

9/11, former head of the Office of Legal Counsel, Jack Goldsmith, summa-rized the sense of panic that prevailed in the government: "It is hard to over-state the impact that the incessant waves of threat reports have on the judgment of people inside the executive branch who are responsible for pro-tecting American lives."[72] The government's threat matrix—a daily summary of threats to the U.S. and its allies—is rife with "nerve-jangling scenarios and maddening" chatter,[73] but devoid of enough detail to tip the government on how exactly to defend against the next attack. The result was that decision makers had "so few good clues" that "everything starts to look suspicious."[74]

Though the expression "everything changed on 9/11" quickly became cli-ché, it did accurately describe the U.S. government's reaction, including how it saw threats and its own vulnerabilities.[75] That post-9/11 mentality had sev-eral consequences. One was the sense that hiding behind Fortress America, a territory isolated by oceans on both sides, suddenly seemed futile. Until 9/11, America's entire experience with foreign policy had been built on the self-limiting and other-limiting notion of geographic isolation. In contrast, the 9/11 attacks had shown the porosity of boundaries. As Robert Keohane foreshadowed, "In the absence of clear and defensible criteria that American leaders can use to distinguish vital from non-vital interests, the United States is at risk of intervening throughout the world in a variety of conflicts."[76]

Unable to distinguish among threats, the United States did adopt a less discriminatory approach to its interests abroad.[77] Every intelligence tip was treated as though it "might be the next World Trade Center attack"; each level of government, from analyst all the way to the president, was fixated on not being responsible for letting the next attack through the cracks. The government would now try to "chase down every lead."[78] Less discriminatory also meant a more expansive response to terrorism. It began with Afghanistan and expanded to include offensive action in the Philippines, the Horn of Africa, and Pakistan. Intervention was just a symptom of the wholesale change in mind-set that followed 9/11.

A second consequence of the post-9/11 world is that the attacks came to loom over every threat that had looked manageable prior to 9/11. Old threats took on greater salience. Saddam Hussein, for example, had been contained during the 1990s, but 9/11 caused President Bush to reevaluate. Defending the decision to go on the offensive, Bush asserted: "After September the 11th, the doctrine of containment just doesn't hold any water as far as I'm concerned."[79] In his remarks to Bob Woodward, he had sounded a similar theme. The attacks of 9/11 led him to take seriously "Saddam Hussein's capacity to create harm...all his terrible features became much more threat-ening. Keeping Saddam in a box looked less and less feasible."[80] Iraq had been a thorn in the side of U.S. interests since the Gulf War, and its ability to threaten the United States took on a whole new plausibility after 9/11.

Secretary of State Colin Powell, who often disagreed with and ultimately left the administration, had a similar explanation about why 9/11 exercised the administration about Iraq. "We went to war on the basis that we have a terrible regime and what makes—it's been terrible forever. What makes it so terrible now, in the aftermath of 9/11, is that they had demonstrated that they will use these weapons.... And that was the precipitating cause."[81] Certainly the evidence connecting Iraq and a nonstate terrorist group—the premise of the argument for invading Iraq—was precarious. For those inside the government, however, even the ability to imagine the scenario was sufficient.

A third consequence of the post-9/11 mind-set was that shortsightedness prevailed over decision making. As President Bush informed the West Point graduating class of 2002, "If we wait for threats to fully materialize, we will have waited too long."[82] Confronting even inchoate threats became the anchor for U.S. security policy after 9/11. Potential threats would be accorded the same attention as those that had already made themselves manifest. In the long term, confronting emerging, unproven threats would be costly, but after the 9/11 attacks, it seemed foolish to think about the long-term conservation of resources. In the aftermath of 9/11, somehow it seemed more reasonable to ask, What if there were no long term? What if getting to 100 percent certainty on threats took too long?[83] Why worry about burning resources and burning bridges with allies if the long term was in doubt?

Time horizon and its effect on decision making implicitly arose frequently after 9/11. In his 2002 State of the Union speech—with its infamous "axis of evil" reference—President Bush asserted that "time is not on our side. I will not wait on events, while dangers gather. I will not stand by, as peril draws closer and closer."[84] That message took shape in the 2002 National Security Strategy, which vowed that "America will act against such emerging threats before they are fully formed. We cannot defend America and our friends by hoping for the best...history will judge harshly those who saw the coming danger but failed to act."[85] In the speech that preceded the intervention, Bush equated acting at that moment with the desire to avoid costly delays on the specific question of Iraq: "We are now acting because the risks of inaction would be far greater. In one year, or five years, the power of Iraq to inflict harm on all free nations would be multiplied many times over.... We choose to meet that threat now, where it arises, before it can appear suddenly in our skies and cities."[86] In an interview on *Meet the Press*, Vice President Cheney echoed these thoughts: "One of the things it [9/11] changed is we recognized that time was not on our side, that in this part of the world, in particular, given the problems we've encountered in Afghanistan, which forced us to go in and take action there, as well as in Iraq, that we, in fact, had to move on it."[87]

Intelligence estimates did little to temper the post-9/11 concerns about Iraq. The 2002 NIE cautioned that "Iraq has continued its weapons of mass destruction programs in defiance of UN resolutions and restrictions...we judge that we are seeing only a portion of Iraq's WMD efforts, owing to Baghdad's vigorous denial and deception efforts."[88] More in line with the concerns prompted by 9/11, the NIE indicated that Saddam "might decide that only an organization such as al Qaeda—with worldwide reach and extensive terrorist structure, and already engaged in a life-or-death struggle against the U.S.—would perpetrate the type of terrorist attack that he would hope to conduct...it would be his last chance to exact vengeance by taking a large number of victims with him."[89]

The caveat that the likelihood of this scenario was low did not feature prominently in the NIE. One important qualifier did make it into a letter from Director of Central Intelligence George Tenet to Senator Bob Graham, chairman of the Senate Committee on Intelligence, on 7 October 2002. Tenet clarified that "Baghdad for now appears to be drawing a line short of conducting terrorist attacks with conventional or CBW [chemical or biological weapons] against the United States." Muddling the message, however, the letter continued that "Saddam might decide that the extreme step of assisting Islamist terrorists in conducting a WMD attack against the United States would be his last chance to exact vengeance by taking a large number of victims with him." The possibility was low, according to a senior intelligence witness who testified to the Senate Committee on Intelligence, but the consequences if Saddam did resort to an attack and used WMD were high.[90]

This line of thinking still resonated with Representative Jane Harman, ranking member on the House Permanent Select Committee on Intelligence, one year into the Iraq conflict. Defending her supportive position on the war on the basis of this NIE, she asserted in 2004 that the 2002 NIE had made two additional statements that varied alarmingly with the previous estimates on Iraq that had been more tepid: "First, that Baghdad possessed chemical and biological weapons, and second, that Baghdad was reconstituting its nuclear weapons program. These were centerpieces of the NIE and of the case for war."[91] Her remarks reflect the basis on which many members of Congress appeared to vote, and that is the 2002 NIE that had struck a startling tone on Iraq's weapons programs. Questions about the haste with which the NIE had been assembled, why this estimate was far more certain than its predecessors, and how to reconstruct postwar Iraq were largely ignored.[92]

Thus, the attacks of 9/11 made manifest the possibility of direct threats against the United States. The future looked less certain and time horizons were short, making it seem unwise to wait until tomorrow to confront the threat either with or without allies. Intelligence estimates on Iraq only served to reinforce these concerns; a slew of intelligence errors added up to a "whole shoddy repertoire of mistakes and techniques that made a hunch about Saddam Hussein seem urgent."[93] The 2002 National Security Strategy presaged how that mentality would affect allies: "While the U.S. will constantly strive to enlist the support of the international community, we will not hesitate to act alone, if necessary, to exercise our right of self-defense."[94] In the event that interests between it and other states diverged, the United States made it clear that it would seek a policy of "as much multilateralism as possible, as much unilateralism as necessary."[95]

This is the message President Bush communicated in a speech to the United Nations on 12 September 2002. "The purposes of the United States should not be doubted. The Security Council resolutions will be enforced—the just demands of peace and security will be met—or action will be unavoidable...we cannot stand by and do nothing while dangers gather."[96] After the UN passed resolution 1441 on 8 November 2002, President Bush voiced a similar concern about delaying action on the disarmament of Iraq: "The world must not lapse into unproductive debates over whether specific instances of Iraqi non-compliance are serious."[97]

The reason President Bush saw additional debate as unproductive is that it stood in the way of intervention. The view was at odds, however, with the majority of the Security Council, which preferred giving inspections more time.[98] Having reached a point of deadlock in the Security Council, the United States and the United Kingdom had two options: they could concede and let inspections continue, delaying an invasion until after the Security Council had arrived at a more definitive conclusion about Iraq's weapons programs. That option spelled an uncertain amount of time. Alternatively, the United States and the United Kingdom could choose not to seek a second resolution and invade alone.[99] That option they could carry out on their own, without further multilateral negotiation and without additional delay.

Iraq as a "Cakewalk"

Expectations about the nature of the war only fanned these go-it-alone flames. If overestimates of the threat made quick and unilateral action seem necessary, then underestimates of the commitment created reassurances that unilateralism would not be costly. The confidence that "even alone, U.S. forces would win this war"[100] guided thinking on whether to expend energy and time collecting allies. Former Deputy National Security Advisor for Iraq and Afghanistan Meghan O'Sullivan noted in an interview that the administration believed that "the absence of a coalition wouldn't hurt" the intervention's outcome.[101]

The reason is that senior policy makers expected that the United States could overthrow the regime "quickly and cheaply"[102] and that the war itself would be "quick and easy."[103] As Gordon and Trainor write in an authoritative account of the conflict, "Rumsfeld and his generals misread their foe...the allied ground forces, as few as they were, expected to run roughshod over the Guard units with a combination of maneuver and firepower and drive directly to Baghdad."[104] Several factors contributed to that misreading.

First, many of the policy makers responsible for the 2003 Iraq war had participated in the crushing victory during Desert Storm a decade or more earlier. They viewed "the invasion of Iraq largely as a continuation of the Persian Gulf War."[105] In the Gulf War, the United States had developed a coalition that had overestimated the number of Iraqi troops, delivering a devastating defeat to an army that was thought to be more numerous and potent than the Iraqi military of 2003. In the Gulf War, "progress was rapid. Iraqi conscripts offered little resistance and surrendered in large numbers as Coalition forces overran the forward defenses."[106] The victory was decisive and contributed to the expectation that the 2003 intervention would yield similar results.

Second, if the United States had experienced overwhelming victory in the Gulf War, it could extrapolate from that encounter and conclude that the victory in Iraq would be overwhelmingly greater. Since then, the United States had embarked on a transformation of its military that had generated an even larger gap between the technology of the United States and that of the Iraqis. Moreover, estimates suggested that the Iraqi military had been degraded since the 1991 Gulf War; the regular army staffing was 40 percent (down 60 percent) from 1991, munitions were down 50 percent from pre-1991 levels, and of the aircraft that Iraq retained from 1991, only about 50 to 60 percent of the planes were serviceable, flown by poorly trained pilots.[107] The military had reorganized after 1991, but through the combination of damage in the previous war, sanctions, and degradation in the intervening years, the Iraqi military did not look nearly as threatening as it had in the run-up to the previous war in the Gulf.[108]

Third, limited human intelligence caused the United States to rely on dubious sources that only reinforced the expectation of ease. One key source for human intelligence (HUMINT) came from Ahmad Chalabi and his organization, the Iraqi National Congress, an exile group that sought regime change in Iraq. The Iraqi National Congress had assured the administration that Iraqis were being oppressed by Saddam Hussein and that U.S. forces would be greeted as "liberators" with "flowers and candy."[109] As a result of the ease, all but 30,000 soldiers might be expected back in the United States by September of the same year.[110] Another now maligned source was "Curveball," an Iraqi defector whose inflated statements of Iraq's WMD programs played into the hands of a U.S. government that was already wary of Saddam's WMD capabilities. That the United States had to rely on a source to which it did not have direct access—Rafid Ahmed Alwan, or "Curveball" was an Iraqi defector working with German intelligence—was dubious but at the time appeared to be the least bad source under conditions of scarce human intelligence.[111]

Fourth, Secretary Rumsfeld seemed convinced that the recent, sweeping experiences in Afghanistan had validated his transformational model of warfare and meant that the approach of using few but agile troops could work as effectively in Iraq.[112] Early in the planning process, when General Franks approached Secretary Rumsfeld with a recommended troop number in the hundreds of thousands, Rumsfeld remarked that the number was too high: "I'm not sure that that much force is needed given what we've learned coming out of Afghanistan."[113] Indeed, the early experiences of Afghanistan and the Afghan Model of light, agile, and transformational forces had given the United States what seemed to be further support for the argument that few forces would be necessary in Iraq[114] and that war could be "speedy *and* lethal."[115]

Kenneth Adelman, a military assistant to Rumsfeld in the 1970s, in the Arms Control Agency in the Reagan administration, and a member of the Defense Policy Board, summed up the prevailing belief that the United States could win on the cheap. In a *Washington Post* op-ed, he wrote: "I believe demolishing Hussein's military power and liberating Iraq would be a cakewalk. Let me give simple, responsible reasons: (1) It was a cakewalk last time; (2) they've become much weaker; (3) we've become much stronger; and (4) now we're playing for keeps."[116] Anything short of quick, decisive victory seemed unrealistic.[117]

Last, the emphasis on troop numbers and quality assumed that to the extent there were challenges, they would be in winning the war, not winning the peace. Vice President Cheney famously asserted, "I really do believe that we will be greeted as liberators"; the absence of civilian resistance was expected to mean that challenges would be concentrated in combat with the Iraqi military, itself eviscerated since 1991, ultimately producing a quick, low-cost intervention with few casualties.[118] Peace would quickly fall into place, according to the civilian leadership. The military side was warier. It anticipated a number of operational and political challenges, including the costs of rebuilding Iraq after regime change.[119]

Over several months and many iterations, the civilian and military leadership reconciled differences between the more cautious larger scale operation advocated by the military and the smaller, "think outside the box" plan advocated by the civilian leadership. The result was an invasion force of 145,000 that the military believed would be a sufficient initial presence but that would accommodate the civilian leadership's goal of avoiding a massive troop build-up.[120] This grand compromise was achieved by "fiddling with the assumptions" of the war's challenges in the conflict and postconflict phases, however.[121] In so doing, defense planners arrived at rosy assumptions about the time line of conflict. In February 2003, before the start of the war, Rumsfeld predicted that the conflict "could last six days, six weeks. I doubt six months."[122] The top military and civilian advisors had similarly low predictions. Chairman of the Joint Chiefs of Staff (CJCS) General Myers estimated 30 days to defeat the Iraqi military; Vice CJCS General Pace expected less than a month. Deputy Secretary of Defense Paul Wolfowitz guessed between 7 days and Wolfowitz's senior military assistant, Lt. Gen. Craddock anticipated 21 days. One military planner said: "MG Petraeus' rush to get me onto his planning team sooner rather than later in spring/early summer 2003 was based on his sense that the entire war might be 'over' by summer's end (the prevailing concern back then was to get over there before it ended!)."[123]

Planning documents declassified in 2007, referred to as "Polo Step Iraq War Planning Slides," reveal the wholesale underestimation of the duration and commitment that the intervention would carry with it. As one example, they show how the United States would have drawn down to 25,000 troops in less than two years and then to 5,000 troops by December 2006,[124] which National Security Archive Executive Director Thomas Blanton referred to as part of the "completely unrealistic assumptions about a post-Saddam Iraq that permeate these war plans."[125] Military planners who generated these plans were actually trying to plan conservatively to "send the message to civilian policy makers that the invasion of Iraq would be a multiyear proposition, not an easy in-and-out war." With the benefit of hindsight, even these conservative estimates look "startlingly unrealistic."[126]

Expectations of a quick, straightforward victory translated into low cost estimates. Office of Management and Budget Director Mitch Daniels said that costs would be in the range of $50 to $60 billion, based in part on estimates from the 1991 Gulf War.[127] Deputy Secretary of Defense Paul Wolfowitz took issue with such high estimates in testimony on 27 March 2003. He argued that estimates of $60 to $90 billion had vastly overstated the likely cost of the war, in part because of revenues from oil that were expected to accrue $50 to $100 billion over two to three years.[128] In his testimony, Wolfowitz asserted that Iraq could finance its own reconstruction through oil revenues. Estimates from the United States Agency for International Development (USAID) were similarly low, around $1.7 billion for the U.S. taxpayers for the entire intervention and reconstruction.[129]

The distinction between the prediction of a swift war and the reality of a longer occupation is important because it is these predictions that, while "wildly off the mark,"[130] determined the U.S. approach to intervention. With the anticipation of a reasonably quick, inexpensive, and manageable war, the United States believed it could intervene alone and succeed. Had it believed that the effort would take the time and resources that it did, the administration, as Grossman indicated, would have been more committed to finding allied support. Without an expectation that allies would bring such value, the administration proceeded with the more unilateral plan, intervening with primarily U.S. troops under the premise that the United States would win easily by relying on its own resources.

ALTERNATIVE ACCOUNTS OF U.S. COOPERATION BEHAVIOR IN IRAQ

Norms in a Post-9/11 World: Or, "I Don't Care What the International Lawyers Say"

There is little evidence to suggest that the United States felt constrained by shared international beliefs about how to use force in the years after 9/11 and leading up to the Iraq War. As Cofer Black, testified to the 9/11 Commission, the "gloves came off" after 9/11, and the government shed any constraints on its ability to prosecute the war on terror.[131] What followed from this shift in strategy—from cautious to bellicose—was not just a more expansive foreign policy but, more generally, "almost unfettered latitude" in how President Bush conducted the so-called war on terror.[132]

The principle of self-defense quickly superseded other norms of war after 9/11.[133] The mantra within the U.S. defense establishment became "What have you done to kill a terrorist today?"[134] Living the mantra itself, the administration made it clear that it would enact "tough new rules of engagement"[135] and resist anything that would stand in its way of prosecuting terrorists. That meant sidestepping its own Constitution's provision of habeas corpus and international norms on when or how to go to war.[136] As Richard Clarke, the administration's counterterrorism czar, reports in his memoir, *Against All Enemies*, Bush responded to his cabinet's legalistic concerns about preemption and unilateralism with the statement that "any barriers in your way, they are gone" after 9/11. He went on to assert that "I don't care what the international lawyers say, we're going to go in and kick some ass."[137]

A number of post-9/11 policies point to the administration's disregard—at least in the initial years immediately after the attacks—for international norms as a general proposition. One of the first and most egregious examples was the treatment of prisoners and use of enhanced interrogation techniques that became common after 9/11. Seeking better and timelier intelligence from prisoners rounded up after the invasion of Afghanistan, the U.S. government engaged in aggressive interrogation of prisoners. The behavior, as a Senate Armed Services Committee investigation found, was not the product of "a few bad apples" but was systematically crafted at the highest levels of government and applied across almost all cases of interrogation.[138]

This shift was grounded in a number of legal opinions advanced throughout 2002. In January 2002, Assistant Attorney General Jay Bybee advised White House Counsel Alberto Gonzales that the United States had "sufficient grounds" to deny detainees the standard entitlements covered under the Geneva Conventions.[139] In February 2002, President Bush accepted the conclusions of the Bybee memo that the Taliban and al Qaeda would not be eligible for Common Article 3 Provisions of the Geneva Conventions,[140] an outcome contradicted by subsequent Supreme Court decisions.[141] Having accepted the limited application of the Geneva Conventions, the Department of Justice went further, drafting a memo dated 1 August 2002 that issued legal guidance on thresholds for torture. The Department of Justice's Office of Legal Counsel suggested that actions "must be equivalent in intensity to the pain accompanying serious physical injury, such as organ failure, impairment of bodily function, or even death" to constitute torture.[142] Almost no behavior could constitute torture under this exceedingly narrow definition; only severe beatings, threats of imminent death, burning, electric shocks to genitalia, rape or sexual assault, and "forcing the prisoner to watch the torture of others" would count as torture. Even these were mere guidelines, since the Office of Legal Counsel advised that existing circumstances might call for suspension of U.S. obligations under international law. The memo's authors, Jay Bybee and John Yoo, determined that "necessity or self-defense may justify interrogation methods that might violate" the sections of the domestic code that implemented the Convention against Torture.[143] This guidance on treatment of detainees, considered deeply flawed by a number of legal scholars, violated both the spirit and letter of norms that had evolved in the five decades since the introduction of the Geneva Conventions in 1949.[144]

Separately, the Defense Department worked to find "increasingly severe" interrogation techniques that would "enhance our efforts to extract additional information" in spite of previous commitments to the Convention against Torture.[145] While many of these memos were careful to parse legal language to conclude that the recommendations were "in accordance" with international law, the interpretations are so liberally divined as to suggest that the administration had clearly made normative prescriptions on appropriate international behavior subordinate to operational effectiveness. Indeed, it is difficult to assess the administration's behavior after 9/11 without concluding that its goal was to obviate international legal norms to the extent necessary as a way to increase its operational autonomy. As the *New Yorker*'s Jane Mayer concludes, the Bush administration implemented "a policy of deliberate cruelty that would've been unthinkable on Sept. 10."[146]

Permitting such liberal interpretations of international law was the extraordinary girth that Congress had granted to the administration on 14 September 2001. The Authorization on the Use of Military Force allowed the president to use whatever means necessary against those actors "he determines planned, authorized, committed, or aided the terrorist attacks that occurred on September 11, 2001, or harbored such organizations or persons, in order to prevent any future acts of international terrorism against the United States."[147] The generously worded authorization permitted President Bush to let the ends justify the means; that is, the president was able to undertake whatever actions he deemed necessary to prevent future attacks. Once the Bush administration had determined that intervening in Iraq was necessary, any lack of multilateral support would not obstruct the approach to intervention. It was clear that the Bush administration was not going to allow some ambiguous cooperation norm to impinge on its counterterrorism strategy.

This is not to say that it was unaware of the norm. In a memo dated 15 October 2002, the Pentagon anticipated a series of possible consequences from an Iraq intervention. One was that "world reaction against preemption or 'anticipatory self-defense' could inhibit U.S. ability to engage [in cooperation with other countries] in the future."[148] It was aware that members of the international community could censure a "preemptive" intervention and that they might then stand on the sidelines, not just for the Iraq intervention but in future engagements. Considering what it expected to be the shorter term impact of not acting, the United States was dismissive of longer term unhelpful consequences of spurning these norms of war.

Granting that norms may have an effect on behavior that falls short of actually constraining actors, did norms shape the modes, means, and course of action that the United States took with respect to the Iraq intervention? If this significantly lower bar is the standard for normative salience and effectiveness, then U.S. behavior with regard to the intervention in Iraq does provide some evidence of normative pull. First, the United States did go to some great lengths to proclaim that its "coalition of the willing" represented 47 states, including a combined population of 1.23 billion people, a combined gross domestic product (GDP) of $22 trillion, and every race, religion, and ethnicity in the world. As the White House reported in its official Web site, "This number is still growing, and it is no accident that many member nations of the Coalition recently escaped from the boot of a tyrant or have felt the scourge of terrorism."[149]

Although such rhetoric was designed to influence domestic opinion favorably by implying that the United States was not assuming the entire burden, it had the added effect of making the intervention appear to be broadly sanctioned, a message clearly intended to politically legitimate the U.S.-led intervention. By repeatedly citing the numbers and robustness of the coalition, the United States was, in effect, arguing that its intentions and actions had been endorsed by the international community and should therefore be accepted as a legitimate use of force.

Second, the type of state that the United States gathered into its coalition also reflects some degree of normative strength. The United States did not seek the support of Palau and Micronesia for their material capabilities or ability to shift the balance of power, but rather for the political validation they—at least in the aggregate—might offer to the coalition. The United States had been unable to channel its intervention through an international organization (IO) and therefore shopped for an alternate method of multilateralism.[150] In this case, the next best form of multilateralism was an ad hoc coalition; that the United States chose this course of action rather than absolute unilateralism does attest to some normative pull, since the United States could have more easily conducted the intervention alone than with less equipped soldiers from Georgia or Azerbaijan, whom the U.S. military considered somewhat of a liability because these troops came unequipped and untrained.[151]

Perhaps the strongest evidence for normative salience is a counterfactual exercise. Had there been no multilateral norm, would the United States have bothered assembling a coalition of the willing comprised of many states that were able to provide little if any material support? Would the United States have been touting the number of states in its coalition as a way to suggest that the action was widely endorsed? While it did not ultimately constrain the U.S. decision to intervene, the multilateral norm did have some effect on the degree to which the United States sought allies and how the United States framed the intervention, in other words, the modes and means of intervention.

In that sense, the case of Iraq is not unlike that of Haiti in terms of the distinctions between the actual degree of multilateralism and the desired perception of multilateralism. In both cases, elites used rhetoric about the collective, multilateral nature of the response, while actual participation in combat operations reflected a much more unilateral strategy (though the obvious difference is that Haiti had UN authorization). These examples set up the possibility of a deep-superficial multilateral distinction in which the rhetoric or political spin is multilateral, suggesting some normative or political interest in appearing to be multilateral, while the actual operational outcome is unilateral, reflecting an unwillingness to let coalition operations hinder effectiveness. I return to this distinction in the conclusion of the book.

THE DOMESTIC AUDIENCE

Despite Iraq's being something of a security nuisance since the 1991 war, President Bush spoke for himself and his predecessor by saying that regime change in Iraq had previously been "more of an attitude than a plan" before 9/11.[152] The same might be said for the American domestic audience. Congress had passed the Iraq Liberation Act in 1998 that called for regime change, and public opinion polls showed that Americans did not like or trust Saddam Hussein, but neither was actually interested in walking this talk of regime change. That attitude became more of a plan after 9/11. The domestic audience quickly favored intervention, though at least in the case of the public, it registered some stipulations on the form of intervention it preferred: multilateral. The administration dismissed these preferences—often verbally denigrating the effect of public opinion—in favor of going alone. Nonetheless, that it went to the UN at all is some evidence of domestic influence. As this section shows, the administration's staunch preference was to avoid the international bureaucracy, but instead it did go through the process, largely because of the influence of Secretary Powell and Prime Minister Blair, who urged a public-friendly path of going through the UN.

The American Public: Saddam = "Evil"

One of the tropes about the Iraq War is that the Bush administration misled the public on the case for war. Threat inflation coming from the Bush administration—as the argument goes—caused an otherwise unperturbed public to follow it into war. Public opinion data tell a different story. Deep and lingering distrust of Saddam Hussein predated the Bush administration. Rather, it followed immediately from the 1991 Gulf War. Between 1991 and 2003, the percentage of Americans who viewed Iraq mostly or very unfavorably never dropped below 85 percent.[153] Views of Saddam Hussein were even more negative. Between 1998 and mid-2002, between 96 and 97 percent of Americans viewed Saddam Hussein unfavorably. Pre-9/11 polls that queried whether Iraq posed a threat detected similarly concerned attitudes. In March 2001, 85 percent of Americans declared Iraq to be a threat, matched by about the same number—86 percent—in December 2001.[154] In short, the public had had serious misgivings about Saddam Hussein and his government for more than a decade before the Iraq War.

Already a distrusted character, Saddam Hussein did not win any additional popularity points after the 9/11 attacks. On the contrary, as Pew Research found in its polling, "America's view of the world changed dramatically, and perhaps permanently, on Sept. 11."[155] What changed in the wake of 9/11 was the salience of terrorism and the sense that threats could come from anywhere and cross any boundaries. Iraq was generically malevolent, according to Americans, but what made it particularly threatening was the imagined plausibility of collusion with terrorist groups, a view that gave rise to the belief that Saddam Hussein had linked up with terrorist groups to carry out the 9/11 attacks. In a February 2002 Gallup Poll, Americans were asked whether they would describe the government of Iraq as "evil." Eighty-two percent of Americans agreed that Saddam's government could best be described as evil.[156] In December 2002, 79 percent of Americans believed that Iraq "is involved in acts of terrorism against the U.S."[157] When asked more explicitly in February 2003 about Iraq's ties with al Qaeda, a full 87 percent of Americans thought it was certain or likely that Iraq was connected with the terrorist group and that this relationship posed a threat to U.S. security.[158] In September 2003, several months after the intervention and the discovery that Saddam did not have WMD, 69 percent of the public still believed in a possible connection between Saddam and the attacks on the World Trade Center and the Pentagon, and 82 percent believed he had provided material assistance to bin Laden and the terrorist network.[159] The public's vilification of Saddam since the 1991 Gulf War had translated into a view that Saddam might be behind anything sinister, including the 9/11 terrorist attacks.

Although Iraq had been a major foreign policy issue throughout the 1990s, and the official U.S. policy after 1998 was regime change in Iraq, domestic commitment to that policy lacked traction until the 9/11 attacks. A public that had been reluctant to use force in the 1990s now thought "twice about the risks inherent in the purely dovish position on Iraq"[160] and became more actively supportive of the use of force. The public supported a renewed sense of international engagement on threats to American security. Iraq appeared to be one of those threats.

Polls taken after 9/11 record that shift. Whereas in February 2001, only 52 percent of the American public supported invading Iraq, in September 2001, 73 percent supported using force against Iraq; support remained high through 2001. It declined into the mid-50s as President Bush began making the case in 2002 and rose again only after Secretary Powell gave his defense to the Security Council in February 2003 and immediately prior to the invasion in the middle of March.[161] Rather than "matching the evolution of the administration's public positions," as some critics have claimed, the public's concern and willingness to use force in Iraq appears to be more directly related to the 9/11 attacks than to the administration's making the case for war.[162]

Political elites of all stripes did little to defuse the public's concern about security, however, or to disavow it of spurious connections between Saddam's propensity for evil and the likelihood of future terrorist attacks. Vice President Cheney said that "it was pretty well confirmed" that 9/11 ringleader Mohammad Atta had met with senior Iraqi intelligence officials. Robert Kerrey, a former Democratic senator from Nebraska and a member of the 9/11 Commission, cited "credible evidence that Iraqi intelligence personnel met with one of the leaders of this attack."[163] President Bush also did not correct the misperceptions of a connection between terrorism and Saddam Hussein and framed the Iraq intervention as the next logical phase in the war on terror. The statement that followed the fall of Baghdad is typical of the administration's rhetoric: "The liberation of Iraq is a crucial advance in the campaign against terror. We've removed an ally of al Qaeda, and cut off a source of terrorist funding."[164] By drawing connections between the 9/11 attacks and intervention in Iraq, political elites helped consolidate support among a public already jolted from the 9/11 attacks and predisposed to loathe Saddam Hussein.

Beyond being generally inclined toward war, the public had a specific leaning toward a multilateral approach. Although as many as 70 percent of Americans supported the intervention in general terms,[165] some of that support was conditional on multilateral sanction. Polls indicated that Americans were less supportive of unilateral intervention than intervening with allies. When asked whether the United States should use force against Iraq even if allies did not "go along," only 38 percent of Americans responded in the affirmative in February 2003;[166] that number was even lower in a separate poll (Chicago–German Marshall Fund), which found only 20 percent of Americans agreeing that the United States should invade Iraq even if the United States had to "go it alone."[167] Even when asked explicitly about the downside of multilateralism taking more time—in the form of inspections—in exchange for allied support, most Americans indicated that they would be willing to wait. Over a period of six months, from August 2002 to February 2003, that question was asked 10 times; support for waiting ranged from 72 percent in February 2002 and decreased slightly until late February 2003, when still 59 percent supported waiting for allies before taking action.[168]

Support for multilateralism in the form of UN authorization was also strong but inconsistently so. When asked if UN Security Council authorization was necessary for invasion, 67 percent of Americans concurred in January 2003, though just 56 percent by February.[169] Yet another poll found that only 22 percent of Americans said the United States should "not use force" if the UNSC did not authorize the intervention.[170] Perhaps one implicit reason is that 68 percent of Americans agreed that UNSC Resolution 1441, which warned of "severe consequences" if Iraq did not cooperate with disarmament, provided adequate UN authorization to proceed with military intervention in Iraq.[171] Another is that the public appeared to look for a good faith effort. That support for intervening "alone" increased 12 percent after Secretary of State Colin Powell's presentation to the UN Security Council suggests that the U.S. public was generally satisfied with such efforts, irrespective of whether that effort actually translated into a Security Council resolution authorizing force.[172] In a somewhat contradictory finding, however, a different poll found that 57 percent of Americans thought that the United States should obtain a second UN resolution before taking action.[173] Capping the series of conflicted opinions, in February 2003, 62 percent of the public expressed willingness to proceed without UN approval, though 61 percent said they would not agree with the decision.[174]

Despite some logical inconsistencies and seeming contradictions across polls, public support for intervening with multilateral support nonetheless tended to be higher than support for acting alone. The ideal intervening condition was one in which the United States had both allies *and* the support of the UN Security Council. In four polls leading up to the intervention, support for military action under these conditions reached 85 percent, compared with median support of 46 percent for "one or two allies" and 35 percent for acting alone.[175]

The U.S. Congress and the Blank Check for War

The public's sense of vulnerability and resulting support for intervention in Iraq was magnified in Congress, which resoundingly endorsed intervention in Iraq. The U.S. House voted 296 to 133, garnering 46 more supporting votes than George H. W. Bush had received to go into the 1991 Gulf War. On 2 October 2002, the Senate voted 77 to 23[176] on the Joint Resolution to Authorize the Use of Force against Iraq, an overwhelming margin,[177] particularly compared with the 52–47 Senate vote that had authorized the Gulf War on 12 January 1991.[178] Toughness on national security had become the dominant political narrative after 9/11, and Democrats wanted to look responsive to the national interest.[179] This was particularly true leading up to the 2002 midterm elections, the first national election after the 9/11 attacks. Legislators therefore voted for the Iraq authorization rather than be accused, just a year after 9/11, of being weak on homeland defense. They gave the president no specific provision for *how* he was authorized to defend against Iraq, leaving him considerable degrees of policy latitude to intervene with as many or few allies as he was able to muster.

The Mixed Effect of the Domestic Audience

Taken together, the domestic environment leading up to the Iraq War paints a mixed picture in terms of its effect on the administration's cooperation strategy. The public was still on edge after 9/11. Having distrusted Saddam Hussein since the 1991 Gulf War, the 9/11 attacks gave them further ammunition to draw sketchy and unwarranted connections between Saddam Hussein and the attacks. They were primed for war. More so than Congress, the public expressed a preference, albeit an equivocating one, for multilateral action over going it alone. In light of these preferences, the decision to intervene without the UN and with one or two allies is inconsistent at least with the public's hopes.

The administration's dismissive rhetoric is consistent with the view of a public opinion discounted by elites. As President Bush responded to antiwar protests in February 2003, "You know, the size of protests is like deciding, well, I'm going to decide policy based upon a focus group.... The role of a leader is to decide policy based upon the security—in this case, the security of the people."[180] Indifference toward public opinion was a running theme with the Bush administration on Iraq. In December of the previous year, he had similarly asserted: "I don't run my administration based upon polls and focus groups."[181] President Bush had anointed himself "the Decider" and was not prone to the distractions and vagaries of public opinion.

Despite rhetoric to the contrary, there is some evidence that the domestic audience—including Congress—was not irrelevant in guiding how the United States went to war. The main evidence for this is that President Bush did not trust the UN to manage inspections or carry out a responsible Iraq policy more generally. Going to the UN at all and seeking authorization to intervene, according to one of Bush's biographers, was not "Bush's idea...he was wary of what the French, the Russians, and the Germans had in store for him. Just as much, he detested what the UN had come to embody. It was all about *process*. As if what counted wasn't action but instead the act of talking...while dangers gathered."[182] Vice President Cheney harbored even more animosity toward the UN. He advocated a streamlined, unilateral approach; he was wary of going to the UN, worried that it would "snag them in a morass of UN debate and hesitation."[183]

A second resolution authorizing force certainly went too far, according to the administration. Under Secretary of Defense Douglas Feith, a Cheney ally, wrote in his memoirs that the vice president was "clearly uneasy with Powell's talk of a second resolution" that would authorize the use of force.[184] Cheney suggested that seeking a second UN resolution would push the United States back into the "hopeless soup of UN process."[185]

Thus, if we start from the premise that many influential administration officials were skeptical of any multilateral involvement on the issue of Iraq, then any action that was marginally multilateral—even simply going to the UN to make the case for the first resolution—may be considered the result of outside pressures.

Those outside pressures came from the domestic audience, both the U.S. and foreign audiences. With Congress having abdicated oversight with its October 2002 authorization, Secretary of State Colin Powell was mainly responsible for advocating on behalf of the U.S. public. He warned President Bush of the upcoming midterm elections in the United States and suggested that voters "were keen to see UN support for U.S. policy."[186] Going through the UN, Powell implied, would reassure voters that the administration was taking their interests into account. Otherwise, he suggested, the administration could expect to suffer in the midterm elections.

Public opinion also imposed pressures in less direct ways. Although general support for intervention was relatively high, the administration had the sense that support might not remain high. Speaking to President Aznar of Spain, Prime Minister Blair, and Portugal's Prime Minister José Manuel Durão, Bush said: "Maybe lightning will strike and Chirac will agree with our co-sponsored resolution," but it was likely that coming to a resolution would take time negotiating. That would mean a delay of "a week or two weeks or three weeks.... Public opinion won't get better and it will get worse in some countries like America."[187] Understanding that public support had a short shelflife, the administration had to advance its case and conduct the intervention in a comparably narrow window. Thus, public opinion may have played a more dominant role with respect to the timing of intervention, which ultimately did put some constraints on the cooperation strategies available to the administration. Multilateral negotiation would take time, and the administration ran the risk that every week of multilateral bargaining would mean less and less public support.

Particularly prior to congressional authorization, the administration was also keenly aware of the potentially constraining effects of the legislative branch. Bush's director of political affairs, Kenneth Mehlman, advised Bush that he needed to "get them on record before the [2002] election...to prod them into passing a resolution authorizing the president to use force."[188] The move was politically adroit: force Congress's hand on the first post-9/11 elections and, in return for the near-certain authorization, be able to say that the United States had intervened with congressional sanction. Once Congress was on the record as supporting the intervention, it would have less leverage on *how* the United States intervened.

Perhaps more so than the U.S. domestic audience, a more relevant reason that the United States channeled its intervention through the UN was because of British pressure. As British Foreign Secretary Jack Straw told Bob Woodward, "If you are really thinking about war and you want us Brits to be a player, we cannot be unless you go to the United Nations."[189] For Britain, UN participation was a way to mollify Blair's domestic audience and own Labour Party, assuaged only once they saw that their government had first cooperated with international institutions before resorting to force.[190] In early September 2002, British Prime Minister Tony Blair publicly urged President Bush to seek authorization from the UN before taking military action. He had previously made private pleas but adamantly and publicly pressed his position that the United States and Britain make a "coordinated effort to get the UN to back us."[191] The British preference for a "legal fig leaf" for intervention prevailed.[192] Thus, to the extent that the United States did seek to present its case to the UN on 12 September 2002 and then 5 February 2003, it is due at least in part to the result of pressure from America's key ally, Britain, not to conduct its intervention without at least a pretense of multilateralism.[193]

THE PERMISSIVE ROLE OF REGIONAL POWERS

The largely unilateral Iraq intervention offers weak support for the regional power argument. Using the 1991 Gulf War as a guide, we might have expected the United States to reach out to similar powerful regional actors. Geopolitics had changed somewhat in the intervening years, of course. In 1990-1991, as the United States was making coalition decisions with respect to the Gulf War, the Soviet Union was still a prominent player in the region, making it politically risky to intervene in Iraq without Soviet backing. By 2002-2003, Russia was still recovering from its serious economic decline of the 1990s and mainly focused inward on domestic demographic, military, and fiscal weakness.[194] Russia certainly did not have the regional influence that had made it useful in the earlier war, so it is not surprising, according to the regional power thesis, that the United States gave short shrift to rallying Russia's support for intervention.

In principle, two other key regional allies from 1991, Turkey and Saudi Arabia, were as important in the run-up to the 2003 war as they had been over a decade earlier. Saudi Arabia had enormous amounts of capital that had made the 1991 war a relative bargain for the United States; it was also home to U.S. military bases, including a command post. Turkey was assumed to be a staging area for the 4th Infantry Division;[195] planners hoped that it would provide a base for 62,000 infantry and for launching air attacks from Incirlik Air Base.[196] Turkey was politically important for Iraq as well, given its history with the Iraqi Kurds in the north and the possibility that Turkey could intervene in northern Iraq and create a "war within a war," destabilizing the north of Iraq.[197]

Despite these countries' potential value and, in the extreme case, the potential for destabilization, the Bush administration was clearly willing to go into Iraq without the active degree of support—or "resource pooling"—that these countries had provided in the previous war or could have provided in 2003. One reason is that both states' support appeared to be fungible. In 2002, the United States began moving assets from Prince Sultan Air Base in Saudi Arabia to Al-Udeid in Qatar, including technology for a combined air operations center (a command post) in Qatar that would enable the United States to coordinate the Iraq War from Qatar, rather than Saudi Arabia, and with greater flexibility than the United States was permitted under the agreement with Saudi Arabia.[198]

Another reason for the willingness to go without Turkey is that the United States believed that Turkey was desirable but not crucial to victory. According to one army colonel who helped plan the Iraq invasion, "We were confident we could take down the regime without an attack out of Turkey."[199] Having a credible entry point from the north would certainly have helped, which is why the United States offered lucrative loans and grants to offset the consequences of war and why the negative vote in the Turkish Parliament came as a disappointment.[200] The 4th Infantry Division, which had been at sea awaiting the decision in the Turkish Parliament, ultimately attacked from the south instead of from Turkey. General Franks and his staff actually claimed that the diplomatic maneuvering with Turkey had been a feint, a "deception campaign" designed to divide Iraqi forces rather than have them concentrated in the south.[201] Though it is difficult to confirm Franks's thesis, it is broadly consistent with the way President Bush characterized Turkey's effect on the Iraq War: "We'll win without Turkey. It would be nice to have Turkey. The issue is how to make sure they don't go into northern Iraq."[202]

Though the first part of the statement is dismissive of the benefits of resource pooling, the last part shows an awareness that counterbalancing behavior could be destabilizing. In this case, too, the possibility of counterproductive influence on the intervention was somewhat less operative for both Turkey and Saudi Arabia. The war-within-a-war scenario could have been destabilizing in the case of Turkey, but it was almost unimaginable that Saudi Arabia would use military force to challenge the U.S. invasion or support Iraq. The United States nonetheless quietly pursued assurances from Saudi Arabia that the United States could undertake operations from Prince Sultan Air Base,[203] which was a requirement even for the U.S. "unilateral" invasion plan.[204] Both regional actors were therefore at least permissive in the 2003 Iraq War and had asserted that they would not actively resist the intervention.[205] The United States was willing to proceed with substitutes to their material support, coupled with tacit assurances that they would not interfere.

By a similar logic as that of Turkey and Saudi Arabia—strong states that border Iraq—we might expect the United States to have been concerned with Iran, less out of the hope of cooperation but more to avoid possible meddling. Iran's border with Iraq is lengthy and disputed, its track record of relations with Iraq stormy, and its arsenal distinguished.[206] As one paper in Asia put it, Iran had an "impressive curriculum vitae of weapons of mass destruction"[207] and was a foremost sponsor of terrorism, which should have elicited concerns about its counterproductive influence. This would have been more of a concern in the 2003 war than in 1991, when more of the fighting was south near Kuwait and war aims were more restrictive than the plans for regime change in 2003. Moreover, in 1991, Iran was still weakened from the eight-year war of the 1980s and probably unwilling to engage voluntarily in a war over Iraq. By 2002, it was no "mystery" that "Iran hankered for America's defeat in Iraq."[208]

Despite the shrouded nature of U.S.-Iran relations, it does appear that the United States sought Iran's noninterference in Iraq. Direct communication was impossible because of the post-1979 diplomatic rift between the two countries that grew worse after the United States designated Iran as an "axis of evil" country. Through indirect exchanges, however, the United States tried to secure assurances from Iran that it would at least remain neutral in the conflict.[209] Throughout the autumn of 2002 and until the 2003 invasion, it appears that Iran expressed an intent to remain neutral.[210]

The U.S. goal of mere permissiveness on the part of key regional powers may therefore suggest a revision to the regional power thesis. While active support from powerful regional allies may be desirable, it may not be a necessary condition for intervention. More necessary may be ensuring that these states simply not interfere. Saudi Arabia, for example, may not have offered financial or troop backing as it had in 1991, but it did give the United States private assurances that the United States would have access to Saudi bases and use of the command post near Riyadh. Similarly, Turkey, though it did not allow the United States to launch an attack from its territory, did offer reassurances that it would not actively obstruct U.S. efforts.[211] A permissive response—that is, an assertion that these states would not actively balance against U.S. actions in the region—was satisfactory.

CONCLUSION

This chapter has argued that two main factors contributed to unilateralism in the Iraq War. The first had to do with the short time horizon that followed 9/11. The attacks of 2001 animated the imagination. Particularly given the nature of the attacks, anything seemed possible after 9/11. Threats that seemed to warrant patience before 9/11 now took on a whole new level of menace. Tomorrow's security seemed uncertain if threats, even inchoate ones, were not addressed today. Iraq, which the United States had considered a security problem for more than a decade, took on greater urgency. Not only would Iraq now take center stage but also the United States would deal with it alone if necessary. It might complicate relations with allies in the process, but waiting for the participation of allies and UN authorization seemed costly to leaders who woke up every day to startling new threat reports.[212]

Further pushing decision makers away from multilateralism was the belief that they could sidestep the multilateral process at little cost. If, as they expected, the war would be quick and inexpensive, then allies and international institutions would serve little purpose and not affect the outcome. It became clear in the years after the invasion that the United States had done insufficient planning for the postwar and therefore ended up with an overly optimistic picture of what it would take to win not only the war but also the peace. The combination of these two factors—short time horizon based on worst-case threat assessments and low operational commitment based on best-case scenario—favored unilateralism over multilateralism. It produced the erroneous view in the administration that the absence of a coalition would not undermine the effort.

Adherence to norms of war weighed lightly on the Bush administration's post-9/11 actions. The case of interrogation illustrated how the gloves came off after 9/11 and how concerns about appropriateness became secondary to military effectiveness narrowly defined. The administration's willingness to intervene in Iraq without UN authorization and a robust coalition is consistent with an administration willing to flout international norms after 9/11. It did seek a nominal coalition of states and try to frame its intervention in multilateral and indeed legal terms, all gestures in the direction of multilateral norms.[213] In its actions, though, the United States was ultimately unwilling to be chastened by international multilateral norms.

Similarly, domestic politics had little bearing on the U.S. cooperation strategy, as President Bush often reminded reporters. He consistently asserted his indifference to polls, whether those regarding support for the war or about support being conditional on multilateral sanction. Despite these assertions to the contrary, it does appear that domestic support affected the timing of intervention. The official U.S. policy toward Iraq in the late 1990s was regime change, but without 9/11 and the public's post-9/11 conflation of terrorism threats with Iraq, U.S. elites would have been unlikely to have the public support they needed to intervene in Iraq. To the extent that public support for intervention after 9/11 was expected to be short-lived, the United States had to circumvent multilateral delays in order to intervene in the short time frame of support that public opinion offered.

The public's specific preference for multilateralism had less of a direct bearing on cooperation strategies but did come into play. The default view of the administration opposed the UN's bureaucratic process not necessarily because they were concerned it would fail but rather that it would succeed in producing additional inspections that might delay the onset of conflict.[214] Two factors prompted the administration to pursue UN channels. First, Colin

Powell advocated going through the UN route to appease voters in the November midterm elections, whom he thought would favor UN support for U.S. policy. Second, the British favored going through the UN, and if the United States wanted British support, it would need to give a nod in the direction of the international institution. Prime Minister Blair's insistence on going through the UN prompted Bush to tell British officials that "your man has got cojones" to ask Bush to take the UN path.[215] The upshot, however, is that Bush complied with that request.

Last, the regional power dynamics hypothesis finds the least support from the Iraq case. Consistent with the thesis, the United States was largely dismissive of Russia, either as a state that could help "pool" regional resources or as one that could obstruct the intervention; in the intervening years since the 1991 war, Russia had lost that regional influence. At odds with the thesis, however, the United States sought but was willing to intervene without the support of key regional actors. If the 1991 Gulf War were any guide to the key regional actors for a war in Iraq, we would expect that the United States would have waited for Saudi Arabia and Turkey to provide support. Instead, it merely sought a permissive role and reassurances that neither would interfere with the intervention. One reason is that other command posts and flexible planning meant that support from Saudi Arabia and Turkey was substitutable as long as they were unlikely to obstruct the intervention. Similarly, the United States also conducted indirect exchanges with Iran to ensure its neutrality. Far from acting as though it needed to pool regional resources, the United States was merely after a hands-off environment in which these actors did not stand in the way of the invasion. The simple interest in permissiveness was derivative of the operational expectations: the United States did not expect to *need* the resources of these regional actors as it had in 1991. It just needed them not to interfere.

8

Conclusion

Multilateralism emerged as one of the few winners of the Iraq War. The lesson that "unilateralism in foreign policy is a bad thing" seemed to grow more salient as the costs of the war mounted in the years after the invasion. Hundreds of billions of dollars and thousands of lives made unilateralism seem like an overdetermined disaster, particularly when the putative threat had turned out to be vastly overestimated. As David Ignatius concluded in a *Washington Post* column, the experience in Iraq spawned a new generation of "born-again multilateralists."[1]

However, showing how prevailing attitudes toward cooperation change—and sometimes change quickly—minilateralism had already become the new multilateralism by 2009. That was just three years after multilateralism had made a resurgence, six years after critics had bemoaned the end of multilateralism, and eight years after columnist Charles Krauthammer had colorfully derided multilateralism as the act of "submerging American will in a mush of collective decision-making."[2] The problem with multilateralism, its newest and vintage critics alike complained, is that it is impossible to produce agreement on anything—finance, proliferation, security, or climate—when almost 200 states have a vote. All have different interests, and negotiations end either in deadlock or some diluted agreement that is toothless. The beauty of minilateralism, its proponents argue, is that it brings "to the table the smallest possible number of countries needed to have the largest possible impact on solving a particular problem."[3]

All of these accounts acknowledge the downsides of alternative cooperation approaches, but they all fail to appreciate fully the disadvantages of their preferred approach to cooperation. Minilateralism may be one way around deadlocked negotiations, but it ignores the reason that multilateralism is seen as legitimate: that it is viewed as an independent, neutral assessment of the lead state's ambitions. The very heterogeneity and veto structure of the UN Security Council means that if an intervention does gain authorization, it has passed a difficult test; the broad sanction legitimizes the action.[4] Minilateralism suffers from similar design flaws as a coalition of the willing: it is almost a hand-picked group of actors that have agreed to agree. It is therefore not particularly neutral and would therefore lack the legitimacy of multilateralism.

As this book has shown, there is no silver bullet approach to cooperation, which is why the views of particular advocates can all seem plausible at one time or another. It is also why states' behaviors vary as much as they do. Even within the same period of U.S. dominance—the post–Cold War period—the United States sometimes intervened with the UN and allies, with the UN and few allies other times, and in some cases with neither the UN nor substantial numbers of allies. That variation cut across political parties and within the same administration. The reason, as this chapter will recapitulate, is that the inputs to cooperation strategy relate to the intervention itself—the time horizon and operational commitment—not to a particular distribution of power, political party, or individual. Alternative accounts about norms, domestic politics, and regional powers mattered at the margins or in some cases were important in explaining a particular cooperation strategy but did not explain strategies across cases. Table 8.1 summarizes the findings across cases.

This concluding chapter begins by discussing how the central argument and alternative hypotheses fared in the case studies. Second, it evaluates how the main argument would apply to states other than the United States, laying out the conditions under which both other powerful states and small states would be expected to act multilaterally or unilaterally. The third part of the chapter uses the argument to consider the factors that might be better suited to cooperation; this section makes the policy case for better intelligence assessments and realism about the costs of war, since the costs of war are systematically underestimated, meaning that cooperation is systematically undervalued. The remaining section of the chapter looks at the future of multilateralism, suggesting that formal multilateralism might be decreasingly workable as relative American power declines. Other forms of multilateralism, whether coalitions or formal institutions other than the UN,

Table 8.1 Salience of Arguments across Cases.

Intervention	Time Horizon/Op Commitment	Multilateral Norms	Domestic Politics	Regional Power Dynamics
Gulf War (1991)	+	−	−	+
Haiti (1994)	+	−	+	−
Afghanistan (2001)	+	−	−	+
Iraq (2003)	+	−	+	−

"+" means there was evidence for that hypothesis; "−" means the absence of strong evidence or that there was evidence to the contrary.

might therefore become increasingly common and legitimate. Hybrid forms of cooperation are even more compatible with a powerful state's interests but require deft statecraft to couch realpolitik missions in politically palatable terms.

OF TIME HORIZONS AND OPERATIONAL COMMITMENTS

If powerful states intervened unilaterally because they could, then the post-Cold War period would have consisted of one unilateral U.S. intervention after another. Instead, the United States adopted multilateral strategies more often than not, and a theoretical analysis helps clarify why. Powerful states act multilaterally as often as possible because multilateralism is a power-conserving strategy. The expansive, imposed use of force, Kissinger observed in his study of nineteenth-century statecraft, could not legitimate itself. Rather, it would trigger resistance that made actions costlier to achieve.[5] Understanding the limits of force, in contrast, would reassure other states that a particular action had been widely sanctioned. It would attract powerful allies and perpetuate a status quo that had favored its rise. These incentives are actually more powerful for states with a number of international interests, for whom the task of policing is otherwise prohibitively costly over time.

The problem, however, is that multilateralism is cumbersome, slow, and sometimes unnecessary. In most cases, a lead intervening state can tolerate these costs, since multilateralism pays over time. When time horizons are short, however, long-term payoffs seem imprudent, and actors favor the near-term gratification of unilateralism. The time horizon shifts when external events introduce new information about the security environment. Thus, a direct, military attack on the homeland creates vast uncertainty about the future, produces infinitely short time horizons, and favors immediate payoffs. These conditions are inhospitable to cooperation. Stable expectations about the future—rising challenges, intermediate-term economic challenges to a third party—create longer time horizons. With the long term in mind, multilateralism looks attractive despite being unwieldy in the short term. With these long time horizons, the lead intervening state will pursue formal multilateral channels, whether the UN or some regional organization.

The form of multilateralism—whether the lead state also seeks allies or instead intervenes with international organization (IO) authorization and few allies—depends on operational commitment. Intervening with a coalition is fraught with coordination difficulties that can produce as many problems as it solves. If the lead state believes it can win quickly or on the cheap, a smaller coalition will look more appealing as a way to reduce coordination challenges. In other cases—the most extreme being a "contested zone" in which the opponent has a numerical advantage—even powerful states will seek help.

Though this argument concedes that there is enormous value to the legitimacy that comes with multilateralism, it challenges normative arguments that assume that legitimacy and appropriateness are ends in themselves. As the cases in the book showed, states would rather be seen as legitimate and appropriate but, contrary to dominant accounts of norms, are generally unwilling to compromise effectiveness for the sake of legitimacy. In case after case, the United States has talked a good game on legitimacy and principled multilateralism but acted primarily on the basis of time horizons and operational commitments, breaching any meaningful constraints in the process.

In the 1991 Gulf War, the United States acted first and obtained authorization later. The surprise military attack on an ally created short time horizons; the second-order effects—an invasion of Saudi Arabia and the strangling of Western economies—reinforced the need to act quickly. The United States deployed hundreds of thousands of troops before asking either the UN or its Congress for authorization to use force, despite the deployment risking immediate combat with the Iraqi military. Only once the deterrent force was in place did the United States sincerely engage a multilateral strategy, and only then because its military planners needed more time and because it needed allies for what was expected to be a tough battle of attrition.

At times throughout the buildup to the intervention, the United States asserted its right and willingness to act unilaterally. Its unilateral deployment of hundreds of thousands of troops at a time when the UN had simply condemned the invasion of Kuwait and well before it authorized "all necessary means" suggests that the assertion to use force unilaterally went beyond mere bravado. It was clear from the outset, however, that despite its power, the United States would be unable to carry out the intervention alone. The "monument to multilateralism" resulted from a genuine concern that the Iraqi Army, the fourth largest in the world and seasoned from its war with Iran, would be formidable and exact considerable costs that the United States would rather share with allies.

The 1994 Haiti intervention illustrated the other end of the time horizon spectrum. After having stalled for years, the United States gradually escalated from diplomatic to economic sanctions and finally military invasion in the early 1990s. With little at stake, pursuing UN authorization seemed obvious; the United States risked little by taking several years to stoke multilateral channels and eventually produce UN authorization for a U.S.-led intervention. Moreover, compared with some of the coordination challenges associated with the Gulf War, the multilateral strategy for Haiti was comparatively easy. In exchange for U.S. authorization of Russian peacekeepers, Russia agreed to authorize American intervention in Haiti. In the operations themselves, the United States kept small Caribbean states at the periphery for the more challenging combat phase and transitioned responsibility to a genuine multilateral force only for the peacekeeping phase, which the United States expected to be open-ended and therefore unpalatable as a long-term commitment. This hybrid approach—few allies early on and fully multilateral in the later postconflict phases—allowed the United States to minimize the coordination challenges in the more difficult phases and maximize the contribution of allies in the far costlier, open-ended peacekeeping phase.

Operations in Afghanistan followed a similar pattern, except that the unilateral offensive counterterrorism operations continued to operate in parallel with the multilateral stabilization and reconstruction operations, rather than as a handoff. Despite the expectation that Afghanistan could be a large-scale, long-enduring commitment, the United States intervened largely alone in the initial phases. The 9/11 attacks created terribly unstable expectations about the future. The next attack seemingly could come from anywhere at any time; the short time horizon created an urgency toward action that made collecting allies unhelpful, even if going it alone could be costly over the long term. The implementation of the Afghan Model—a transformational model of warfare—called for small numbers of agile forces and made the go-it-alone approach seem less onerous.

Having addressed the initial threats in Afghanistan and realizing that the commitment would be years and not months, the United States eventually transitioned to a multilateral strategy for the open-ended reconstruction and stabilization phases. The hybrid strategy—in which the United States would continue with unilateral counterterrorism operations outside the multilateral force—reflected differences in time horizons across the two types of operations. Counterterrorism operations addressed the high-value threats—major Taliban or al Qaeda leaders—and in that sense dealt with the short-term security pressures. Stabilization operations addressed underlying economic and development issues over longer time horizons, making them better suited to a multilateral approach.

In the Iraq case, the United States was even more dismissive of multilateral principles, barely nodding in the direction of the UN before deciding it could wait no longer and intervening largely alone. Scarred after the 9/11 attacks, the United States came to obsess about "wild conceptual and strategic twists" on old threats. The attacks caused American leaders to "unshackle their thinking and disregard no possibility because it seems unlikely."[6] Containing Iraq had seemed possible before 9/11 but, took on greater plausibility after 9/11. Time horizons appeared short, making deadlock in the UN look unsatisfactory. Going with a cobbled-together coalition of the willing seemed sufficient because planners expected Iraq to be an easy victory. The overestimated threat and underestimated commitment made multilateralism seem both unnecessary and potentially costly.

ALTERNATIVE ACCOUNTS OF COOPERATION BEHAVIOR

The Effect of Norms on Intervention

As this book has argued from the outset, even powerful states generally seek multilateral strategies for foreign military interventions but not as lofty ends in themselves. Multilateralism is often not about principles but about conserving power, reassuring other states, and getting help on costly interventions. Going to great lengths to obtain UN authorization and collect allies because this is the appropriate way to intervene does not describe U.S. behavior during this period.[7] In the 1990s, UN authorization was practically a rubber stamp for U.S. interests, to the chagrin of critics of U.S. hegemony who saw the United States draping its "hegemonic tactics" in the blue flag of the UN and intervening under the pretense of multilateralism.[8] With some logrolling in the UN Security Council (UNSC), the United States was fairly easily able to obtain UNSC resolutions for its interventions. The ease of generating IO authorization during this period meant there were fewer up-front coordination costs of multilateralism; moreover, since the United States avoided operating under UN command, it further minimized many of the potential operational costs of multilateralism. Far from requiring that the United States go to great lengths, multilateralism was reasonably accessible at relatively low cost and therefore an obvious strategy for a powerful state.

The cases in this book also challenge the argument that states are willing to go multilaterally even when "doing so compromises the effectiveness of the mission," a normative account of cooperation behavior. On the contrary, only because the U.S. military has developed accommodation strategies has it been willing to intervene multilaterally with less capable allies. In the Gulf War, for example, the United States created separate chains of command, one for the United States and European allies, the other for Arab states. In the Iraq War, the United States carved out an area for coalition members to minimize interoperability, language, and information exchange difficulties. In interventions such as Haiti and Afghanistan, the United States largely conducted the challenging phases unilaterally and the post-conflict phases multilaterally.[9] Coalition operations do present some challenges, but these are challenges to which the U.S. military has adapted. During an interview, one CENTCOM planner explained that "we are a top-down organization. There is no pushback in the military; we do what our leadership tells us to do, which means we adapt when our leadership tells us to work within a coalition framework."[10] Former Under Secretary of Defense for Policy Douglas Feith went further and said that the U.S. military had become so accustomed to coalition options that "military officers' default position is to operate multilaterally. They think every operational problem has a coalition solution."[11]

Interviews with a number of senior military leaders suggested that the military appreciates the political benefits of being seen as acting multilaterally and has found accommodation strategies to minimize the operational cost. In addition to having dual command structures, the military has also institutionalized coalition operations through organizations such as the Coalition Coordination Center (CCC) at CENTCOM. Stood up in Tampa soon after 9/11, the CCC includes representation from 65 countries, with the purpose of coordinating not only military but also political, economic, and social strategies for counterterrorism. Initially somewhat cumbersome, the institutionalization over time has streamlined collective decision making on both military and nonmilitary approaches to terrorism.[12]

These accommodation strategies and institutions provide further insight into the motivations behind multilateralism. Contrary to the suggestion that the United States acts multilaterally even when it compromises operational effectiveness, this analysis shows that the United States will *rarely* act with a large coalition of states unless there is some way to minimize coalition inefficiencies. Only because it has devised ways to do that is it willing to intervene multilaterally.

Even the multilateral experience from which the norm ostensibly arose— the 1991 Gulf War—stemmed from instrumental, means-ends calculations about why multilateralism might be a more effective approach to intervention. To generate support from key allies, including France, Canada, and the Soviet Union, whom the United States sought for material reasons and for whom UN authorization was a prerequisite for offensive action, the United States had to work through the UN. The United States therefore went through the UN in part as a means by which to secure the allies' participation. Formal multilateralism appeared to beget participatory multilateralism, since several allies conditioned their support on Security Council authorization.[13] Authorization served the purpose of generating support from allies whose material assets or cooperation in enforcing sanctions the United States would need.

In what had been an improvised approach to the Gulf War, driven by instrumental calculations rather than idealistic ends, multilateralism became a more common practice after that conflict, reinforcing the argument that any multilateral pattern of behavior that followed was not created out of a sense of idealistic appropriateness but rather for instrumental effectiveness. Based on the same logic that led Stanley Hoffmann to predict collective security's demise based on what he anticipated would be a dismal showing of multilateralism in the Gulf War, the success of multilateralism in the Gulf War created a renaissance for collective security. Henceforth, motivated by a sense that IO authorization was both easy and effective, the UN became an obvious stop for coalition building on the way to war.

In spite of the preceding critique of existing multilateral normative claims, it is fair to say that the multilateral norm may have conditioned the mode by which the United States intervened during this period. For example, it is unlikely that the United States would have sought support from states such as the Barbados to intervene in Haiti had there been no multilateral norm. As with Palau, Poland, and Portugal with respect to the Iraq War, Barbados did little to shift the balance of power in Haiti and, in fact, required U.S. matériel and funding to conduct the operations in which it did participate. As one marine colonel who operated in Panama, the Gulf War, Somalia, Haiti, and Iraq said in reference to this type of coalition partner: "more often than not they seem to take on more of a window dressing for political cover than anything else. Rarely can they sustain themselves and usually they end up relying exclusively on our capabilities."[14]

These states do help an administration build a case that the intervention is multilateral and therefore legitimate. That the United States seeks these states for its interventions finds support in the perceived political legitimation that those states—at least in the aggregate as part of an ad hoc coalition— may confer. As another marine colonel operating in Iraq, characterized coalition operations, "As you have no doubt found, the political benefit of maintaining a coalition is the true rationale for it vice its effectiveness in the field. Effectiveness is really a bonus."[15]

In short, the constructivist argument explains why the United States puts on a good political show regarding allies. When President Bush went out of his way to tout the number of states in the coalition of the willing, he did that because those states had implicitly sanctioned the action. That 47 states had done so, a fact he pointed out repeatedly, meant broader sanctioning and greater legitimacy for the behavior. That the United States wanted credit for intervening multilaterally—particularly in the case of the Iraq War, where there was sharp criticism about whether and how it intervened—acknowledges the presence of a multilateral norm. Its adherence appears to be based more on convenience than on actual commitment to the norm, however; it comes in the form of cheap talk about the multilateral coalition and the collection of what the military calls "window dressing" allies that contribute little materially, operate at the periphery, and therefore avoid interfering with U.S. combat operations.[16]

The multilateral rhetoric or coalition of the willing veneer that an executive applies to what is otherwise a largely unilateral intervention shows that evidence of normative strength should not be considered dichotomous: whether the norm is proscriptive or not, or whether it ultimately constrains a state from acting unilaterally or not. Rather, we could envision the strength of the norm as affecting behavior across a continuum. On one end of the continuum would be complete unilateralism and disregard for a multilateral norm. On the other end would be the unwillingness to act without multilateral consensus—either formal or with allies—on a particular intervention. In practice, neither of these two extremes describes typical U.S. behavior. Indeed, the United States is generally willing to operate without UN authorization but will forum shop for alternate IOs such as NATO or resort to an ad hoc coalition, with each forum conferring less and less legitimacy, but also less and less constraint.

Where the U.S. approach is likely to be situated on that spectrum is highly contingent on time horizon and operational commitment, both factors that vary depending on the security environment. The shorter the time horizon, the greater the incentive to circumvent the costly delays of multilateralism. The expectation of low operational commitment of multilateralism—such as that expected for an airstrike, a quick in-and-out operation, or special operations mission—would also create incentives for unilateralism. We would still expect to see some pretense of trying to secure IO authorization and generate multinational participation, but there would be little patience for costly delay and a greater likelihood that the United States would be closer to the unilateralism end of the spectrum. Normative pressures might then shape the way the United States formulated its response, whether in seeking an ad hoc coalition of like-minded states rather than intervening entirely alone or by framing its intervention in multilateral terms.

For example, the cases of Iraq, Haiti, and the Gulf War show that the United States may go to great lengths to pitch the missions as multilateral even when the coalition contributions themselves are largely unilateral, bilateral, or minilateral. Combat operations, a more substantive indicator of behavior than rhetoric, however, are more likely to reflect calculations of consequences even if the rhetoric may reflect an understanding of appropriateness. Cooperation behavior may therefore be a tiered approach, with the contents determined by consequences and the framing by appropriateness. Consequences on the ground dominate but tend to operate with a superficial multilateral shroud as a nod to the normative pressures for multilateralism.

The Effect of Domestic Politics

In surveying the effect of domestic politics on foreign policy, James Fearon investigates "how domestic-political interactions lead a state to choose bad or foolish foreign policies, relative to some normative standard."[17] This research finds little support for the proposition that domestic politics—whether in the form of public opinion or legislative pressures—systematically distort how leaders pursued their foreign policy choices.

In some cases, leaders patently ignored domestic preferences. Public support for intervention in Haiti was minimal, yet the Clinton administration nonetheless intervened. Public support for multilateralism in Iraq was high compared with going alone, yet the Bush administration intervened with a feeble coalition of the willing. Legislative preferences were often similarly shunned. In the 1991 Gulf War, the Bush administration continuously asserted that it did not need congressional authorization. Its actions were consistent with that dismissive rhetoric. President Bush did not consult with Congress, and he did not ask for approval until after he deployed half a million troops and obtained UN authorization, effectively leaving Congress no option other than to go along with the intervention. In the Haiti intervention, the president's own party was vociferously opposed to the intervention, and yet he undertook it nonetheless. In the post-9/11 environment, Congress was a nonplayer, deferring major foreign policy interventions to the executive and offering little oversight on military actions abroad, including Afghanistan and the 2003 Iraq conflict.

Despite these significant decisions to sidestep domestic audiences, there is some evidence that leaders considered domestic preferences when making intervention decisions. The Clinton administration may have ignored domestic disdain for intervening in Haiti but extinguished some of the domestic heat from the intervention by going multilaterally. The particular benefit was that the United States could quickly transfer responsibility to the UN and allies just six months after intervening, meaning that public censure, while strong, would at least be short-lived. In the 1991 Gulf War, the Bush administration manipulated congressional reluctance to buy more financial support from abroad, despite its own willingness to resist congressional preferences for restraint. In the run-up to the 2003 Iraq conflict, Colin Powell urged that the administration go through the UN to appease U.S. domestic audiences ahead of the 2002 midterm elections. Though its multilateral approach reflected a mind made up by time horizons and the expected ease of intervention, the decision to seek UN authorization—cursory as it was—took into account domestic preferences.

Beyond the effect of U.S. domestic preferences, in some cases foreign domestic audiences had an impact on how the United States intervened. In the 1991 Gulf War and 1994 Haiti conflict, the United States sought allies for operational reasons, and the only way it could co-opt certain states was to intervene with UN authorization. In the former case, France, Egypt, and Turkey were emphatic that the operation go through the UN, and in the latter, France and Canada resisted participation unless it went through the UN. Similarly, the British were adamant that the United States and the United Kingdom seek UN authorization for the 2003 Iraq War. It appears that Prime Minister Blair's preference held sway and accounted for the decision to seek the first resolution (1441) and attempt a second resolution prior to intervening. To the extent that the United States hopes to form a multilateral coalition that includes certain states such as France, Canada, Turkey, and Germany, it needs to secure UN authorization. Then UN authorization becomes an instrumentally useful way to generate the support of the states for whom IO authorization is a necessary condition.

Regional Politics

According to the regional power account of multilateralism, the lead intervening state would more likely go unilaterally in the absence of great powers and multilaterally in a region with great powers. Challenging the expectations, *either* the absence or presence of regional powers made multilateralism somewhat more likely, though for different reasons. Far from explaining when the United States had license to intervene unilaterally, the absence of regional powers acted as green lights for multilateralism. Despite Mexico, Brazil, and Uruguay's opposition to the Haiti intervention, none of these states had the clout or institutional power to block the UN resolution that authorized U.S. intervention. A region without powers meant a region without the influence to block a UN resolution that the United States had foisted onto the multilateral organization. It made some form of multilateralism *more* likely.

The presence of a regional power did, however, influence how the United States intervened in certain regions and informed which states were particularly valuable in a coalition. In the 2001 invasion of Afghanistan, for example, the United States made a concerted effort to enlist support from the central Asian countries bordering Afghanistan. One of the sources of delay leading up to the invasion was that the United States was still working out basing and overflight agreements with Uzbekistan and Tajikistan, without which it would not have the close air support it needed for operations in Afghanistan. The United States sought Russian support to ensure support from central Asian countries but also to reduce the likelihood of counterproductive activities in Afghanistan.[18]

The 1991 Gulf War tells a similar story; the United States was as aware of recruiting the USSR to forestall any counterbalancing as it was of obtaining UN authorization. With its historical ties to Iraq, the Soviet Union could otherwise have played a counterproductive role. As a result of laudable diplomatic efforts, the Soviets were essentially paid billions of dollars to sit on the sidelines and play a passive, nonintrusive role in the intervention. By 2002–2003, Russia had experienced 10 years of decline, and the United States was far less concerned about unwanted meddling effects; the United States exerted almost no energy trying to recruit Russia's support for the Iraq intervention.

Based on the regional power account of cooperation, we should have seen more effort to recruit Saudi Arabia and Turkey in the 2003 Iraq War. The position of the two countries was similar to the 1991 intervention, but in the earlier case the United States was concerned with incorporating those states, and in the latter it was more willing to find substitutes as long as they would provide tacit support for the operation. The similarities in positions and the varying cooperation approaches with respect to these states suggest that above a certain threshold of support—tacit rather than active material support—operational imperatives rather than concern with regional politics will dominate. In the latter case, the United States expected a considerably easier victory and had fewer incentives to pool regional resources. Only if the regional power poses the possibility of actively counterbalancing the intervention will the United States seriously consider those states' opposition as a potential cost of intervention and be deterred from intervening without them.

UNILATERALISM FOR STATES BIG AND SMALL?

As this book claimed toward the outset, the United States may currently be the most visible state to act unilaterally, but that choice is open to states other than the United States. Since the end of the Cold War, the United Kingdom and France have unilaterally sent their militaries into former African colonies such as Sierra Leone and Ivory Coast, Russia into Chechnya and Georgia, and Australia into East Timor. Since it appears that other major powers are willing to intervene unilaterally, the question is how they make the choice of going it alone and whether the argument advanced in this book applies to all states, just to great powers, or to a subset of great powers.

Brief consideration of state behavior suggests that the argument would likely apply to other great powers with some form of unilateral option that would allow them to circumvent multilateral channels, albeit under a more limited set of circumstances. As with the U.S. cases, direct threats would produce short time horizons, giving powerful states the motivation to act quickly and therefore unilaterally to secure their interests rather than wait to build consensus for collective action. As recently as the attempted coup in the Ivory Coast in September 2002, the French acted unilaterally that same month to stabilize the security situation of a former

colony, deploying 1,000 troops well before the West African regional organization or the UN decided to send troops. Once there, France brought in
reinforcements in December 2002, and having brought some stability to
the country, France proceeded to make the case for UN action. French
Foreign Minister Dominique de Villepin, who had opposed the unilateral
U.S. intervention in Iraq, made the case—*ex post*—for multilateral intervention in the Ivory Coast. He argued that "the threats weighing on the
whole region due to the Ivory Coast crisis justify a collective mobilization
and call for everyone to face their responsibilities."[19] The UN mission in
Côte d'Ivoire did not arrive until May 2003, and an actual peacekeeping
operation did not arrive until April 2004, almost two years after France
had unilaterally deployed its forces to the Ivory Coast.[20]

The French experience demonstrates that cooperation choices are in part
a function of power projection. A middle-size to large state with a reasonably
powerful military such as France can deploy troops unilaterally on a regional
level to address short-term challenges such as political and economic instability in a former colony. Rather than wait to make the case to the UN as
security degenerated in the country, the French undertook the initial
responses alone. While it was powerful enough to deploy its small peacekeeping force regionally, however, it would probably lack the power to do so
globally. Thus, time horizons work in tandem with operational commitments
for great powers other than the United States. The United States can unilaterally deploy anywhere in response to short time horizons and then later (as
in the case of the 1991 Gulf War) assemble a robust coalition to confront
large operational challenges. France has that capacity at the regional level,
but the operational challenges of a global response would limit its ability to
respond unilaterally when time horizons are short if the task is global.
Perhaps it can intervene unilaterally with a small force in a region close to it,
but it is unable to deploy a large force in a region far beyond.

At a nonmilitary level, Japan demonstrated a similar logic after North
Korea conducted a missile test in 2006. Japan imposed unilateral sanctions
on Pyongyang rather than waiting for the international community to generate its own set of sanctions. For Japan, whose constitution permits only a
self-defense capacity, economic sanctions were the most robust form of retaliation allowed; Japan conducted this form of retaliation unilaterally out of
the recognition that it was uniquely positioned to be vulnerable to a North
Korean attack. Rather than wait for the potentially costly delays of generating a multilateral set of sanctions, which may not ultimately have matched
the level of punishment that Japan felt was necessary, Japan instead acted
unilaterally.[21] Although it used sanctions rather than force, Japan's choice of
unilateral retaliation illustrates how the logic of time horizons could apply to
states other than the United States.

The argument about time horizons and operational commitment has inverse effects on smaller states whose unilateral options are limited. Faced with a remote threat and thus longer time horizons, a small state may attempt to tackle a threat unilaterally—most likely with tacit U.S. acceptance—gradually employing the material power it does have against the rising challenger. With more direct threats and shorter time horizons, however, a smaller state could not hope to chisel away at the challenge on its own but would favor a multilateral response, which would be more reliable than the response that it could assemble on its own. In 1990, for example, a unilateral response to Iraq's invasion was unavailable to Kuwait. Even Saudi Arabia was unable to respond unilaterally. With time horizons short, these states could not act unilaterally and instead relied on multilateral strategies for confronting Iraq.

The preceding discussion suggests that the argument may be generalizable beyond the case of the United States. These generalized propositions, however, make certain theoretical assumptions about factors that may be distinctive and culture-specific in practice. For example, it assumes a universality of time horizons. In other words, faced with the same types of threats, leaders across cultures should have a preference for survival and will act quickly and unilaterally if their material capabilities allow. Comparative studies of business cultures suggest that such universality may not hold. Whereas U.S. business managers tend to value "short-run profits," for example, Japanese counterparts "are considered to adopt a very long time horizon in their decisions. They build on long-term relationships...and long-term organization of relationships...characteristic of 'Japanese-style capitalism.'"[22]

Applying this comparison to security, we might expect time horizons of cultures other than the United States to be calibrated differently; the effect would be a lower propensity to act quickly irrespective of their threat environment. On the other hand, business considerations may not be relevant at all in the context of security. Whether the assumption about universal time horizons would actually also apply to security is unclear, given the one-country scope of this study. Nonetheless, potential variations in time horizon by culture are worth considering before concluding definitively that this framework applies to states other than the United States.[23]

MULTILATERALISM AS AN END IN ITSELF

In 2007, former Deputy Secretary of State Strobe Talbott's postmortem of Iraq consisted of a one-word villain: "unilateralism."[24] According to this argument, unilateralism was responsible for the Iraq "quagmire" and a myriad of other failed American foreign policies, from climate change to the

International Criminal Court and the Anti-Ballistic Missile Treaty. The argument may have overstated the point but generally seemed to be on the right side of history. If the argument that more multilateralism is better is correct, then it bears mentioning how more multilateralism might be possible. The way to think about that question is to consider the factors that affect whether states are inclined to cooperate. The argument in this book says something about when that happens and how those conditions could be expanded.

The first way has to do with time horizons. If short time horizons are more likely to produce unilateral outcomes, is there some way to extend a state's time horizon and create incentives for multilateralism? Since the inputs for time horizon involve assessments about threat, then the instinctive answer might be negative. Threats are threats, and artificially extending the time line on which a threat is operative would be risky and unwise. But the response is more nuanced than that. Leaders make decisions on the basis of intelligence assessments, which themselves are an aggregation of objective inputs such as technical evaluations of weapons' development. Assessments are also based on softer assessments about adversaries' intentions and motivations.[25]

Intelligence failures, in which threats were either underestimated or overestimated, are endemic to history. Famously, U.S. leaders dismissed a "mass and variety of signals" that foretold the attacks on Pearl Harbor.[26] More than 60 years later, the United States read the signals on Iraq with gravity that appears unwarranted in retrospect and that led to a costly conflict. As Robert Jervis has observed, "The very fact that intelligence failures have occurred in all countries and all eras indicates that while there may be better or worse systems in terms of accuracy, errors are likely to be frequent even if we do better."[27]

Though the prognosis is not optimistic, some methods might be implemented that would more accurately gauge threat. For example, assessments on Iraq were relatively cursory and did not engage methods of alternative hypothesis testing, which might have revealed and challenged existing biases. Nor did they offer estimates of relative certainty—or uncertainty, as it were—that might give consumers of intelligence pause with respect to the credibility of a particular estimate. Unfortunately, intelligence reforms that would address these shortcomings have been tried "for years and the fact that several alternatives have been tried and abandoned indicates the depth of the difficulties."[28] Thus the prospects in terms of assessing threat—which produces the primary input to time horizon—correctly more often are not sanguine.

Possibilities for greater multilateralism are more viable in terms of the second factor, expectations of operational commitment. The reason is that though there are cases in which the United States overstates the operational challenges, as in the 1991 Gulf War, when it expected a costly battle that ended in just six weeks, most cases show that the United States tends to underestimate the costs of conflict. Though not a case study in this book, the war in Kosovo is also a good example. The NATO intervention was expected to be a short bombing campaign operation against Serbia, three days of air-strikes that would convince Milosevic to negotiate on NATO's terms. Instead, the operation became much more protracted, lasting 78 days and incurring considerably higher costs, thousands of Serbian casualties, and hundreds of thousands of dislocations.[29] Somalia was more onerous than the simple food relief mission that had been envisioned at the outset and turned into a blood-bath. European and American forces remained in the Balkans more than a decade after arriving. The costs of stabilizing Iraq and Afghanistan have risen steadily despite earlier, more optimistic expectations about what it would take to "win."[30] Thus, to the extent that any bias appeared in a repeated fashion, it is the propensity for the United States to underestimate these operational challenges, particularly in terms of what it takes to win the peace and conduct successful postconflict reconstruction operations.[31]

In his book on the causes of war, Stephen Van Evera hypothesizes that "war is more likely when states fall prey to false optimism about its out-come."[32] A corollary of that argument is that *unilateralism* is more likely when states fall prey to false optimism about its outcome. Underestimating the cost of war makes the burden seem more manageable by fewer partici-pants. This bias has the effect of undervaluing allies. Unfortunately, history— not just that of the United States but of states in general—is littered with instances in which states initiated what they expected to be quick military adventures only to be mired in a protracted, costly conflict. In his book *Causes of War*, Geoffrey Blainey concludes that "faith in victory and indeed a quick victory seems to characterize the leaders of the clashing nations on the eve of each war."[33] Among a number of similar tales, Van Evera quotes a Prussian leader telling his troops not to overprepare for the fight against Revolutionary France in 1792. He advises that they not "buy too many horses, the comedy will not last long. The army of lawyers will be annihilated in Belgium and we shall be home by autumn."[34] The revolutionary wars with France lasted on and off until 1801.

The American experience with war has fallen into similar traps over time, but its more recent planning fallacy has been the expectation that peace follows smoothly from war. The problem is not that the United States misreads the balance of power in combat, but that it expects that its strength can also win the peace.[35] What it has found, but evidently not internalized, is that David can sometimes defeat Goliath, particularly through asymmetric means. The clear policy implication that follows is that giving more attention to the possible costs, particularly in the longer and costlier postconflict phase, may bring estimates closer in line with reality. The likely effect is to produce greater interest in sharing what is often a lengthy and costly burden of intervention.

WHERE DOES MULTILATERALISM GO FROM HERE?

One of the many concerns about the Iraq War is that it had ushered in a new era of unilateralism. Though some of the concern had to do with individual ideologies, the concern with more enduring implications was the structural argument: that unilateralism is a temptation of unipolarity.[36] If this were the case, then enduring power asymmetries would cause the United States to continue sidestepping multilateral channels. The future of international cooperation would look very bleak.

This book showed why those concerns were on shaky ground. It showed in theoretical terms that there are a number of reasons to expect multilateralism despite power asymmetries. First, the brazen use of force would be likely to trigger costly resistance, which would be counterproductive. Rather, acting in coordination with other states would reassure others of benign intentions and perpetuate a status quo that favors its dominance. Second, unipolarity means that this state de facto has more interests, so the policing effort is considerably costlier than for powerful states with fewer international interests. Working with allies is another way to conserve rather than overextend power.

Empirically, the book showed that concentrated power actually has led more often to multilateralism than to unilateralism in the post–Cold War period.[37] Power asymmetries relative to possible allies and institutions gave the United States what other states wanted: debt relief for rotating Security Council members, political support for maligned regimes, and power to approve or veto other states' military adventures. The United States has employed all of these to coax states into sanctioning its interventions. Thus, unipolarity put the United States in a position of global leadership to craft multilateral solutions that might not otherwise have been possible. As former Director of Policy Planning Richard Haass summarized, "Hard-headed multilateralism is not an alternative to leadership, but its manifestation."[38] Power meant that the United States went *multi*laterally, not unilaterally because it could.

Nonetheless, the high-water mark for the UN Security Council—the period immediately following the Gulf War until the debacles in Rwanda and Bosnia—may not return. Because preponderant power has been associated more with multilateralism than with unilateralism, the relative decline in U.S. power could actually lead to a *decrease* in certain forms of multilateralism. For example, with a resurgent Russian power and rising China, Security

Council authorization would become increasingly difficult to obtain. Some of those patterns are already becoming apparent. For example, at the outset of the 1990s, Russia was voting with the United States in the General Assembly 89 percent of the time compared with 40 percent of the time by the end of the decade.[39] Stronger veto players with increasingly divergent interests would make multilateralism slower and compromises costlier.

A continuation of this trend would prompt the United States to shop for a multilateral forum other than the UN, one that "maximizes decision-making legitimacy while ensuring the preferred outcome" of the United States.[40] After the UN, NATO would be a next obvious forum, but it, too, comes with its own set of baggage in terms of acting as a multilateral authorizing institution. With its accession to 28 states, NATO has found itself increasingly perplexed with regard to any coherent strategic concept, according to NATO Director of Policy Planning Jamie Shea. He admitted that NATO is driven by events rather than by a well-conceived set of criteria for action, an admission of the ad hoc way NATO governs itself. Shea acknowledges that without a more coherent strategic concept, NATO member countries will find it more convenient to make a "series of bilateral agreements that meet individual states' needs better," as the United States did with its intervention in Afghanistan.[41]

The result of these factors—enduring incentives for multilateralism and more powerful veto players—may mean that participatory multilateralism, in which states operate without an IO mandate but with a robust coalition of states, becomes more common. Depending on the area of intervention, the United States would be expected to collect relevant regional actors, as well as reliable European (e.g., the United Kingdom and Poland) and Pacific (e.g., Japan and Australia) partners. In other words, we may expect to see the United States shopping for "ever changing" coalitions of the willing or "multilateralism à la carte" if the UN becomes unworkable, as it was during the first four decades after its establishment.[42]

A strategy that appeared to serve the United States well and might therefore continue is a hybrid approach to cooperation. As several of the cases in this book have shown, the typical policy debates that frame cooperation strategies as a "dispute between . . . a nationalist, unilateralist version of hegemony, and a liberal, multilateral version"[43] may miss the point. Cooperation strategies are rarely a dichotomous proposition between *either* multilateralism *or* unilateralism. In practice, a wise strategy—given U.S. material power and the benefits of burden-sharing—may be a hybrid approach, one that is largely unilateral, bilateral, or minilateral in early phases and then multilateral for postcombat phases of operations.

First, the United States gains relative autonomy up-front, when time horizons are likely to be shortest. If the unilateralism extends to combat operations, then the lead state has autonomy for operations that can produce interoperability among militaries that have different types of capabilities or national caveats about where and how they can fight that could otherwise impose grave consequences. Second, it receives multilateral assistance in the stabilization and reconstruction phases, where it becomes comparatively easier to integrate less advanced militaries for operations that can last indefinitely and pose high opportunity costs if the United States has to commit large numbers of troops for missions that other militaries are capable of conducting. If the "most basic test of international arrangements" is that they be "incentive compatible,"[44] then the hybrid approach to intervention passes this test with flying colors.

This hybrid approach may look iron fisted, however, and indeed it is a tenuous proposition if the iron fist is not covered with a velvet glove. As the 1991 Gulf War and Haiti cases show, the reason states may be willing to sit on the sidelines in the early phase and participate in later postconflict phases is because of savvy U.S. diplomacy. George H. W. Bush only earned his nickname "mad dialer" after exhaustive diplomatic efforts to convince allies to authorize an intervention that the United States had already begun. He and President Clinton turned the crank on Haiti in the early 1990s, gradually building international support for an intervention it had planned and would undertake regardless of how many "flags" participated in it.

By contrast, in the run-up to the 2003 Iraq conflict, the Bush administration perfected the knack of needling even friendly states—for example, Secretary of Defense Rumsfeld's New Europe versus Old Europe distinction—to the point of alienation. Being dismissive came from the erroneous belief that the United States needed to act quickly and that it did not need much help, but it only served to poison the well and make later recruitment of allies virtually impossible. According to diplomat Dennis Ross, who had worked in the George H. W. Bush and Bill Clinton administrations, a key difference among these administrations and that of George W. Bush was not goals but statecraft: the ability to listen, appreciate other arguments, and ultimately persuade other states. Presidents George H. W. Bush and Clinton reassured other states of benign U.S. intentions, even if the intentions were not, and effectively persuaded other states to go along with what the United States had already decided. In contrast, President George W. Bush bothered little with reassurances, making it more difficult and costly to implement U.S. foreign policy goals.[45]

For even the most seemingly clear-cut cases of intervention, statecraft is paramount, not just for obtaining multilateral support but for obtaining it generally on the lead state's terms. If anything then, this is the resounding policy implication of this book. Even under the best circumstances, multilateralism is not easy. It becomes far more difficult, however, when leaders take off the velvet gloves.

Notes

CHAPTER 1

1. Paul Kennedy, "The Eagle Has Landed," *Financial Times*, 2 February 2002. For earlier pessimism, see his concerns about "a vast array of strategical commitments" that made the United States prone to "imperial overstretch," in *Rise and Fall of Great Powers: Economic Change and Military Conflict from 1500 to 2000* (New York: Vintage, 1987).

2. Charles Krauthammer, "The New Unilateralism," *Washington Post*, 8 June 2001.

3. Lisa Martin, "Interests, Power, and Multilateralism," *International Organization* 46, no. 4 (1992): 792.

4. Quoted in Philippe Girard, *Clinton in Haiti: The 1994 US Invasion of Haiti* (Houndmills, England: Palgrave Macmillan, 2004), 75.

5. Arthur Stein, *Why Nations Cooperate: Circumstance and Choice in International Relations* (Ithaca, NY: Cornell University Press, 1990), 3; Robert Axelrod and Robert O. Keohane, "Achieving Cooperation under Anarchy: Strategies and Institutions," *World Politics* 38, no. 1 (1985): 226–254; Robert Axelrod, *The Evolution of Cooperation* (New York: Basic Books, 1984); Thomas Schelling, *The Strategy of Conflict* (Cambridge, MA: Harvard University Press, 1980).

6. Robert Jervis, "Unipolarity: A Structural Perspective," *World Politics* 61, no. 1 (2009): 196.

7. Robert Jervis, "The Compulsive Empire," *Foreign Policy* 61, no. 1 (2003): 83–87.

8. Stephen Brooks and William Wohlforth, "International Relations Theory and the Case against Unilateralism," *Perspectives on Politics* 3, no. 3 (2005): 519.

9. Max Boot, "The Doctrine of the 'Big Enchilada,'" *Washington Post*, 14 October 2002.

10. Martha Finnemore, *The Purpose of Intervention: Changing Beliefs about the Use of Force* (Ithaca, NY: Cornell University Press, 2003), 80.

11. David Skidmore, "Understanding the Unilateralist Turn in U.S. Foreign Policy," *Foreign Policy Analysis* 1, no. 2 (2005): 207–228.

12. This is similar to the approach followed in Henry Nau, *At Home Abroad: Identity and Power in American Foreign Policy* (Ithaca, NY: Cornell University Press, 2002), introduction. I thank Peter Katzenstein for bringing this to my attention.

13. Henry Kissinger, *A World Restored: Metternich, Castlereagh and the Problems of Peace, 1812-22* (Boston: Houghton Mifflin, 1957), 25.

14. Paul W. Schroeder, *Metternich's Diplomacy at Its Zenith 1820-1823* (Austin: University of Texas Press, 1962), 4, 8.

15. Kissinger, *A World Restored*, 26.

16. Social constructivists tend to view experiences as historically contingent and might therefore take issue with the notion of moving seamlessly across centuries. Martha Finnemore suggests that it is "risky" to generalize patterns of behavior beyond a particular historical context and actor's identity. See Martha Finnemore, "Legitimacy, Hypocrisy, and the Social Structure of Unipolarity: Why Being a Unipole Isn't All It's

Cracked Up to Be," *World Politics* 61, no. 1 (2009): 59. My analysis challenges the notion that a different frame is needed for each historical period and actor; rather, I submit that there is a timelessness to the idea that states will tend to come together to balance against aggressors.

17. I thank Randall Schweller for bringing this formulation to my attention.

18. E. H. Carr, *The Twenty Years Crisis* (Houndmills, England: Palgrave Macmillan, 2001), 92.

19. Robert O. Keohane, "The Contingent Legitimacy of Multilateralism," Garnet Working Paper, no. 09/06, September 2006. Michael Barnett and Martha Finnemore point to some of these deficiencies in "The Politics, Power, and Pathologies of International Organizations," *International Organization* 53, no. 4 (1999): 699-732.

20. Barry Posen, "Command of the Commons: The Military Foundations of U.S. Hegemony," *International Security* 28, no. 1 (2003): 32.

21. Ibid., 24.

22. Colin Powell, quoted in declassified minutes of the 3 August 1990 National Security Council meeting.

23. George H. W. Bush and Brent Scowcroft, *A World Transformed* (New York: Knopf, 1998), 327.

24. Ian Hurd, "Legitimacy and Authority in International Politics," *International Organization* 53, no. 2 (1999): 379-408.

25. This is also referred to as within-case variation; the "before" and "after" refer to the cooperation strategy before and after it shifted. For more on this type of case study, see John Gerring, *Case Study Research: Principles and Practice* (New York: Cambridge University Press, 2007), 30-31.

26. See, inter alia, John Ikenberry, "Is American Multilateralism in Decline?" *Perspectives on Politics* 1, no. 3 (2003): 533-550; David M. Malone and Yuen Foong Khong, *Unilateralism and U.S. Foreign Policy: International Perspectives* (Boulder, CO: Lynne Rienner, 2003); Lisa L. Martin, "Self-Binding: How America Benefited from Multilateralism—and the Cost We Bear by Going It Alone in a Risky New Century," *Harvard Magazine*, September–October 2004.

27. *Forum shopping* means that a state can pursue its interests not just in one central international organization but in smaller regional organizations or even no IO at all. For a discussion of forum shopping, see Marc L. Busch, "Overlapping Institutions, Forum Shopping, and Dispute Settlement in International Trade," *International Organization* 61, no. 4 (2007): 735-761.

28. For a quantitative comparison of U.S. interventionism versus other major powers, see Jeffrey Pickering and Emizet F. Kisangani, "The International Military Intervention Dataset: An Updated Resource for Conflict Scholars," *Journal of Peace Research* 46, no. 4 (2009): 589-599.

29. Arthur Stein, "Incentive Compatibility and Global Governance: Existential Multilateralism, a Weakly Confederal World, and Hegemony," in *Can the World Be Governed? Possibilities for Effective Multilateralism*, ed. Alan S. Alexandroff (Waterloo, ON: Wilfrid Laurier University Press, 2008), 17-84.

30. The special issue of *World Politics* (vol. 61, no. 1, January 2009) is a notable attempt to close this theoretical gap. Similarly, Stephen Brooks and William Wohlforth also seek to close the theoretical gap with *World Out of Balance* (Princeton, NJ: Princeton University Press, 2008).

31. G. John Ikenberry, Michael Mastanduno, and William C. Wohlforth, "Introduction: Unipolarity, State Behavior, and Systemic Consequences," *World Politics* 61, no. 1 (2009): 1-27.

CHAPTER 2

1. William C. Wohlforth, "The Stability of a Unipolar World," *International Security* 24, no. 1 (1999): 9.
2. Christopher Layne, "The Unipolar Illusion," *International Security* 17, no. 4 (1993): 13.
3. Stephen Brooks and William Wohlforth, *World Out of Balance* (Princeton, NJ: Princeton University Press, 2008), 13.
4. Brooks and Wohlforth, *World Out of Balance*.
5. Sarah Kreps, "American Grand Strategy after Iraq," *Orbis* 53, no. 4 (2009): 629-645.
6. Brooks and Wohlforth, *World Out of Balance*.
7. G. John Ikenberry, Michael Mastanduno, and William C. Wohlforth, "Introduction: Unipolarity, State Behavior, and Systemic Consequences," *World Politics* 61, no.1 (2009): 1; Brooks and Wohlforth, *World Out of Balance*, chapter 2.
8. Christopher Layne, "The Unipolar Illusion Revisited: The Coming End of the United States' Unipolar Moment," *International Security* 31, no. 2 (2006): 11.
9. A *combat-ready force* is one "prepared to engage in battle if they encounter resistance." See Patricia L. Sullivan and Michael T. Koch, "Military Intervention by Powerful States, 1945-2003," *Journal of Peace Research* 46, no. 5 (2009): 707-718.
10. For similar reasons, the strikes against Iraq in the 1990s are considered interventions, since their goal was to coerce Saddam Hussein into cooperating with weapons inspectors.
11. Nora Bensahel, "Humanitarian Relief and Nation Building in Somalia," in *The United States and Coercive Diplomacy*, ed. Robert J. Art and Patrick M. Cronin, 21-56 (Washington, DC: United States Institute of Peace, 2003), 35.
12. Robert Antony Pape, *Bombing to Win* (Ithaca, NY: Cornell University Press, 1996), 12-13.
13. For additional justification, see Elizabeth Saunders, "Transformative Choices: Leaders and the Origins of Intervention Strategy," *International Security* 34, no. 2 (2009): 119-161.
14. Ariel Levite, Bruce W. Jentleson, and Larry Berman, *Foreign Military Intervention: The Dynamics of Protracted Conflict* (New York: Columbia University Press, 1992), 6.
15. Robert O. Keohane, "Multilateralism: An Agenda for Research," *International Journal* 45, no.4 (1990): 731.
16. White House Web site, available from http://georgewbush-whitehouse.archives.gov/news/releases/2003/03/20030327-10.html.
17. John Ruggie, "Multilateralism: Anatomy of an Institution," *International Organization* 46, no. 3 (1992): 561; Martha Finnemore, *The Purpose of Intervention: Changing Beliefs about the Use of Force* (Ithaca, NY: Cornell University Press, 2003), 81.
18. Richard Haass, "The Age of Nonpolarity: What Will Follow U.S. Dominance," *Foreign Affairs* 87, no.3 (2008): 44-56. In his neoconservative postmortem, Francis

Fukuyama challenges the "coalitions of the willing" approach but acknowledges that the international system lacks institutions that "confer legitimacy on collective action." In particular, the UN may be adequate for peacekeeping but lacks legitimacy and the effectiveness to deal with issues in the security arena. A multi-multilateral world has emerged because of deficiencies in a variety of international institutions. See his "After Neoconservatism," *New York Times*, 19 February 2006.

19. Alexander Thompson, "Coercion through IOs: Security Council and the Logic of Information Transmission," *International Organization* 60, no.1 (2006): 1–34.

20. Ibid. NATO also qualifies as multilateral for similar reasons; heterogeneous interests of constituent states contribute to diffuse reciprocity and leadership among the members. See Stephen Weber, "Shaping the Balance of Power: Multilateralism in NATO," *International Organization* 46, no. 3 (1992): 633–680.

21. Gary Williams, "Prelude to an Intervention," *Journal of Latin American Studies* 29, no.1 (1997): 131–169; H. W. Brands Jr., "Decisions on American Armed Intervention: Lebanon, Dominican Republic, and Grenada," *Political Science Quarterly* 102, no. 4 (Winter 1987–1988): 607–624.

22. Abraham Lowenthal, quoted in Yale H. Ferguson, "The 1965 Dominican Intervention: Recent Interpretations," *International Organization* 27, no.4 (1973): 528–529.

23. Kenneth Oye, "Explaining Cooperation under Anarchy: Hypotheses and Strategies," *World Politics* 38, no.1 (1985): 19.

24. See, for example, Stephen D. Krasner, "Regimes and the Limits of Realism: Regimes as Autonomous Variables," *International Organization* 36, no. 2 (1982): 499.

25. Barbara Koremenos, Charles Lipson, and Duncan Snidal, "The Rational Design of International Institutions," *International Organization* 55, no.4 (2001): 792.

26. Thomas L. Friedman, "Running the Gulf Coalition Is a Tricky Business," *New York Times*, 23 September 1990.

27. Koremenos et al., "Rational Design," 778.

28. Joseph Jupille and Duncan Snidal, "The Choice of International Institutions: Cooperation, Alternatives, and Strategies," working paper, 19 2005 December 24.

29. Koremenos et al., "Rational Design," 774.

30. Thomas A. Keaney and Eliot A. Cohen, *Gulf War Air Power Survey Summary Report*, 1993; United States Central Command's Operation Desert Shield/Desert Storm (Washington, DC: National Security Archive, 1991).

31. Greg Sheridan, "America's Luckiest Ally: The View from Australia," *Australian*; International Security Program seminar series at the Center for Strategic and International Studies, 15 November 2006.

32. Miles Kahler, "Multilateralism with Small and Large Numbers," *International Organization* 46, no. 3 (1992): 681–708; Beth V. Yarbrough and Robert M. Yarbrough, "Regionalism and Layered Governance: The Choice of Trade Institutions," *Journal of International Affairs* 48, no. 1 (1994): 102.

33. Ruth Wedgwood makes a similar argument about power politics and UNSC paralysis in "Unilateral Action in a Multilateral World," in *Multilateralism and U.S. Foreign Policy*, ed. Stewart Patrick and Shepard Forman, 167–189 (Boulder, CO: Lynne Rienner, 2002).

34. Erik Voeten, "Outside Options and the Logic of Security Council Action," *American Political Science Association* 95, no. 4 (2001): 845–858; Alex Bellamy, Paul

Williams, and Stuart Griffin, *Understanding Peacekeeping* (London: Wiley-Blackwell, 2004); Jerzy Ciechanski, "Enforcement Measures under Chapter VII of the UN Charter: UN Practice after the Cold War," *International Peacekeeping* 3, no. 4 (1996): 82–104; Kathryn Talentino similarly finds that multilateral interventions after the Cold War increased 365 percent; see her *Military Intervention after the Cold War: The Evolution of Theory and Practice* (Athens: Ohio University Press, 2005), 29.

35. David M. Malone, *The UN Security Council: From the Cold War to the 21st Century* (Boulder, CO: Lynne Rienner, 2004), 8.

36. Samuel Huntington, "The Lonely Superpower," *Foreign Affairs* 78, no. 2 (1999): 39.

37. Jerzy Ciechanski, "Enforcement Measures"; Talentino, *Military Intervention*, 29.

CHAPTER 3

1. Robert Keohane, *After Hegemony* (Princeton, NJ: Princeton University Press, 1984).

2. Stephen Brooks and William Wohlforth, "International Relations Theory and the Case against Unilateralism," *Perspectives on Politics* 3, no. 3 (2005): 514.

3. Robert Kagan, "Interview: Robert Kagan and Joseph Nye Weigh the Option of a Military Campaign against Iraq," NPR Transcript, 21 September 2002.

4. E. H. Carr, *The Twenty Years Crisis* (Houndmills, England: Palgrave Macmillan, 2001), 92.

5. For the tip on this historical analogy, I am indebted to Randall Schweller, who points to Napoleon and Metternich's respective approaches to statecraft in "A Tale of Two Realisms: Expanding the Institutions Debate," *Mershon International Studies Review* 41, no. 1 (1997): 1–32. I develop the logic further in these pages.

6. Algernon Cecil, *Metternich 1773-1859: A Study of His Period and Personality* (London: Eyre and Spottiswoode, 1947), 91.

7. Ibid., 131.

8. Henry Kissinger, *A World Restored: Metternich, Castlereagh and the Problems of Peace, 1812-22* (Boston: Houghton Mifflin, 1957), xx.

9. For more on Napoleon's strategies, successes, and failures, see, inter alia, Gregory Fremont-Barnes and Todd Fisher, *The Napoleonic Wars: The Rise and Fall of an Empire* (Oxford: Osprey, 2004); William O'Connor Morris, *Napoleon, Warrior and Ruler, and the Military Supremacy of Revolutionary France* (London: Putnam, 1893); David G. Chandler, *The Campaigns of Napoleon* (New York: Scribner, 1973); Charles Esdaile, *Napoleon's Wars: An International History: 1803-1815* (New York: Viking, 2008).

10. Kissinger, *A World Restored*, 1, 6.

11. Ibid., 17.

12. Ibid., 6, 17, 4–7.

13. Schweller and Priess, "A Tale of Two Realisms."

14. Ibid., 18.

15. Kissinger, *A World Restored*, 199.

16. Robert Jervis, "Unipolarity: A Structural Perspective," *World Politics*, 61, no. 1 (2009): 211. Stephen Walt has also made this point that balancing stems less from who the United States is than what it does; accordingly, the United States should strive to "be welcomed rather than feared." See "Taming American Power," *Foreign Affairs* 84, no. 5 (2005): 105.

17. See troop and financial contributions at http://www.globalsecurity.org/military/ops/desert_storm-allied.htm and http://www.globalsecurity.org/military/ops/desert_storm-finan.htm.

18. Julian E. Barnes, "Cost of Iraq War Will Surpass Vietnam's by Year's End," *Los Angeles Times*, 11 April 2009.

19. Francis Fukuyama, "Nation-Building 101," *Atlantic Monthly*, January–February 2004.

20. See the Iraq Casualty Count at http://icasualties.org/Iraq/index.aspx; Afghanistan at http://icasualties.org/OEF/index.aspx.

21. National Security Advisory Group, *The U.S. Military: Under Strain and at Risk*, January 2006; available at http://merln.ndu.edu/merln/mipal/reports/US_Military_Under_Strain_and_at_Risk.pdf.

22. An *opportunity cost* is defined as the "foregone opportunities that have been sacrificed." Paul Samuelson, *Economics: An Introductory Analysis*, 7th ed. (New York: McGraw-Hill, 1967), 443.

23. Operations Northern and Southern Watch, which followed the 1990–1991 Gulf War, ended at the beginning of the 2003 Iraq War and would likely otherwise have continued. See *The Cost of War and Reconstruction: An Update* (An Analysis by the House Budget Committee Democratic Staff), 23 September 2003, available at http://www.house.gov/budget_democrats/analyses/iraq_cost_update.pdf.

24. Steven R. Bowman, "Bosnia: U.S. Military Operations," CRS Brief for Congress, 8 July 2003, available at http://www.au.af.mil/au/awc/awcgate/crs/ib93056.pdf; "United States to Withdraw All Troops from Bosnia before 2007," BBC, 30 August 2006; "U.S. Troops Mark End of Mission in Bosnia," *Washington Post*, 25 November 2004.

25. Dan Bilefsky, "Tensions Rise in Fragile Bosnia as Country's Serbs Threaten to Seek Independence," *New York Times*, 27 February 2009.

26. Robert Gilpin, *War and Change in World Politics* (London: Cambridge University Press, 1981), 106–107.

27. Robert Jervis, "The Compulsive Empire," *Foreign Policy*, no. 137 (July–August 2003): 84.

28. Churchill, quoted in Lord Renwick of Clifton, "Can the 'Special Relation' Survive into the 21st Century?" Third Annual Douglas W. Bryant Lecture; British Library, 14 October 1998, available at www.bl.uk/eccles/pdf/dwbryant/renwick.pdf.

29. James Fearon identifies this phrase, *costly delays*, in "Bargaining, Enforcement, and Cooperation," *International Organization* 52, no. 2 (1998): 274, 277; Abhinay Muthoo, "A Non-Technical Introduction to Bargaining Theory," *World Economics* 1, no. 2 (2000): 147.

30. Daniel Poneman, "Multilateralism: Lessons from Iraq," in *Iraq and America: Choices and Consequences*, ed. Ellen Laipson and Maureen S. Steinbrunner (Washington, DC: Stimson Center, 2006).

31. Elaine Sciolino, *The Outlaw State: Saddam Hussein's Quest for Power and the Gulf Crisis* (New York: John Wiley and Sons, 1991), 321; see also Dennis Ross, *Statecraft, and How to Restore America's Standing in the World* (New York: Farrar, Straus and Giroux, 2007), 89–90.

32. H. W. Brands, "George Bush and the Gulf War of 1991," *Presidential Studies Quarterly* 31, no. 1 (2004): 113–131.

33. For more on the horse-trading that took place to acquire Security Council votes, see James Baker III, *The Politics of Diplomacy* (New York: Putnam, 1995), 305–328. See also Guy Dinmore and Mark Turner, "US Persuades with Economic Muscle," *Financial Times*, 11 February 2003.

34. George H. W. Bush and Brent Scowcroft, *A World Transformed* (New York: Knopf, 1998), 464.

35. Hans Morgenthau, *Politics among Nations: The Struggle for Power and Peace*, 5th ed. (New York: Knopf, 1978), 181.

36. Amy Belasco, *The Cost of Iraq, Afghanistan, and Other Global War on Terror Operations since 9/11*, CRS Report 33110, 14 July 2008.

37. Stephen Brooks, "Dueling Realisms," *International Organization*, 51, no. 3 (1997): 445, 450.

38. For more on the security application of a discount rate, see ibid., 450.

39. Bruce Russett and Miles Lackey, "In the Shadow of the Cloud: If There's No Tomorrow, Why Save Today?" *Political Science Quarterly* 102, no. 3 (1987): 259.

40. Author's e-mail correspondence with Jack Levy, Rutgers University, 8 April 2007. See also Herbert A. Simon, "Rationality in Political Behavior," *Political Psychology* 16, no. 1 (1995): 50; Monica Duffy Toft, "Issue Indivisibility and Time Horizons as Rationalist Explanations for War," *Security Studies* 15, no. 1 (2006): 34–69.

41. Thomas Risse, *Cooperation among Allies* (Princeton, NJ: Princeton University Press, 1995), 20.

42. Robert Bushman, Raffi J. Indjejikian, and Abbie Smith, "CEO Compensation: The Role of Individual Performance Evaluation," *Journal of Accounting and Economics* 21 (1996): 172.

43. Philip Streich and Jack Levy, "Time Horizons, Discounting, and Intertemporal Choice," *Journal of Conflict Resolution* 51, no. 2 (2007): 199–226.

44. See discussion in the "Round Table on Measurement of Expectations," Franco Modigliani and discussion by Avram Kosselgoff, Report of the Boston Meeting of the Econometric Society, 26–29 1951 December 481–483.

45. John Rae, quoted in Shane Frederick, George Loewenstein, and Ted O'Donoghu, *Journal of Economic Literature* 40 (June 2002): 353. For more on the relationship between uncertainty and choice, see Leonard Green and Joel Myerson, "A Discounting Framework for Choice with Delayed and Probabilistic Rewards," *Psychological Bulletin* 130, no. 5 (2004): 769–792.

46. Thomas J. Christensen, *Useful Adversaries: Grand Strategy, Domestic Mobilization, and Sino-American Conflict, 1947-1958* (Princeton, NJ: Princeton University Press, 1996), 27–28. Christensen uses this typology to illustrate how easily decision-making elites will be able to mobilize domestic audiences; I apply the typology differently, arguing that directness of threat affects how states view their security futures, which in turn translates into a state's time horizon.

47. The term is used more frequently in the militaries of Commonwealth countries. See, for example, interview with Air Chief Marshal Sir Graham Erik Stirrup, UK Chief of Defense Staff, "Military Matters," 11 November 2007, available at http://news.bbc.co.uk/2/hi/programmes/andrew_marr_show/7089432.stm.

48. Lisa Martin, "Interests, Power, and Multilateralism," *International Organization* 46, no. 4 (1992): 792.

49. Renwick, "Can the 'Special Relation' Survive into the 21st Century?"

50. Kenneth Waltz, *Theory of International Politics* (Reading, MA: Addison-Wesley, 1979), 166.

51. Cecil, *Metternich*, 141.

52. In the initial engagement, Austria had 25,000 soldiers, including 10,000 cavalry, to France's 4,000. See David Chandler, *The Campaigns of Napoleon* (New York: Macmillan, 1966), 402.

53. Ibid.

54. For more on the strategic and operational dynamics within the Third Coalition, see Frederick C. Schneid, *Napoleon's Conquest of Europe* (Santa Barbara, CA: Greenwood, 2004), 77–144; David Chandler, *The Campaigns of Napoleon*, 381–442.

55. Transformation of U.S. military forces, for example, has created gaps in capabilities that make coalition operations more difficult. See, for example, David C. Gompert and Uwe Nerlich, *Shoulder to Shoulder: The Road to U.S.-European Military Cooperability: A German-American Analysis* (Santa Monica, CA: RAND, 2002).

56. Barry Posen, "Command of the Commons: The Military Foundation of U.S. Hegemony," *International Security* 28, no. 1 (2003): 22.

57. *The World Fact Book* (Washington, DC: Central Intelligence Agency, 2010), data on Iran and North Korea.

58. Posen, "Command of the Commons," 32.

59. Bob Woodward, *The Commanders* (New York: Simon and Schuster, 1991), 285.

60. Gordon, "Bush's Aims: Deter Attack, Send a Signal," *New York Times*, 8 August 1990. The army also had almost 500,000 in the Army National Guard and 300,000 in the Army Reserve, bringing the total force up to about 1.6 million, but half of this total were soldiers who would have to be activated and were less immediately available. For force structure comparisons between the Cold War and the 1990s, see "A Changed Army," available at http://www.army.mil/aps/98/chapter2.htm.

61. James Baker III, *The Politics of Diplomacy* (New York: Putnam, 1995), 279.

62. This logic is similar to the institutional choice logic in Joseph Jupille and Duncan Snidal, "The Choice of International Institutions: Cooperation, Alternatives and Strategies," 19 December 2005 working paper.

63. Brooks, "Dueling Realisms," 450.

64. Milton Bearden, "Afghanistan, Graveyard of Empires," *Foreign Affairs* 80, no. 6 (2001): 17–29.

65. This is the central puzzle of G. John Ikenberry, *After Victory: Institutions, Strategic Restraint, and the Rebuilding of Order after Major Wars* (Princeton, NJ: Princeton University Press, 2000).

66. Thus, the conclusion that multilateralism is more likely than not is similar to neoliberal arguments, but I arrive at it differently. Like scholars such as John Ikenberry, I agree that multilateralism provides incentives to cooperate, but I disagree that it "locks in" the United States, particularly because the forms of multilateralism we each discuss are different. His deals with alliances such as NATO and institutions such as the post–World War II UN, International Monetary Fund, and World Bank. The subject of multilateralism for this book is more discrete, dealing with multilateral arrangements that change depending on the intervention. Therefore, these coalitions would be associated with dynamics different from those associated with alliances, whether chain-gaining, buck-passing, abandonment, and entrapment, all of which have received considerable scholarly attention. Whether the lead state

sought multilateralism in this form would depend on the security conditions surrounding the intervention rather than on some "grand strategic bargain" that is set in motion and expected to endure and lock states in for decades. See G. John Ikenberry, *Liberal Order and Imperial Ambition: Essays on American Power and International Order* (Cambridge: Polity, 2006), 91–92. See, for example, Glenn Snyder, *Alliance Politics* (Ithaca, NY: Cornell University Press, 2007); Thomas Christensen and Jack Snyder, "Chain Gangs and Passed Bucks: Predicting Alliance Patterns in Multipolarity," *International Organization* 44 (1990): 137-168.

67. Martha Finnemore, *The Purpose of Intervention: Changing Beliefs about the Use of Force* (Ithaca, NY: Cornell University Press, 2003), 128.

68. Theo Farrell, *The Norms of War* (Boulder, CO: Lynne Rienner, 2005), 1; I am also thankful for Farrell's insights in my subsequent correspondence with the author; Washington, DC, 25 April 2007.

69. Finnemore, *The Purpose of Intervention*, 80-82.

70. Ibid., 80.

71. Peter J. Katzenstein, *The Culture of National Security: Norms and Identity in World Politics* (New York: Columbia University Press, 1996), 5.

72. Martha Finnemore, *National Interests in International Society* (Ithaca, NY: Cornell University Press, 1996), 3.

73. James March and Johan Olsen, "The Institutional Dynamics of International Political Orders," *International Organization* 52, no.4 (1998): 951-952.

74. Jeffrey T. Checkel, "The Constructivist Turn in International Relations Theory," *World Politics* 50, no. 2 (1998): 324-348.

75. See James Fearon, quoted in Martha Finnemore and Kathryn Sikkink, "International Norm Dynamics and Political Change," *International Organization* 52, no. 4 (1998): 891-892.

76. Finnemore, *The Purpose of Intervention*, 134.

77. James Fearon, "Domestic Politics, Foreign Policy, and Theories of International Relations," *Annual Review of Political Science* (1998): 291, 304.

78. John H. Aldrich, Christopher Gelpi, Peter Feaver, Jason Reifler, and Kristin Thompson Sharp, "Foreign Policy and the Electoral Connection," *Annual Review of Political Science* 9 (2006): 496. See also, inter alia, H. S. Foster, *Activism Replaced Isolationism: U.S. Public Attitudes 1940-1975* (Washington, DC: Foxhall, 1983); R. S. Beal and R. H. Hinckley, "Presidential Decision Making and Opinion Polls," *Annals* 472, no.1 (1984): 72; Leslie Gelb, "The Essential Domino: American Politics and Vietnam," *Foreign Affairs* 50, no.3 (1972): 459; Ole Holsti, "Public Opinion and Foreign Policy: Challenges to the Almond-Lippmann Consensus," *International Studies Quarterly* 36, no.4 (1992): 439.

79. Joseph R. Biden Jr., *To Stand against Aggression: Milosovic, the Bosnian Republic, and the Conscience of the West*, report prepared for the Senate Committee on Foreign Relations, 103rd Cong., 1st session, 1993, Committee Print 103-33, 3.

80. William Drozdiak, "France Puts Force under U.S. Command," *Washington Post*, 17 January 1991.

81. Terrence L. Chapman and Dan Reiter, "The United Nations Security Council and the Rally Round the Flag Effect," *Journal of Conflict Resolution* 48, no. 6 (2004): 886-909; Steven Kull, I. M. Destler, and Clay Ramsey, *The Foreign Policy Gap: How Policymakers Misread the Public* (College Park, MD: Program on International Policy Attitudes, 1997).

82. Bruce Jentleson and Rebecca Britton, "Still Pretty Prudent: Post–Cold War American Public Opinion on the Use of Military Force," *Journal of Conflict Resolution* 42 (1998): 406–407.

83. Kenneth Schultz, "Tying Hands and Washing Hands," in *Locating the Proper Authorities: The Interaction of Domestic and International Institutions*, ed. Daniel Drezner (Ann Arbor: University of Michigan Press, 2003), 109, 118–119.

84. For more on hand tying, see Judith Goldstein and Joanne Gowa, "US National Power and the Post-War Trading Regime," *World Trade Review* 1, no. 2 (2002): 153–170.

85. Marc Hetherington and Michael Nelson, "Anatomy of a Rally Effect: George W. Bush and the War on Terrorism," Political Science and Politics 36 (2003): 37. See also John Mueller, War, Presidents, and Public Opinion (New York: Wiley, 1973).

86. Alexander Thompson, "Screening Power: International Organizations as Informative Agents," in *Delegation and Agency in International Organizations*, ed. Darren Hawkins, David Lake, Daniel Nielson, and Michael Tierney (New York: Cambridge University Press, 2006), 372. Mearsheimer makes a similar argument in chapter 6, *The Tragedy of Great Power Politic* (New York: W. W. Norton, 2001).

87. Telegram No. 35678 from Stalin to Shtykov, the 8th Department of the General Staff of the Armed Forces of the USSR, 6 July 1950.

88. William Whitney Stueck, *The Korean War: An International History* (Princeton, NJ: Princeton University Press, 1997).

89. David Lake, *Entangling Relations: American Foreign Policy in Its Century* (Princeton, NJ: Princeton University Press, 1999), 7.

90. Ibid., 51, 161, 201, 286–287. If the intervention is in the region of other powerful states, opportunism—or free riding—by the somewhat smaller states might also be more difficult to achieve. This general expectation of free riding draws on Mancur Olson Jr. and Richard Zeckhauser, "An Economic Theory of Alliances," *Review of Economics and Statistics* 48, no. 3 (1966): 266–279, which suggests that the largest states (in terms of GDP) pay a disproportionate share of nonexcludable goods such as defense costs. Todd Sandler shows that there is a greater willingness of small states to contribute if there are "substantial excludable benefits" and "joint products are present," which might be more likely if an intervention were in their region. See Todd Sandler, "An Economic Theory of Alliances," *Journal of Conflict Resolution* 37, no. 3 (1993): 447. See also "On the Economic Theory of Alliances," *Journal of Conflict Resolution* 19, no. 2 (1975): 330–348.

91. Galia Press-Barnathan makes this point in *Organizing the World: The United States and Regional Cooperation in Asia and Europe* (New York: Routledge, 2003), 26–29.

92. Kenneth Waltz, *Man, the State and War* (New York: Columbia University Press, 1959), 16.

93. Stephen Walt, *Taming American Power: The Global Response to U.S. Primacy* (New York: W. W. Norton, 2005), 30–31.

94. Paul A. Papayoanou, "Intra-Alliance Bargaining and U.S. Bosnia Policy," *Journal of Conflict Resolution* 41, no. 1 (1997): 105.

95. "Clinton's Statement on War Crimes Court," BBC, 31 December 2000.

96. "Madeline Albright," *News Hour*, 6 March 1997, transcript available at http://www.pbs.org/newshour/bb/fedagencies/march97/albright_3-6.html.

97. Author's exchange with Dr. Thomas Christensen; Ithaca, NY; 26 April 2009.

98. Andrew Bennett illustrates the learning thesis with the experience of Soviet interventionism between 1973 and 1996; see *Condemned to Repetition? The Rise, Fall, and Reprise of Soviet-Russian Military Interventionism, 1973-1996* (Cambridge, MA: MIT Press, 1999).

99. James M. Goldgeier and Steven Weber, "Getting to No: The Limits of Multilateralism," *National Interest* 82 (Winter 2005-2006): 69-76.

100. For coding of intervention failure, see Michael W. Doyle and Nicholas Sambanis, *Making War and Building Peace* (Princeton, NJ: Princeton University Press, 2006); see also Lise Morjé Howard, *UN Peacekeeping in Civil Wars* (Cambridge: Cambridge University Press, 2008).

101. This literature includes, inter alia, Randall L. Schweller, "Bandwagoning for Profit: Bringing the Revisionist State Back In," *International Security* 19, no. 2 (1994): 72-107; Andrew Bennett, Joseph Lepgold, and Danny Unger, "Burden-Sharing in the Persian Gulf War," *International Organization* 48, no. 1 (1994): 39-75. Along the lines of security guarantees as a lure for bandwagoning, see Victor D. Cha, "Abandonment, Entrapment, and Neoclassical Realism in Asia: The United States, Japan, and Korea," *International Studies Quarterly* 44, no. 2 (2000): 261-291; Glenn Snyder, "The Security Dilemma in Alliance Politics," *World Politics* 36, no. 4 (1984): 461; Thomas Risse-Kappen, *Cooperation among Democracies*: The European Influence on American Foreign Policy (Princeton, NJ: Princeton University Press, 1995).

102. An exception is Alexander Thompson, *Channels of Power: The UN Security Council and U.S. Statecraft in Iraq* (Ithaca, NY: Cornell University Press, 2009). See also Galia Press-Barnathan, "The Changing Incentives for Security Regionalization: From 119 to 911," *Cooperation and Conflict* 40, no. 3 (2005): 281-304.

103. As the phrase suggests, a most likely case is one in which a dominant theory—in this case, structural realism—predicts that a certain behavior unilateralism is most likely for a particular state (the United States). For more on most likely cases, see Harry Eckstein, "Case Study and Theory in Political Science," in *Handbook of Political Science*, ed. Fred Greenstein and Nelson Polsby, 79-137 (Reading, MA: Addison-Wesley, 1975), 118.

104. John Gerring, *Case Study Research: Principles and Practice* (New York: Cambridge University Press, 2007), 115.

105. For justification of the United States as an enduring unipolar power, see Stephen Brooks and William Wohlforth, *World Out of Balance* (Princeton, NJ: Princeton University Press, 2008).

106. Alexander George and Andrew Bennett, *Case Studies and Theory Development in the Social Sciences* (Cambridge, MA: MIT Press, 2005), 67.

107. Ian Hurd, *After Anarchy: Legitimacy and Power in the United Nations Security Council* (Princeton, NJ: Princeton University Press, 2007), 39.

108. James G. March and Johan P. Olsen, "The Institutional Dynamics of International Political Orders," *International Organization* 52, no. 4 (1998): 949.

109. Jon Elster, "Social Norms and Economic Theory," *Journal of Economic Perspectives* 3, no. 4 (1989): 99-117.

110. Richard N. Haass, "We Can't Meet Most of the Challenges We Face on Our Own," interview with the Council on Foreign Relations, 7 July 2003, available at http://www.cfr.org/publication.html?id=6107.

111. Ian Hurd, "Legitimacy and Authority in International Politics," *International Organization* 53, no. 2 (1999): 387.

112. Andrew Cortell and James Davis Jr., "Understanding the Domestic Impact of International Norms: A Research Agenda," *International Studies Review* 2, no. 1 (2000): 70. For more on framing effects, see James N. Druckman, "On the Limits of Framing Effects: Who Can Frame?" *Journal of Politics* 63, no. 4 (2001): 1041.

113. Nina Tannenwald faces a similar problem of overlapping predictions and relies in part on leaders using "taboo talk" to justify their nonuse of nuclear weapons. "Multilateral talk" is this study's equivalent. See Nina Tannenwald, *The Nuclear Taboo: The United States and the Non-Use of Nuclear Weapons since 1945* (Cambridge: Cambridge University Press, 2007), 54–55.

114. This follows Ian Hurd's suggestion of using a counterfactual question to compare the behavior under the norm with behavior that would have resulted in the absence of the norm. See Ian Hurd, "Legitimacy and Authority in International Politics," *International Organization* 53, no. 2 (1999): 379–408.

115. George W. Downs, David M. Rocke, and Peter N. Barsoom, "Is the Good News about Compliance Good News about Cooperation?" *International Organization* 50, no. 3 (1996): 379–406.

116. Jason Seawright and John Gerring, "Case Selection Techniques in Case Study Research: A Menu of Qualitative and Quantitative Options," *Political Research Quarterly* 61, no. 2 (2008): 301–302. According to a number of qualitative method scholars, this is a legitimate case of selecting on the dependent variable (as long as this is not the only case study), since doing so serves the purpose of identifying factors that lead to the outcome of interest. See, for example, George and Bennett, *Case Studies and Theory Development in the Social Sciences*, 23–24.

117. For more on easy versus hard cases, see George and Bennett, *Case Studies and Theory Development in the Social Sciences*, 121–122.

118. John Gerring, *Case Study Research: Principles and Practice* (New York: Cambridge University Press, 2007), 31–32.

CHAPTER 4

1. Strobe Talbott, "Status Quo Ante: The United States and Its Allies," in *After the Storm: Lessons from the Gulf War*, ed. Joseph S. Nye and Roger Smith (New York: Madison, 1992), 4.

2. Ibid.

3. James Baker III, *The Politics of Diplomacy* (New York: Putnam, 1995), 331.

4. Article 51 of the Charter of the United Nations, available at http://www.un.org/aboutun/charter/chapter7.shtml.

5. Margaret Thatcher, "Argentina Invades the Falklands," in *The Downing Street Years* (New York: Harper Collins, 1993), 173–185.

6. "No Time to Go Wobbly," discussions between Margaret Thatcher and President George Bush, available at http://www.margaretthatcher.org/archive/us-bush.asp. For more on British preferences, see also Steve A. Yetiv, *Explaining Foreign Policy: U.S. Decision-Making and the Persian Gulf War* (Baltimore, MD: Johns Hopkins University Press, 2004), 46.

7. Baker, *The Politics of Diplomacy*, 304; Dennis Ross, *Statecraft: And How to Restore America's Standing in the World* (New York: Farrar, Straus and Giroux, 2007), 80.

8. Among those who were opposed to a tough Arab response were Jordan, Libya, Sudan, Palestine, Mauritania, and Yemen. See John Kifner, "Arabs to Convene on Iraqi Invasion," *New York Times*, 4 August 1990; "Iraqi Newspaper Rejects Arab League Resolution," *INA*, 8 August 1990.

9. Elaine Sciolino, *The Outlaw State: Saddam Hussein's Quest for Power and the Gulf Crisis* (New York: John Wiley and Sons, 1991), 233.

10. George H. W. Bush, "Address before a Joint Session of the Congress on the Persian Gulf Crisis and the Federal Budget Deficit," 11 September 1990; available at http://bushlibrary.tamu.edu/research/papers/1990/90091101.html.

11. *Conduct of the Persian Gulf War: Final Report to Congress* (Washington, DC: Department of Defense, 1992), chapter 2, "The Response to Aggression."

12. Ibid., 59.

13. "The Gulf War," *Time*, 27 May 1991; "Allied Troop Contributions," Global Security, http://www.globalsecurity.org/military/ops/desert_storm-allied.htm. The contributions would have amounted to the third largest defense budget at the time, according to the *Conduct of the Persian Gulf War*, 59–60. Andrew Bennett, Joseph Lepgold, and Danny Unger, "Burden-Sharing in the Persian Gulf War," *International Organization* 48, no.1 (1994): 48–50.

14. Khaled bin Sultan, *Desert Warrior: A Personal View of the Gulf War by the Joint Forces Commander* (New York: Harper Perennial, 1996). Syria's decision-making influence came in part from asserting that its participation was contingent on Israel not participating. As a result, the United States accepted Syrian troops and asked Israel to remain on the sidelines.

15. Declassified minutes from the 3 August 1990 National Security Council meeting.

16. *Conduct of the Persian Gulf War*, 19.

17. Howard Teicher and Gayle Radley Teicher, *Twin Pillars to Desert Storm: America's Flawed Vision in the Middle East from Nixon to Bush* (New York: William Morrow, 1993).

18. Walid Khalidi, "The Gulf Crisis: Origins and Consequences," *Journal of Palestine Studies* 20, no. 2 (1991): 11. See also Yetiv, *Explaining Foreign Policy*, 22.

19. For original documents on the early 1980s, see http://www.gwu.edu/~nsarchiv/NSAEBB/NSAEBB82/. For a thorough and scathing attack of U.S. support for Iraq in the 1980s, see Murray Waas, "What Washington Gave Saddam for Christmas," in *The Iraq War Reader: History, Documents, Opinions*, ed. Micah Sifry and Christopher Cerf, 30–40 (New York: Simon & Schuster, 2003).

20. Declassified National Security Directive 26, "US Policy toward the Persian Gulf," 2 October 1989, available at www.fas.org/irp/offdocs/nsd/nsd26.pdf.

21. George H. W. Bush and Brent Scowcroft, *A World Transformed* (New York: Knopf, 1998), 307.

22. Baker, *The Politics of Diplomacy*, 271.

23. Ibid.

24. Michael R. Gordon, "Pentagon Objected to Bush's Message to Iraq," *New York Times*, 25 October 1992.

25. Yetiv, *Explaining Foreign Policy*, 23.

26. Michael R. Gordon and Bernard E. Trainor, *The Generals' War: The Inside Story of the Conflict in the Gulf* (New York: Little, Brown, 1995), 22. President Bush defends Glaspie's response; the conventional wisdom that she gave a green light, he argues, is wrong. See Bush and Scowcroft, *A World Transformed*, 311.

27. The invasion was particularly surprising, given Saddam's reassurances the previous week that Iraq was "sick of war" and wanted "friendship" with the United States. See "U.S. Embassy Baghdad to Washington" memo (Saddam's message of friendship to George Bush) of 25 July 1990. See also Jean Edwards Smith, *George Bush's War* (New York: Henry Holt, 1992), 14.

28. Bush and Scowcroft, *A World Transformed*, 317.

29. Ibid.

30. 3 August 1990 NSC meeting; Bush and Scowcroft, *A World Transformed*, 317.

31. Gulf War: Bush-Thatcher phone conversation, 26 August 1990, quoted in Margaret Thatcher, *The Downing Street Years*, 823–824.

32. Geoffrey Leslie Simons, *Iraq: From Sumer to Saddam* (New York: Palgrave, 1996), 353–355. See also Bush and Scowcroft, *A World Transformed*, 325. States such as Egypt, Turkey, and Yemen were also reluctant; all but Yemen traded economic assurances from the United States for their support in the Gulf. Yemen ultimately voted against Resolution 678, prompting one senior U.S. diplomat to say that it "was the most expensive no vote you ever cast," as it led to the termination in $70 million in U.S. foreign aid to Yemen (Simons, *Iraq*, 358).

33. David Hoffman, "Shevardnadze Repeats Kremlin Preference for Political Solution," *Washington Post*, 8 November 1990.

34. Thomas Friedman, "How U.S. Won Support to Use Mideast Forces," *New York Times*, 2 December 1990.

35. By 5 August 1990, these battle groups were positioned for long-range strikes, and by 8 August, they were on station prepared for closer range air strikes. See *The U.S. Navy in Desert Shield/Desert Storm* (Washington, DC: Department of the Navy, 1991).

36. The 3 August 1990 declassified minutes of the National Security Council meeting on Iraq.

37. Molly Moore and Patrick E. Tyler, "U.S. Deployment May Reach More Than 200,000 Troops," *Washington Post*, 11 August 1990.

38. Michael R. Gordon, "Bush Sends U.S. Force to Saudi Arabia as Kingdom Agrees to Confront Iraq," *New York Times*, 8 August 1990; Paul Bedard, "Cheney Considers Asking Bush to Call Reserve Forces," *Washington Times*, 15 August 1990; Juan J. Walte, "100,000 U.S. Troops Are Facing 200,000 Iraqis," *USA Today*, 20 August 1990.

39. This provision allows the commander in chief to order reserve members to active duty without congressional authorization, up to 200,000 at one time; see http://www4.law.cornell.edu/uscode/html/uscode10/.

40. *Conduct of the Persian Gulf War*, 80.

41. Rowan Scarborough, "Force Passes 200,000," *Washington Times*, 15 October 1990.

42. "Too Far Too Fast in the Gulf," *New York Times*, 11 November 1990; Thomas W. Lippman, "New Troop Deployment Elicits Muted Public Response," *Washington Post*, 9 November 1990.

43. Bush and Scowcroft, *A World Transformed*, 329.

44. Ibid, 328.

45. Lawrence J. Korb, "We Can Afford to Fight Iraq," *New York Times*, 21 August 1990; Representative Pat Schroeder held representative views on the burden-sharing issue, suggesting that allies "have let Uncle Sucker do their heavy lifting for them again." Quoted in John Harwood, Jean Heller, and David Dahl, "Gulf Issue: Who Goes, Who Pays?" *St. Petersburg Times*, 14 September 1990.

46. "U.S. Asks NATO for Help in Gulf," *Toronto Star*, 8 December 1990.

47. Bush and Scowcroft, *A World Transformed*, 327.

48. This is consistent with military classification of the phases of conflict in which Phase I is the "halting the invasion" and phase II is "force buildup/deploy decisive force," leading to phase III of combat operations and phase IV of postcombat. All four are part of an intervention, even if all are not associated with bloodshed; see http://www.globalsecurity.org/military/ops/mtw-phases.htm.

49. Herbert Tillema, "Foreign Overt Military Intervention in the Nuclear Age: A Clarification," *Journal of Peace Research* 26 (November 1989): 181.

50. I thank Professor Elizabeth Saunders, George Washington University, in thinking through this point. Personal exchange, 14 May 2009.

51. This period of mobilization and deployment corresponds with phases I and II of major theater war (see note 49).

52. The 3 August 1990 declassified NSC minutes, 3–4.

53. Michael R. Gordon, "Iraq Bolsters Invasion Force, Adding to Worry on Saudis," *New York Times*, 4 August 1990; Khaled, *Desert Warrior*, 12. Steven Metz makes a similar assertion about imminent invasion of Saudi Arabia in *Iraq and the Evolution of American Strategy* (Dulles, VA: Potomac, 2008), 21.

54. Deputy Secretary Eagleburger had first raised this prospect in the 3 August 1990 National Security Council meeting. According to the principals in this meeting, the leaders of Jordan, Egypt, and Yemen were consumed with "hand wringing" over whether their countries would also be targets. See Bush and Scowcroft, *A World Transformed*, 335; see also Steven Metz, *Iraq and the Evolution of American Strategy*, 22.

55. Bush and Scowcroft, *A World Transformed*, 328.

56. Khaled, *Desert Warrior*, 11.

57. *Conduct of the Persian Gulf War*, 58–59.

58. Norman Friedman, *Desert Victory: The War for Kuwait* (Annapolis, MD: Naval Institute Press, 1991), 40–41, 224.

59. Dennis Ross, *Statecraft: And How to Restore America's Standing in the World* (New York: Farrar, Straus and Giroux, 2007), 75.

60. *Conduct of Persian Gulf War*, 58; Governor Sununu's comment in 3 August 1990 declassified NSC minutes.

61. Deputy Secretary of State Lawrence Eagleburger, quoted in 3 August 1990 NSC minutes.

62. General Scowcroft, in 3 August 1990 NSC minutes.

63. *Conduct of Persian Gulf War*, 82.

64. Fred Kaplan, "Biggest Fear: Quick Strike by Saddam," *Boston Globe*, 8 August 1990.

65. General Powell, quoted in 3 August 1990, NSC minutes.

66. Webster, quoted in Bush and Scowcroft, *A World Transformed*, 334.

67. *United States Central Command, Operation Desert Shield/Desert Storm* (Tampa, FL: CENTCOM, 1991), 6.

68. Ibid.

69. See 3 August 1990 NSC declassified minutes.

70. *Conduct of the Persian Gulf War*, 82; Guy Gugliotta, "Top Marine Sees 'Fairly Brutal' War," *Washington Post*, 18 December 1990.

71. "America's Best Weapon: Patience," *New York Times*, 2 October 1990.

72. Bush and Scowcroft, *A World Transformed*, 381.

73. Lawrence Freedman and Efraim Karsh, "How Kuwait Was Won: Strategy in the Gulf War," *International Security* 16, no. 2 (1991): 5.

74. Quoted in Bush and Scowcroft, *A World Transformed*, 327.

75. Jane Edward Smith, *George Bush's War* (New York: Henry Holt, 1992), 18.

76. Colin Powell, quoted in 3 August 1990 NSC meeting minutes.

77. *Conduct of the Persian Gulf War*, 48.

78. Dilip Hiro, *Desert Shield to Desert Storm: The Second Gulf War* (New York: Harper Collins, 1992), 2, 43; Chris Hedges, "A Million Strong? Some Experts Question Iraq's Military Strength," *New York Times*, 11 August 1990.

79. *Conduct of the Persian Gulf War*, 308.

80. "Iraqi Use of Chemical Weapons," Department of State Action Memo, 21 November 1983; "Saddam's Chemical Weapons Campaign: Halabja, 16 March 1988," Department of State's Bureau of Public Affairs, 14 March 2003. The declassified National Security Directive 54 of 15 January 1991—entitled "Responding to Iraqi Aggression in the Gulf"—reports that the objective of U.S. and coalition efforts was to "destroy Iraq's chemical, biological, and nuclear capabilities" and "discourage Iraqi use of chemical, biological, or nuclear weapons," suggesting that the United States believed that Iraq had those capabilities and might be inclined to use them. Available at the National Security Archive: http://www.gwu.edu/~nsarchiv/NSAEBB/NSAEBB39/document4.pdf.

81. Glenn Frankel, "British Commander Says Gulf Casualties May Be Very High," *Washington Post*, 30 November 1990.

82. Norman Schwarzkopf, *It Doesn't Take a Hero: The Autobiography of General H. Norman Schwarzkopf* (New York: Bantam, 1993), 356.

83. "Cost of War in Persian Gulf Put at 65,000 Lives, $50 Billion," Reuters, 19 November 1990.

84. Colin Nickerson, "U.S. Military Medical Crews Prepare for War's Casualties," *Boston Globe*, 25 December 1990.

85. Michael R. Gordon, "Troop Moves Show Hussein Wants to Fight, Many U.S. Officials Say," *New York Times*, 15 January 1991. These estimates proved to be vastly inflated. For more discussion of "hyperbole" in estimates, see Jacob Weisberg, "Gulfballs: How the Experts Blew It, Big-Time," *New Republic*, 25 March 1991, 17-19.

86. David H. Marlowe, *Psychological and Psychosocial Consequences of Combat and Deployment with Special Emphasis on the Gulf War* (Santa Monica, CA: RAND, 2001), 117. An outlier view was that of John Mearsheimer, who thought that the prevailing view was "unduly pessimistic." Mearsheimer, however, was commenting on the expectations of a ground war after three weeks of an air war that had produced little resistance. See "Will Iraq Fight or Fold Its Tent? Liberation in Less Than a Week," *New York Times*, 8 February 1991.

87. Bush and Scowcroft, *A World Transformed*, 327.

88. Schwarzkopf, *It Doesn't Take a Hero*, 385, 390, 404.

89. United States Central Command's *Operation Desert Shield/Desert Storm*, 8.

90. David Nyhan, "Bush Turned the Odds Upside Down," *Boston Globe*, 28 February 1991.

91. General Schwarzkopf briefing on 27 February 1991, in Richard Pyle, *Schwarzkopf: The Man, the Mission, the Triumph* (London: Mandarin, 1991), 194-195.

92. Cortell and Davis, "Understanding the Domestic Impact of International Norms," 70.

93. Lyndon B. Johnson: "Radio and Television Report to the American People on the Situation in the Dominican Republic," 2 May 1965, available at the American Presidency Project: http://www.presidency.ucsb.edu/ws/index.php?pid=26932&st=&st1=.

94. Max Frankel, "Latins' Aid Asked," *New York Times*, 3 May 1965; see also Thomas J. Hamilton, "Uruguay Assails New U.S. 'Doctrine'" *New York Times*, 5 May 1965.

95. Text of Reagan's "Announcement of Invasion," reprinted in *New York Times*, 26 October 1983.

96. Isaak I. Dore, "The U.S. Invasion of Grenada: Resurrection of the 'Johnson Doctrine'?" *Stanford Journal of International Law* 20, no. 1 (1984): 173–189.

97. Bush and Scowcroft, *A World Transformed*, 370.

98. Secretary Baker's address to the members of the Security Council, November 1990. Available at http://www.bakerinstitute.org/vrtour/gulf_war_col_tour/baker21_full.html.

99. Margaret Thatcher, 2 August 1990 speech, extracted from *The Downing Street Years* (London: Smithmark, 1995), 816–820.

100. Cortell and Davis, "Understanding the Domestic Impact of International Norms," 70. For more on framing effects, see James N. Druckman, "On the Limits of Framing Effects: Who Can Frame?" *Journal of Politics* 63, no.4 (2001): 1041.

101. Martha Finnemore, *The Purpose of Intervention: Changing Beliefs about the Use of Force* (Ithaca, NY: Cornell University Press, 2003).

102. National Security 45 Directive 20 August 1990, available at the National Security Archive, http://www.gwu.edu/~nsarchiv/NSAEBB/NSAEBB39/document2.pdf.

103. PBS *Frontline*, "The Gulf War," transcript available at http://www.pbs.org/wgbh/pages/frontline/gulf/script_a.html.

104. Linda Diebel, "Anti-War Mood Growing among Americans," *Toronto Star*, 28 October 1990.

105. Thomas L. Friedman, "Selling Sacrifice: Gulf Rationale Still Eludes Bush," *New York Times*, 16 November 1990; President Bush, televised speech, 23 October 1990.

106. Elaine Sciolino, "The UN's Watershed," *New York Times*, 30 August 1990.

107. Ibid.

108. "Bush Is Losing Patience with Iraq: U.S. President Claims Authority to Act without UN Concurrence," *Financial Post (Toronto)*, 26 November 1990.

109. Bob Woodward, *The Commanders* (New York: Simon and Schuster, 1991), 169–171.

110. Elaine Sciolino, "The UN's Watershed"; Baker, *The Politics of Diplomacy*, 305.

111. Barker, *The Politics of Diplomacy*, 315.

112. Quoted in Alexander Thompson, "Coercion through IOs: The Security Council and the Logic of Information Transmission," *International Organization* 60 (Winter 2006): 23.

113. Lucia Mouat, "Prestige High, UN Looks Stronger," *Christian Science Monitor*, 11 March 1991.

114. British Ambassador to the UN Sir David Hannay, quoted in Jonathan Schacter, "The UN's New Image," *Jerusalem Post*, 8 March 1991.

115. Stanley Hoffmann, "The Price of War," *New York Review of Books* 38, nos. 1–2 (17 January 1991).

116. David Malone, *The International Struggle over Iraq: Politics in the UN Security Council 1980-2005* (Oxford: Oxford University Press, 2006), 265.

117. Everett Carll Ladd, "Iraq: Good Policy Is Good Politics," *Christian Science Monitor*, 7 September 1990.

118. Gallup poll, August 9-12, 1990.

119. ABC News poll, August 17-20, 1990.

120. ABC News/*Washington Post*, November 14-15, 1990.

121. Gallup Poll, November 29-2 December 1990.

122. John Mueller, "A Review: American Public Opinion and the Gulf War," *Public Opinion Quarterly* 57, no. 1 (1993): 82.

123. David Hoffman, "Messages as Mixed as Audiences: President Struggles to Articulate Goals," *Washington Post*, 15 November 1990.

124. Jim Hoagland, "The Gulf: Right Policy, but Wrong President?" *Washington Post*, 4 November 1990.

125. CBS-*New York Times* survey, November 1990. Quoted in Richard Morin and E. J. Dionne, "Vox Populi: Winds of War and Shifts of Opinion," *Washington Post*, 23 December 1990.

126. Former Defense Secretary James Schlesinger and two former CJCSs argued that giving sanctions a year or more would gradually diminish Iraq's military powers. See Michael R. Gordon, "Quayle Says Delaying War Would Increase Risks," *New York Times*, 30 November 1990.

127. "Gephardt Warns of Cuts in Financing if Bush Orders Attack Alone," *St. Louis Post-Dispatch*, 30 December 1990.

128. Senator Ernest Hollings, Supporting the Actions Taken by the President with Respect to Iraqi Aggression against Kuwait (Senate, 2 October 1990).

129. Mary Curtius, "Aspin Calls for More Troops, Money from Gulf Allies," *Boston Globe*, 16 November 1990.

130. R. W. Apple Jr., "Two-Front Campaign," *New York Times*, October 14 1990.

131. Baker, *The Politics of Diplomacy*, 288.

132. Ibid., 299.

133. On playing international and domestic negotiations off each other, see Robert D. Putnam, "Diplomacy and Domestic Politics: The Logic of Two-Level Games," *International Organization* 42 (1988): 427-460.

134. Louis Fisher, "Presidential Wars," in *The Domestic Sources of American Foreign Policy*, ed. Eugene R. Wittkopf and James McCormick (Lanham, MD: Rowman and Littlefield, 1999), 160-161.

135. Bush and Scowcroft, *A World Transformed*, 389-390.

136. President Bush, quoted in Martin J. Medhurst, *The Rhetorical Presidency of George H. W. Bush* (College Station: Texas A&M Press, 2006), 70.

137. Smith, *George Bush's War*, 106-107.

138. Stephen L. Carter, "Going to War over War Power: Congressional Critics of Bush's Gulf Moves are Looking at the Wrong Constitutional Clause," *Washington Post*, 18 November 1990.

139. Quoted in Smith, *George Bush's War*, 108.

140. Joan Hoff, *A Faustian Foreign Policy from Woodrow Wilson to George W. Bush* (Cambridge: Cambridge University Press, 2007), 135; Anthony Lewis, "Presidential Power," *New York Times*, 14 January 1991.

141. R. W. Apple Jr., "Confrontation in the Gulf: Bush's Limited Victory," *New York Times*, 13 January 1991.

142. David Gergen, "America's Missed Opportunities," *Foreign Affairs*, December–January 1991-1992.

143. Bush and Scowcroft, *A World Transformed*, 395.

144. See H.J.Res. 77, *Authorization for Use of Military Force against Iraq Resolution*. Available at the Library of Congress, http://thomas.loc.gov/cgi-bin/query/z?c102:H.J.RES.77.

145. Kenneth Schultz, "Tying Hands and Washing Hands," in *Locating the Proper Authorities*, ed. Daniel Drezner (Ann Arbor: University of Michigan Press, 2003), 110-111.

146. Charles Krauthammer, "The Unipolar Moment," *Foreign Affairs* 70, no. 1 (Winter 1990-1991): 23-33.

147. See Mearsheimer's section on "structure and peace in the 1990s," in *The Tragedy of Great Power Politics* (New York: W. W. Norton, 2001), 380-383.

148. William Pfaff, "Redefining World Power," *Foreign Affairs* 70, no. 1 (Winter 1990-1991): 34.

149. Secretary Baker indicates that he saw the international system as a "relaxed bipolar world" in 1990-1991. See *The Politics of Diplomacy*, 323.

150. The 3 August 1990 NSC meeting minutes.

151. Oles M. Smolansky, *The USSR and Iraq: The Soviet Quest for Influence*, (Durham, NC: Duke University Press, 1991).

152. Glenn Frankel, "War with Iraq: Is It Inevitable? Europeans Fear That Americans Think So," *Washington Post*, 26 August 1990; see also Baker, *The Politics of Diplomacy*, 278.

153. Ross, *Statecraft*, 81.

154. For more on the Soviet influence in the Middle East, see "Response to Invasion," in Lawrence Freedman and Efram Karsh, *The Gulf Conflict, 1990-1991: Diplomacy and War in the New World Order* (Princeton, NJ: Princeton University Press, 1993), 76-80.

155. Baker, *The Politics of Diplomacy*, 281.

156. Brent Scowcroft argued that Soviet military participation in the coalition would actually create domestic political problems for the United States, with the public and Congress still reticent about the idea of U.S.-Soviet cooperation. See *A World Transformed*, 357-388.

157. Freedman and Karsh, *The Gulf Conflict*, 148.

158. David Lake, *Entangling Relations: American Foreign Policy in Its Century* (Princeton, NJ: Princeton University Press, 1999), 260-261.

159. Khalid, *Desert Warrior*, 38.

160. Robert H. Scales, *Certain Victory* (Dulles, VA: Potomac, 1993), 140.

161. Baker, *The Politics of Diplomacy*, 283-285.

162. Ibid., 281.

163. Bush and Scowcroft, *A World Transformed*, 360.

164. Baker, *The Politics of Diplomacy*, 305.

165. H. W. Brands, "George Bush and the Gulf War of 1991," *Presidential Studies Quarterly* 31, no. 1 (2004): 113-131.

166. Erik Voeten, "The Political Origins of the UN Security Council's Ability to Legitimize the Use of Force," *International Organization* 59 (Summer 2005): 527, 531.

CHAPTER 5

1. United States Arms Control and Disarmament Agency, *World Military Expenditures and Arms Transfers 1995* (Washington, DC: U.S. Government Printing Office, 1996).

2. Philippe R. Girard, *Clinton in Haiti* (New York: Palgrave, 2004), 2.

3. Hans Schmidt, *The U.S. Occupation of Haiti, 1915-1934* (Trenton, NJ: Rutgers University Press, 1995), 6.

4. See Alexander Thompson, "Screening Power: International Organizations as Informative Agents," in *Delegation and Agency in International Organizations*, ed. Darren Hawkins, David Lake, Daniel Nielson, and Michael Tierney (New York: Cambridge University Press, 2006), 372.

5. Mary A. Renda, *Taking Haiti: Military Occupation and the Culture of U.S. Imperialism, 1915-1940* (Chapel Hill: University of North Carolina Press, 2001); see also Chetan Kumar, "Sustaining Peace in War-Torn Societies," in *Military Intervention: Cases in Context for the Twenty-First Century*, ed. William J. Lahneman, 105-132 (New York: Rowman and Littlefield, 2004); Hans Schmidt, *The U.S. Occupation of Haiti*, 6.

6. See the State Department's statement on the Good Neighbor Policy at http://www.state.gov/r/pa/ho/time/id/17341.htm.

7. President Bush issued an executive order that would exempt U.S.-affected industries from the embargo. See David Malone, "Haiti and the International Community: A Case Study," *Survival* 39, no. 2 (1997): 129.

8. Kumar, "Sustaining Peace in War-Torn Societies," 115.

9. Executive Order 12853—Blocking Government of Haiti Property and Prohibiting Transactions with Haiti, 30 June 1993, available at http://www.presidency.ucsb.edu/ws/index.php?pid=61548.

10. United Nations Mission in Haiti background, available at http://www.un.org/en/peacekeeping/missions/past/unmihbackgr2.html.

11. Ian Martin, "Haiti: Mangled Multilateralism," *Foreign Policy*, no. 95 (Summer 1994): 72.

12. Ibid.

13. John M. Goshko, "Effects of Shifts on Haiti Unclear," *Washington Post*, 13 May 1994.

14. Ibid.

15. Douglas Jehl, "Boutros-Ghali Says Sanctions on Haiti Need 'Several Weeks,'" *New York Times*, 28 May 1994; for more on potential allies' positions on Haiti, see William Drozdiak, "Allies Hail Haiti Pact, Pledge Aid," *Washington Post*, 20 September 1994.

16. United Nations, Resolution 940 of 31 July 1994, available at www.un.org/Docs/scres/1994/scres94.htm.

17. Vote on UN Resolution 940 available at http://www.unhchr.ch/Huridocda/Huridoca.nsf/50b01c101750f048c1256610002c88a4/b3358a1b8c77b21e802566fa00 50ac7a?OpenDocument.

18. See, for example, Girard, *Clinton in Haiti*, 39, who writes of Clinton's efforts to build on the "new world order" spirit of his predecessor, President George H. W. Bush.

19. Ibid., 206, note 1.

20. Walter E. Kretchik, "Planning for 'Intervasion': The Strategic and Operational Setting for Uphold Democracy," in *Invasion, Intervention, "Intervasion": A Concise History of the U.S. Army in Operation Uphold Democracy* (Ft. Leavenworth, KS: Command and General Staff College Press, 1998).

21. Chetan Kumar and Elizabeth M. Cousens, *Peacebuilding in Haiti* (IPA Policy Briefing Series, April 1996).

22. Kretchik, "Planning for 'Intervasion.'"

23. For a thorough analysis of the effect of domestic politics and lobbying on the decision to intervene, see the "Domestic Politics" and "Haiti Lobbying" chapters in Girard, *Clinton in Haiti*.

24. Ronald H. Cole, "Grenada, Panama, Haiti," *Joint Force Quarterly*, no. 20 (Autumn–Winter 1998-1999): 62–63.

25. Kretchik, "Planning for 'Intervasion.'"

26. Richard Haass, *Intervention: The Use of American Military Force in the Post-Cold War World* (Washington, DC: Carnegie Endowment for International Peace, 1999), 25.

27. "Eastern Caribbean Countries Asked U.S. to Act against Grenada," *Associated Press*, 25 October 1983.

28. "Lead Caribbean Nations Commit to Haitian Invasion Force," *Deutsche Presse-Agentur*, 31 August 1994.

29. "Training Planned for Haiti Intervention," *St. Petersburg Times*, 31 August 1994; Peter Grief, "Caribbean Grabs Clinton Attention as U.S. Finalizes Haiti Invasion Plan," *Christian Science Monitor*, 6 September 1994, 3; Eric Schmitt, "Legislators in U.S. Differ over Haiti," *New York Times*, 1 September 1994.

30. "Lead Caribbean Nations Commit to Haritian Invasion Force," *Dentsche Presse-Agrentur*, 31 August 1994.

31. Douglas Jehl, "France Says It Won't Support Military Intervention in Haiti," *New York Times*, 13 May 1994.

32. Haass, *Intervention*, 158.

33. Cole, "Grenada, Panama, Haiti," 63.

34. From Kretchik, Figure 7, "Multinational Force, Haiti, 15 Oct 1994," in *Intervasion*.

35. See Table 4 in Kretchik, "MNF, Haiti, 13 Jan 1995," in *Intervasion*.

36. Girard, *Clinton in Haiti*, 76.

37. Ibid., 66.

38. Michael Kramer, "The Case for Intervention," *Time*, 26 September 1994.

39. Michael Kramer, "The Case against Invading Haiti," *Time*, 19 September 1994.

40. William J. Clinton, "Address to the Nation on Haiti," 15 September 1994, available at http://www.presidency.ucsb.edu/ws/index.php?pid=49093.

41. With U.S. support, the Security Council praised the work of 1,600 Russian peacekeepers operating in Georgia and an expanded UN observer mission. Ten days later, Russia offered its support for the Clinton-sponsored Haiti mission. See editorial, *Washington Post*, 24 July 1994; Lally Weymouth, "Yalta II," *Washington Post*, 24 July 1994; "A U.N. License to Invade Haiti," *New York Times*, 2 August 1994.

42. Douglas Jehl, "France Says It Won't Support Military Intervention in Haiti," *New York Times*, 13 May 1994.

43. Douglas Jehl, "Clinton Seeks UN Approval of Any Plan to Invade Haiti," *New York Times*, 22 July 1994.

44. "No Good Reason to Invade Haiti," *New York Times*, 13 July 1994.

45. "Clinton Will Ask You to Back Haiti Invasion," *St. Petersburg Times*, 14 September 1994.

46. Kretchik, *Intervasion*.

47. John Goshko, "Clinton's Haiti Course Is Seen as Irreversible," *Washington Post*, 12 September 1994.

48. Thomas Lippman, "Pentagon Method of Calculation Minimizes Cost of Haiti Operation," *Washington Post*, 17 September 1994.

49. Powell, quoted in David Halberstam, *War in a Time of Peace: Bush, Clinton, and the Generals* (New York: Scribner, 2002), 268.

50. William M. Welch, "Relief amid New Fears in Congress," *USA Today*, 20 September 1994.

51. Thomas L. Friedman, "Is the U.S. President Trying to Conduct Foreign Policy by the Standards of Mother Teresa?" *Globe and Mail*, 8 December 1995.

52. Michael Mandelbaum, "Foreign Policy as Social Work," *Foreign Affairs* 75, no.1 (1996): 16–32.

53. Gabriel Escobar, "Argentina Won't Join Invasion; Policy Feud Prompts Government Reversal," *Washington Post*, 5 August 1994; "Canada Bows Out of Possible Invasion," *Ottawa Citizen*, 3 August 1994.

54. For more on the role of foreign troops in Haiti, see J. Jeffrey Smith, "Multinational Forces Fly to Puerto Rico for Peacekeeping Training," *Washington Post*, 13 September 2005.

55. Deputy Secretary of State Strobe Talbott, Statement before the Senate Foreign Relations Committee, 9 March 1995. Available at http://dosfan.lib.uic.edu/ERC/bureaus/lat/1995/950309TalbottHaiti.html.

56. Author's correspondence with Lt. Col. Walter Kretchik, May 2006.

57. Quoted in Jonathan Schacter, "The UN's New Image," *Jerusalem Post*, 8 March 1991.

58. Smith, "Multinational Forces Fly to Puerto Rico for Peacekeeping Training."

59. Thomas W. Lippman, "Pentagon Method of Calculation Minimizes Cost of Haiti Operation," *Washington Post*, 17 September 1994.

60. Sebastian von Einsiedel and David M. Malone, "Haiti," in *United Nations Interventionism, 1991-2004*, ed. Mats Berdal and Spyros Economides (Cambridge: Cambridge University Press, 2007), 472-473. Russia had also requested that France be more accepting of its peacekeeping mission in Georgia, since Russia had supported Operation Turquoise, a Chapter VII peacekeeping mission to Rwanda in the months following the 1994 genocide.

61. Diego Ribadeneira, "Vote on Haiti Stirs Latin America Fears," *Boston Globe*, 7 August 1994.

62. Danilo Zolo, *Cosmopolis: Prospects for World Government* (Cambridge, MA: Polity, 1997), xiii.

63. Ibid., 164.

64. Ibid., 122.

65. Neil Fenton, *Understanding the UN Security Council: Coercion or Consent?* (Burlington, VT: Ashgate, 2004), 124.

66. Michael K. Gigot, "Haiti Politics: It's No Cuban Missile Crisis," *Wall Street Journal*, 16 September 1994.

67. "Still a U.S. Invasion. Still Wrong." *New York Times*, 2 September 1994.

68. Bill Gertz, "Invasion Force Heads for Haiti; Opposition Grows as Carrier Leaves," *Washington Times*, 14 September 1994.

69. Helen Dewar, "Senators Back Troops, Urge Withdrawal," *Washington Post*, 21 September 1994.

70. William M. Welch, "Lawmakers Push Haiti Debate," *USA Today*, 15 September 1994.

71. Michael Hedges, "U.S. Sends Haiti Mixed Messages on Military's Fate; Christopher, Albright Disagree," *Washington Times*, 12 September 1994.

72. *Time*/CNN poll of 21 September 1994.

73. *Newsweek* poll of 19 September 1994 (more frequent responses were human rights at 41 percent and "Clinton will have political problems if he doesn't carry out his threat to invade" at 32 percent).

74. *New York Times*/CBS News poll, 19 September 1994.

75. ABC News poll of 11 September 1994.

76. Author's interview with Anthony Lake, 30 May 2006, Washington, DC.

77. Michael Hedges, "U.S. Sends Haiti Mixed Messages on Military's Fate," *Washington Times*, 12 September 1994.

78. William M. Welch and Tony Mauro, "Republicans Move to Block President on Invasion of Haiti," *USA Today*, 13 September 1994.

79. Katherine Q. Seelye, "Few Opinions, Pro or Con, Seem to Change in Congress," *New York Times*, 16 September 1994.

80. Carl McClendon, "Administration Critic Praises Clinton's Plan to Invade Haiti," *St. Petersburg Times*, 17 September 1994; Halberstam, *War in a Time of Peace*, 268, 278.

81. See, for example, the *Washington Post*/ABC News poll of 7 August 1994.

82. For an excellent treatment of public support for the Haiti intervention, see Kenneth Schultz (especially figure 2, multilateralism and support for the Haiti operation, 1994), "Tying Hands and Washing Hands," in *Locating the Proper Authorities: The Interaction of Domestic and International Institutions*, ed. Daniel Drezner (Ann Arbor: University of Michigan Press, 2003), 122.

83. Ibid., 121.

84. "J-7 Operational Plans and Interoperability Directorate, Military Operations Other Than War," available at http://www.dtic.mil/doctrine/jrm/mootw.pdf, 3.

85. Anthony Lake cites the need for an "international face" on the intervention as a way to increase the likelihood of acceptance by the local government. Author's interview, 30 May 2006.

86. In his work, Phillip Cunliffe asks why the United States would seek the "patina of UN legitimacy" for a practice in which the United States had historically engaged. This domestic politics explanation would seem to address that conundrum. See Cunliffe, "Uniting the World, Dividing the Nations: Agency in Global Governance," paper prepared for the ISA Convention, San Diego, CA, 2006.

87. For Mexico's statement, see S/PV.3413, pp. 4–5; Uruguay's, S/PV.3413, p. 7; and Brazil's, S/PV.3413, pp. 9–10. For a summary of the meeting, see Chapter 11, "Consideration of the Provisions of Chapter VII of the Charter," United Nations *Repertoire*, Twelfth Supplement (1993-1995).

88. Karen A. Mingst and Margaret P. Karns, "Actors in the UN System," in *The United Nations in the 21st Century* (Boulder, CO: Westview, 2006), 54.

CHAPTER 6

See Secretary of Defense Donald Rumsfeld's press conference of 18 October 2001, available at http://transcripts.cnn.com/TRANSCRIPTS/0110/18/se.23.html.

1. For the verbiage of 1368, see http://www.un.org/News/Press/docs/2001/
SC7143.doc.htm; in this statement, the council notes that the "members departed
from tradition and stood to unanimously adopt resolution 1368, by which they
expressed the Council's readiness to take all necessary steps to respond to the attacks
of 11 September and to combat all forms of terrorism in accordance with its Charter
responsibilities," 12 September 2001. For a more comprehensive listing of IO
reactions, see "International Organizations Respond to Sept 11 Attacks," available at
http://usinfo.org/wf-archive/2001/010925/epf213.htm.

2. UNSC Resolution 1368, available at http://www.un.org/News/Press/docs/
2001/SC7143.doc.htm.

3. Benjamin Lambeth, *Airpower against Terror: America's Conduct of Operation
Enduring Freedom* (Santa Monica, CA: RAND, 2005), 54.

4. See, inter alia, Malcolm Yapp, *Strategies of British India: Britain, Iran, and
Afghanistan, 1798-1850* (Oxford: Oxford University Press, 1980); Patrick Macrory,
Kabul Catastrophe: The Story of the Disastrous Retreat from Kabul, 1842 (Oxford:
Oxford University Press, 1986); Michael A. Gress, *The Soviet-Afghan War: How a
Superpower Fought and Lost* (Lawrence: University Press of Kansas, 2002); Brian
Robson, *The Road to Kabul: The Second Afghan War 1878-1881*, new ed. (Staplehurst,
UK: Spellmount, 2003); Brian Robson, *Crisis on the Frontier: The Third Afghan War
and the Campaign in Waziristan 1919-20* (Staplehurst, UK: Spellmount, 2004).

5. Artyom Borovik, *The Hidden War: A Russian Journalist's Account of the Soviet
War in Afghanistan* (New York: Grove, 2003); Vladislav Tamarov, *Afghanistan: A
Russian Soldier's Story* (Berkeley, CA: Ten Speed Press, 2005); Colonel A. Jalali and
Lt. Col. L. W. Grau, *The Other Side of the Mountain: Mujahideen Tactics in the Soviet
Afghan War* (Quantico, VA: United States Marine Corps, Studies and Analysis
Division, 1999); Peter Hopkirk, *The Great Game: The Struggle for Empire in Central
Asia* (reprint; New York: Kodansha International, 1992).

6. For a useful historical overview of Afghanistan in relation to foreign militaries, see Milton Bearden, "Afghanistan, Graveyard of Empires," *Foreign Affairs* 80,
no. 6 (2001): 17-31.

7. Lambeth, *Airpower against Terror*, 37.

8. T. F. Reid, "Blair Campaigns for War Support," Washington Post, 31 October
2001.

9. "Friends and Allies," *New York Daily News*, 8 October 2001.

10. Thomas Friedman, "We Are Alone," *New York Times*, 26 October 2001.

11. For more on U.S. risk aversion before 9/11, see Steve Coll, *Ghost Wars: The
Secret History of the CIA, Afghanistan, and Bin Laden, from the Soviet Invasion to 10
September 2001* (New York, Penguin, 2004).

12. Ron Suskind, *The One Percent Doctrine: Deep Inside America's Pursuit of Its
Enemies Since 9/11* (New York: Simon and Schuster, 2006), 52.

13. President Bush's remarks at National Day of Prayer and Remembrance,
Address at the National Cathedral, delivered 14 September 2001, available at http://
archives.cnn.com/2001/US/09/14/bush.memorial/.

14. Richard W. Stewart, *The United States Army in Afghanistan: Operation Enduring
Freedom* (Carlisle, PA: Center for Military History, 2004).

15. Stephen Biddle, *Afghanistan and the Future of Warfare: Implications for Army
and Defense Policy* (Carlisle, PA: Strategic Studies Institute, 2002), 11. For other chro-
nological accounts, see Global Security, *Operation Enduring Freedom*, "Planning and

Implementation" and "Initial Deployments," available at www.globalsecurity.org/ military/ops/enduring-freedom.htm; see also Suskind, *The One Percent Doctrine*, 53.

16. "Marines enter Kandahar airport," available at http://www.defenselink.mil/ news/newsarticle.aspx?id=44361.

17. Bob Woodward, *Bush at War* (New York: Simon and Schuster, 2003), 179-180.

18. Alan Sipress and Peter Finn, "U.S. Says 'Not Yet' to Patrol by Allies," *Washington Post*, 30 November 2001.

19. Quoted in Nora Bensahel's treatment of coalition cooperation in Afghanistan and Operation Enduring Freedom more broadly. See *The Counterterror Coalitions: Cooperation with Europe, NATO, and the European Union* (Arlington, VA: RAND, 2003), 7-8.

20. Judy Dempsey and Alexander Nicoll, "NATO Leaders Warm to US Flexibility," *Financial Times*, 27 September 2001.

21. Paul Wolfowitz, press conference at Luns Press Theatre, NATO Headquarters, 26 September 2001; transcript at http://www.defenselink.mil/transcripts/transcript. aspx?transcriptid=1935.

22. Quoted in Sipress and Finn, "U.S. Says 'Not Yet' to Patrol by Allies."

23. Michael Dobbs, "Britain Prepares to Announce Plans for Ground Forces in Afghanistan," *Washington Post*, 26 October 2001; Laurence McQuillan, "Britain Says Ground Troops Are Available, 'Ready to Go,'" *USA Today*, 23 October 2001.

24. Rachel Donnelly, "UK Troops Will Not Be Involved 'for Some Time,'" *Irish Times*, 30 October 2001.

25. Gary Bernsten, *Jawbreaker: The Attack on Bin Laden and Al Qaeda: A Personal Account by the CIA's Key Field Commander* (Westminster, MD: Crown, 2005), 210.

26. T. R. Reid, "Blair Denies Split with Bush over War," *Washington Post*, 22 November 2001; Warren Hoge, "British Defense Secretary Says Troops for Afghanistan Are Being Taken off High Alert," *New York Times*, 27 November 2001.

27. David Wastell, "How 680 Paras Drove a Wedge between London and Washington," *Sunday Telegraph*, 25 November 2001.

28. Michael Gordon, "U.S. and Britain at Odds over Use and Timing of Peacekeeping Troops," *New York Times*, 2 December 2001; see also Michael Gordon, "Afghans Block Britain's Plan for Big Force," *New York Times*, 20 November 2001, in which he quotes a Pentagon official who doubts that there will at any point be some role for British and French forces around Kabul.

29. Sipress and Finn, "U.S. Says 'Not Yet' to Patrol by Allies."

30. Paul Koring, "Foreign Troops Ready to Set Up Afghan Bases," *Globe and Mail*, 22 November 2001.

31. Chip Cummins and Jeanne Cummings, "U.S. Reliance on Northern Rebels May Dilute Support from Pakistan," *Wall Street Journal*, 30 October 2001.

32. Biddle, *Afghanistan and the Future of Warfare*, 24.

33. Charles H. Briscoe, Richard Kiper, James A. Schroder, and Kalev I. Sepp, *Weapon of Choice: Army Special Operations Forces in Afghanistan* (Ft. Leavenworth, KS: CGSC Press, 2004).

34. "The Limits of Intervention," *Independent*, 23 December 2001.

35. See NATO's International Security Assistance Force fact sheet, available at http://www.nato.int/isaf/docu/epub/pdf/placemat.html.

36. Hy S. Rothstein makes a similar argument about the two phases of the Afghanistan campaign in *Afghanistan and the Troubled Future of Unconventional Warfare* (Annapolis, MD: U.S. Naval Institute Press, 2006).

37. For more on the distinction between the American OEF mission and NATO ISAF, see Colonel Michael L. Everett, *Merging the International Security and Assistance Force (ISAF) and Operation Enduring Freedom (OEF): A Strategic Imperative* (Carlisle, PA: Army War College, 2006). As of early 2007, about 14,000 Americans participated under NATO-ISAF; another 11,000 continued participating in counterterrorism operations and police training. See Carlotta Gall, "American Takes Over Command of NATO Force in Afghanistan," *New York Times*, 5 February 2007.

38. See "NATO in Afghanistan," available at http://www.nato.int/cps/en/natolive/topics_8189.htm.

39. "NATO Agrees to ISAF Expansion across Afghanistan," NATO Update, available at http://www.nato.int/docu/update/2006/09-september/e0928a.htm.

40. See speech by NATO Secretary General Jaap de Hoop Scheffer, 20 July 2006, available at http://www.nato.int/docu/speech/2006/s060720d.htm. Indeed, there is a considerable difference that has created problems in the alliance; see Sarah Sewall, "A Heavy Hand in Afghanistan," *Boston Globe*, 15 June 2007.

41. Retired Lieutenant Colonel Conrad Crane makes a similar argument about the possible overlap between Phases III and IV in "Phase IV Operations: Where Wars Are Really Won," *Military Review* (May–June 2005): 27–36.

42. In a speech, General James L. Jones, former Supreme Allied Commander Europe, defined a national caveat as "generally a formal written restriction that most nations place on the use of their forces." He went on to say that "Collectively, these restrictions limit the tactical commanders' operational flexibility." See "Prague to Istanbul: Ambition versus Reality," speech at the Center for Strategic Decision Research, available at http://www.csdr.org/2004book/Gen_Jones.htm. See also David Auerswald and Stephen M. Saideman, "Caveats Emptor: Multilateralism at War in Afghanistan," forthcoming, *International Studies Quarterly*.

43. For more on the operational distinctions between counterterrorism and stabilization and reconstruction operations, see Lt. Gen. Ethem Erdagi, "The ISAF Mission and Turkey's Role in Rebuilding the Afghan State," *Policy Watch #1052*, Special Forum for the Washington Institute for Near East Policy, 18 November 2005; available at http://www.washingtoninstitute.org/templateC05.php?CID=2403.

44. "Statement of Cofer Black: Joint Investigation into September 11: 26 September 2002."

45. Daniel Benjamin and Steven Simon, *The Age of Sacred Terror: Radical Islam's War against America* (New York: Random House, 2003), 290–295, 291; see also Steve Coll, *Ghost Wars: The Secret History of the CIA, Afghanistan, and bin Laden, from the Soviet Invasion to 10 September 2001* (New York: Penguin, 2004).

46. *The 9/11 Commission Report: Final Report of the National Commission on Terrorist Attacks upon the United States* (New York: W. W. Norton, 2004), 213. Chapter 6, "From Threat to Threat," presents an excellent review of the nonsystematic nature of counterterrorism policy leading up to the 9/11 attacks.

47. "Testimony of Richard A. Clarke before the National Commission on Terrorist Attacks upon the United States," 24 March 2004, available at http://www.9-11commission.gov/hearings/hearing8/clarke_statement.pdf. On risk aversion, see transcript of Clarke's question and answer, available at "Transcript: Wednesday's 9/11 Commission Hearings," *Washington Post*, 24 March 2004; http://www.washingtonpost.com/wp-dyn/articles/A20349-2004Mar24.html.

48. Vice President Richard Cheney, quoted in Woodward, *Bush at War*, 291.

49. Suskind, *The One Percent Doctrine*, 50.

50. Ibid., 34.

51. *Campaign Planning Primer 2006*, Department of Military Strategy, Planning and Operations, the U.S. Army War College.

52. For more on some of the interagency challenges, see Woodward, *Bush at War*, 126–170, 136.

53. Author's interview with lead CENTCOM planner, Colonel John Agoglia, 17 April 2007.

54. Milan Vego, "What Can We Learn from Enduring Freedom?" *U.S. Naval Institute Proceedings* 128, no. 7 (2002): 28–33.

55. David C. Gompert and Uwe Nerlich, *Shoulder to Shoulder: The Road to U.S.-European Military Cooperability: A German-American Analysis* (Santa Monica, CA: RAND, 2002).

56. Gompert and Nerlich, p4.

57. Author's interview with U.S. Army special forces officer Kalev Sepp, 12 June 2007.

58. Ibid.

59. Seymour Hersh, "The Other War: Why Bush's Afghanistan Won't Go Away," *New Yorker*, 12 April 2002.

60. For an excellent discussion on the basis and employment of the Afghan Model, see forum on "The Afghan Model and Its Limits" in the 2005–2006 *International Security*: Richard B. Andres, Craig Wills, and Thomas E. Griffith, "Winning with Allies: The Strategic Value of the Afghan Model" and "Allies, Airpower, and Modern Warfare: The Afghan Model in Afghanistan and Iraq."

61. Thomas Ricks, "War Plan for Iraq Is Ready, Say Officials," *Washington Post*, 10 November 2002.

62. Author's interview with then Lt. Col. Michael Fleck, Secretary of the Air Force/Legislative Liaison, 20 September 2006.

63. For a full account of OEF operations in Afghanistan, see Biddle, *Afghanistan and the Future of Warfare*, 8.

64. Woodward, quoted in Richard B. Andres, Craig Wills, and Thomas E. Griffith Jr., "Winning with Allies," *International Security* 30, no. 3 (Winter 2005–2006): 131.

65. Department of Defense News Briefing—Secretary Rumsfeld and General Richard Myers, 8 October 2001, available at http://www.defense.gov/Transcripts/Transcript.aspx?TranscriptID=2032.

66. Barton Gellman, "Secret Unit Expands Rumsfeld's Domain," *Washington Post*, 23 January 2005.

67. Andres et al., "Winning with Allies."

68. This estimate is based on United States Special Operations Command's 2006 Posture, which notes that the 2006 totals of 52,846 represent a 1,400-person increase from 2005 and a 1,500-person increase from 2004; though the rates of growth for 2002 and 2003 are not included, they were unlikely to exceed 1,500 because the post-9/11 increase in SOF training did not begin bearing results until a year or two into recruiting and training. Nonetheless, a conservative estimate for 2001 (fiscal year 2002) would therefore be about 46,846.

69. Gary Schoen, *First in, Last Out* (New York: Ballantine, 2005), particularly parts 3 to 5, which discuss the way special forces developed contacts in and around Afghanistan.

70. Thomas E. Ricks and Vernon Loeb, "Special Forces Open Ground Campaign; Small Numbers Are Said to Be Operating to Aid CIA Effort in Southern Afghanistan," *Washington Post*, 19 October 2001.

71. Kathleen T. Rhen, "Rumsfeld Lauds U.S. Special Ops Forces in Afghanistan," *American Forces Press Service*, 19 November 2001, available at www.defenselink.mil/news/Nov2001/n11192001_200111195.html.

72. That amounts to about 0.4 percent of the SOF totals, compared with about 12 percent of the total army and marine forces that have been involved in Iraq over a period of four years. While the 12 percent has certainly stretched the forces, these two services have nonetheless found ways to keep combat brigades rotating through theater. See Congressional Budget Office, *Some Implications of Increasing U.S. Forces in Iraq*, April 2007, available at http://www.cbo.gov/doc.cfm?index=8024. For more on the Operational Detachment Alpha structure and the early months of Afghanistan, see Max Boot, "Special Forces and Horses," *Armed Forces Journal* (November 2006).

73. Michael Gordon, "Fielding an Afghan Army Is Months Off, U.S. Finds," *New York Times*, 21 March 2002.

74. Michael Gordon, "Where Does Phase 2 Start? In Afghanistan," *New York Times*, 10 March 2002.

75. Bryan Bender and Ellen Barry, "U.S. Troops on Ground in Afghanistan; Rumsfeld Says Effort Aiding Rebel Forces," *Boston Globe*, 31 October 2001.

76. Anthony Cordesman points out that some of the reliance on the Northern Alliance was merely accidental, the result of being unable to deploy large numbers of mountain-capable special forces troops in a relatively short amount of time. See Anthony H. Cordesman and Patrick Baetjer, *The Ongoing Lessons of Afghanistan: Warfighting, Intelligence, Force Transformation, and Nation Building* (Washington, DC: CSIS, 2004), 18. See also Michael O'Hanlon, "A Flawed Masterpiece," *Foreign Affairs* 81, no. 3 (2003), 47–63.

77. Lambeth, *Airpower against Terror*, 60. For more on the objective to minimize collateral damage with an eye toward reconstruction, see Thomas E. Ricks and Alan Sipress, "Attacks Restrained by Political Goals," *Washington Post*, 23 October 2001.

78. Author's correspondence with Army historian Conrad Crane, 14 June 2007.

79. Woodward, *Bush at War*, 275–276.

80. The first sign that the United States was looking at building a new government in Afghanistan was the appointment of James Dobbins as a special envoy to opposition parties in Afghanistan in November 2001. See, for example, "Dobbins Named U.S. Envoy to Opposition in Afghanistan," *Washington Post*, 6 November 2001; Robert D. McFadden, "Seeking a Kabul Coalition, Killings in Kunduz and Bodies in the Rubble," *New York Times*, 19 November 2001.

81. Conrad Crane's presentation, "U.S. Military Operations in Iraq: Planning, Combat, and Occupation," 2 November 2005, held at the School of Advanced International Studies (rapporteur's notes). Separately, Colonel Isaiah Wilson confirmed that there was "no original Phase IV planning of any kind" in Afghanistan. This view found support in interviews with key CENTCOM planners conducted between March and June 2007. Phase IV refers to postconflict operations, which include the transition back to peace and civilian government control. For more on postconflict operations, see Conrad C. Crane, "Phase IV Operations: Where Wars Are Really Won," *Military Review* (May–June 2005): 27–36.

82. Memo from Douglas J. Feith, Under Secretary of Defense for Policy to Secretary of Defense, 11 October 2001.

83. Internal Army War College memo, quoted in Thomas E. Ricks, *Fiasco: The American Military Adventure in Iraq* (New York: Penguin, 2006), 70.

84. "Franks Vows: 'No U.S. Occupying Force in Afghanistan,'" available at http://www.defenselink.mil/news/newsarticle.aspx?id=44355.

85. James Fallows, *Blind into Baghdad: America's War in Iraq* (New York: Vintage, 2006), 128.

86. "Defense Department Lauds Transfer in Afghanistan as Milestone," *Armed Forces Press Service*, 5 October 2006.

87. Richard Haass's testimony to Senate Foreign Relations Committee, 6 December 2001.

88. Quoted in Linda D. Kozaryn, "Marines Enter Kandahar Airport," 14 December 2001, available at http://www.defenselink.mil/news/newsarticle.aspx?id=44361.

89. Admiral Gregory G. Johnson, "Examining the SFOR experience," *NATO Review* (Winter 2004).

90. Karl Eikenberry, "Combined Forces Command-Afghanistan Campaign Assessment," Center for Peace and Security Studies seminar at Georgetown University, 21 September 2006.

91. General James L. Jones Jr., "From Coalition to ISAF Command in Afghanistan: The Purpose and Impact of the Transition," hearing before the Committee on Foreign Relations, United States Senate, 21 September 2006.

92. Author's interview (11 September 2006) with Rian Harris, the Economic Officer (Commercial Section) in the U.S. Embassy, Kabul, Afghanistan, between September 2005 and August 2006.

93. "Gates Says NATO Force Unable to Fight Guerrillas," *Los Angeles Times*, 16 January 2008.

94. James March and Johan Olsen, "The Institutional Dynamics of International Political Orders," *International Organization* 52, no.4 (1998): 949-953.

95. Finnemore, *The Purpose of Intervention*.

96. Ibid., 952.

97. The 9/11 death toll actually exceeded that of Pearl Harbor. For more on the way the 9/11 attacks changed the country, see "A Nation Transformed," within the *9/11 Commission Report*, available at http://www.9-11commission.gov/report/911Report_Exec.htm.

98. On the preeminence of economic security issues, see Brad Roberts, *New Forces in the World Economy* (Cambridge, MA: MIT Press, 1996); on humanitarian and peacekeeping missions as a development of the post–Cold War, see Michael Doyle and Nicholas Sambanis, *Making War and Building Peace: UN Peace Operations* (Princeton, NJ: Princeton University Press, 2003).

99. For a ranking of military and police contributions to UN operations, see http://www.un.org/Depts/dpko/dpko/contributors/2007/dec07_2.pdf.

100. Former Director of Strategic Planning for the UN Abiodun Williams says that often these states come without sufficient equipment and do not send their best troops. Author's interview, 17 January 2008.

101. Colum Lynch, "UN Votes 2,100 More Troops for Congo Force," *Washington Post*, 29 July 2003; for more analysis on the increase in UN peacekeeping after the Cold War, see John Ruggie, "The UN and the Collective Use of Force: Whither or Whether?" *International Peacekeeping* 3, no. 4 (1996): 1-20.

102. Eric Schmitt, "Many Eager to Help, but Few Are Chosen," *New York Times*, 30 November 2001.

103. Secretary of Defense Donald Rumsfeld news transcript, 16 November 2001, available at http://www.defense.gov/transcripts/transcript.aspx?transcriptid=2453.

104. See Rumsfeld interview with *Chicago Sun Times* editorial board, ibid.

105. Secretary Rumsfeld and General Franks news briefing, 27 November 2001, available at http://www.defenselink.mil/transcripts/transcript.aspx?transcriptid=2465.

106. Finnemore, *Intervention*, 134.

107. Mark Memmott, "Poll: Americans Believe Attacks 'Acts of War,'" *USA Today*, 12 September 2001.

108. "American Psyche Reeling from Terror Attacks," Pew Research Center, available at http://people-press.org/reports/display.php3?PageID=30.

109. Jim Drinkard, "America Ready to Sacrifice," *USA Today*, 17 September 2001.

110. Memmott, "Poll"; see also Drinkard, "America Ready to Sacrifice."

111. It should be noted that there was little polling on Afghanistan after 2003, presumably because the polling resources went toward the Iraq War. For additional polls, see http://www.afghanconflictmonitor.org/polls/.

112. David Rohde and David E. Sanger, "How a 'Good War' in Afghanistan Went Bad," *New York Times*, 12 August 2007.

113. See S.J. Res. 23, Joint resolution to authorize the United States Armed Forces against those responsible for the recent attacks launched against the United States, 14 September 2001, available at http://thomas.loc.gov/cgi-bin/query/z?c107:S.J.RES.23. ENR:.

114. *Afghanistan: Key Issues for Congressional Oversight* (Washington, DC: General Accountability Office, 2009; GAO-09-473SP).

115. "The Costs of Soviet Involvement in Afghanistan," February 1987, Director of Intelligence, CIA, available at http://www.gwu.edu/~nsarchiv/NSAEBB/NSAEBB57/us.html.

116. See, for example, "Russia Won't Join Any US Retaliation," *St. Petersburg (Russia) Times*, 15 September 2001; see also Susan Glasser, "Russia Rejects Joint Military Action with United States," *Washington Post*, 15 September 2001.

117. Woodward, *Bush at War*, 116, 118.

118. Carla Anne Robbins and Jeanne Cummings, "Powell's Caution against Quick Strike Shapes Bush Plan; Conservative Aides Bristle as Secretary of State Puts Faith in a Coalition," *Wall Street Journal*, 21 September 2001.

119. Howard Fineman, "Bush's 'Phase One,'" *Newsweek*, 15 October 2001.

120. Mark Helprin, "What to Do in Afghanistan, and Why," *Wall Street Journal*, 3 October 2001.

121. Robin Wright, "Kyrgyzstan Agrees to Continuing U.S. Military Presence at Key Air Base," *Washington Post*, 12 October 2005; Edmund L. Andrews, "A Bustling U.S. Air Base Materializes in the Mud," *New York Times*, 27 April 2001; Thomas E. Ricks and Susan B. Glasser, "U.S. Operated Secret Alliance with Uzbekistan," *Washington Post*, 14 October 2001.

122. Woodward, *Bush at War*, 164.

123. Alexander Cooley writes that the United States paid $21 million in weapons transfers and military assistance. See "Base Politics," *Foreign Affairs* 84, no. 6 (2005): 79-92; Michael Gordon, "U.S. May Gain Use of More Air Bases to Strike Taliban," *New York Times*, 5 November 2001.

124. Edwin Chen and Maura Reynolds, "Russia to Aid Anti-Terror Effort," *Los Angeles Times*, 25 September 2001; see also Woodward, *Bush at War*, 118; Lambeth, *Airpower against Terror*, 30; Robin Wright, "Response to Terror; Coalition of Exceptional Depth Is Forming," *Los Angeles Times*, 30 September 2001.

125. The National Security Archive has stocked numerous cables attesting to Pakistan's support for the Taliban during the 1990s. See, for example, declassified Department of State Report, "Pakistan-Afghanistan Relations," January 1996; U.S. Embassy (Islamabad) Cable, "Bad News on Pak Afghan Policy: Government of Pakistan Support for the Taliban Appears to Be Getting Stronger," 1 July 1998 confidential report. All relevant documents may be found at the National Security Archive's "The Taliban File Part III."

126. Peter Fritsch, "Pakistan Gives Crucial Boost to Coalition," *Wall Street Journal*, 5 October 2001.

127. Greg Jaffe and Steve LeVine, "U.S. Strikes Pound Taliban Forces as Powell Tries to Woo Moderates," *Wall Street Journal*, 17 October 2001; John F. Burns, "Pakistan Conducts Several Nuclear Tests; U.S. Orders Sanctions to Chastise Pakistan," *New York Times*, 2 May 1998.

128. Lambeth, *Airpower against Terror*, 67.

129. See "Iranian Support to the Afghan Resistance," *Afghanistan: Lessons from the Last War* (Washington, DC: National Security Archive, 2001).

130. Scott Neuman, Peter Fritsch, Hugh Pope, Greg Jaffe, and Chip Cummins, "U.S. Gains More Support against Afghanistan," *Wall Street Journal*, 26 September 2001.

131. For more on hard-versus-easy test cases for theories, see Alexander George and Andrew Bennett, *Case Studies and Theory Development in the Social Sciences* (Cambridge, MA: MIT Press, 2005), 121-122.

132. Anne Penketh, "Annan: UN Must Have Role in Fight against Terrorism," *Independent*, 25 September 2001.

CHAPTER 7

1. "The Last Judgment," *Economist*, 27 June 2009.

2. Hans Blix, *Disarming Iraq* (New York: Pantheon, 2004), 11.

3. Dennis Ross, *Statecraft, and How to Restore America's Standing in the World* (New York: Farrar, Straus and Giroux, 2007), 125.

4. Thomas E. Ricks, *Fiasco: The American Military Adventure in Iraq* (New York: Penguin, 2006), 59.

5. Author's interview with Under Secretary of State for Political Affairs Marc Grossman, Washington, DC, 17 January 2007.

6. *Tradecraft* is defined as "the way analysts think, research, evaluate evidence, write, and communicate." This phrase and definition are used in the "Report of the Commission on the Intelligence Capabilities of the United States Regarding Weapons of Mass Destruction," 12, 50; available at http://www.gpoaccess.gov/wmd/index.html.

7. For an account of the first and second Gulf Wars, see Dilip Hiro, *The Longest War: The Iran-Iraq Military Conflict* (New York: Routledge, 1991) and *Desert Shield to Desert Storm: The Second Gulf War* (New York: Routledge, 1992).

8. Ricks, *Fiasco*, 5.

9. For an overview of the international response to Iraq between the 1991 Gulf War and the Iraq War in 2003, see David M. Malone, *The International Struggle over Iraq* (New York: Oxford University Press, 2006). According to Malone, these postwar strategies, particularly the no-fly zones, were evidence of "creeping unilateralism" that would culminate in the 2003 war. See 84–113.

10. Kenneth Pollack, *The Threatening Storm* (Washington, DC: Council on Foreign Relations, 2002), xxiv.

11. Iraq Liberation Act of 1998, available at http://thomas.loc.gov/cgi-bin/query/z?c105:H.R.4655.ENR:.

12. President Clinton's Address on Operation Desert Fox, 16 December 1998, available at http://www.cnn.com/US/9812/16/clinton.iraq.speech/.

13. Secretary of State Madeline Albright interview, *News Hour with Jim Lehrer*, 17 December 1998.

14. Several scholars and former policy makers issued an open letter to President Clinton in which they expressed their support for a more assertive Iraq policy, to include a "complement of diplomatic, political and military efforts." See 26 January 1998 letter to President Clinton available at http://www.newamericancentury.org/iraqclintonletter.htm.

15. UN Security Council 687 Resolution 8 April 1991.

16. Kenneth Katzman, *Iraq: Weapons Threat, Compliance, Sanctions, and U.S. Policy* (Washington, DC: Congressional Research Service, 2003).

17. Security Council Resolution 1284 of 17 December 1999 created UNMOVIC as an entity that would ensure Iraq's compliance with the post–Desert Storm Resolution 687 that mandated disarmament. Hans Blix served as the executive chairman of UNMOVIC from March 2000 to June 2003 and was responsible for the final inspections that preceded the Iraq War. For more background, see the official UNMOVIC site at www.unmovic.org.

18. Malone, *The International Struggle over Iraq*, 114–184; "Very Well Done, Alone—Dealing with Iraq," *Economist*, 15 March 2003; John M. Goshko, "Security Council Debate Reflects Continued Split on Iraq," *Washington Post*, 19 December 1997.

19. "George Bush Takes His Case against Iraq to the United Nations," *Economist*, 12 September 2002; Charles A. Duelfer, "Hide and Seek," *New York Times*, 23 June 2009. Kenneth Pollack writes that "our allies proved perfidious, feckless, or outright duplicitous" during this period. While he is not explicit with his references, we might infer from this statement that he is alluding to behavior such as that of France. See Pollack, *The Threatening Storm*, xxiv.

20. Hans Blix, the director of UNMOVIC, addressed the Washington Institute for Near East Policy's Special Policy Forum on 17 January 2002. The summary of his remarks may be found on the institute's Web site at http://www.washingtoninstitute.org/templateC05.php?CID=1472.

21. Blix, *Disarming Iraq*, 11.

22. Authorization for Use of Military Force against Iraq Resolution of 2002, available at www.c-span.org/Content/PDF/hjres114.pdf.

23. Resolution 1441, UN Security Council, 8 November 2002.

24. Katzman, *Iraq: Weapons Threat*.

25. Blix, *Disarming Iraq*, 11.

26. Secretary of Defense Donald H. Rumsfeld, U.S. Department of Defense briefing, 12 February 2002, available at http://www.defenselink.mil/transcripts/transcript.aspx?transcriptid=2636.

27. Duelfer, "Hide and Seek."

28. For a comparison of the contributions of the Gulf War and those for the 2003 Iraq War, see Alexander Thompson, *Channeling Power* (Ithaca, NY: Cornell University Press, 2009).

29. See "Compartmented Plan Update," 15 August 2002, from the declassified Top Secret/Polo Step slides; available at http://www.gwu.edu/~nsarchiv/NSAEBB/NSAEBB214/index.htm.

30. This overreaction is consistent with the expectations laid out in Charles Kupchan, *Vulnerability of Empire* (Ithaca, NY: Cornell University Press, 1994).

31. Ian Lustick, *Trapped in the War on Terror* (Philadelphia: University of Pennsylvania Press, 2006), 5.

32. James Mann, *Rise of the Vulcans: The History of Bush's War Cabinet* (New York: Viking, 2004), x. George Packer articulates a similar account in *The Assassin's Gate: America in Iraq* (New York: Farrar, Straus and Giroux, 2005); Ron Suskind also makes this point in *The One Percent Doctrine*, 34, 64.

33. Project for the New American Century letter to President Clinton, 26 January 1998, available at http://www.newamericancentury.org/iraqclintonletter.htm.

34. Chalmers Johnson, *The Sorrows of Empire: Militarism, Secrecy, and the End of the Republic* (New York: Macmillan, 2004), 61.

35. John J. Mearsheimer and Stephen Walt, "An Unnecessary War," *Foreign Policy*, January–February 2003.

36. Variations of this argument include Jon Western, "The War over Iraq: Selling War to the American Public," *Security Studies* 14, no. 1 (2005): 106–139; Chaim Kaufmann, "Threat Inflation and the Failure of the Marketplace of Ideas: The Selling of the Iraq War," *International Security* 29, no. 1 (2004): 5–48; Joseph Cirincione, Jessica T. Mathews, and George Perkovich, *WMD in Iraq: Evidence and Implications* (Washington, DC: Carnegie, 2004); Michael Isikoff, *Hubris: The Inside Story of Spin, Scandal, and the Selling of the Iraq War* (New York: Three Rivers Press, 2007); Sheldon Rampton and John Clyde Stauber, *Weapons of Mass Deception: The Uses of Propaganda in Bush's War on Iraq* (New York: Penguin, 2003).

37. Ross, *Statecraft*, 104.

38. For more information on this episode, see Shirley Kan, Richard Best, Christopher Bolkcom, Robert Chapman, Richard Cronin, Kerry Dumbaugh, Stuard Goldman, Mark Manyin, Wayne Morrison, Ronald O'Rourke, and David Ackerman, *China-U.S. Aircraft Collision Incident of April 2001: Assessments and Policy Implications* (Washington, DC: Congressional Research Services, 10 October 2001).

39. Ricks, *Fiasco*, 12; see also 13–15, 26–28; and Lawrence Freedman, "War in Iraq: Selling the Threat," *Survival* 46, no. 2 (2004): 7–50.s

40. Memo on Iraq from Donald Rumsfeld to the Honorable Condoleezza Rice, 27 July 2001, accessed as Appendix 3 of Douglas Feith, *War and Decision: Inside the Pentagon at the Dawn of the War on Terrorism* (New York: Harper, 2008), 535–537.

41. Blix, *Disarming Iraq*, 56.

42. "Struggling on Iraq," *Washington Post*, 27 May 2001; Aram Roston, *The Man Who Pushed America to War: The Extraordinary Life, Adventures, and Obsessions of*

Ahmad Chalabi (New York: PublicAffairs, 2009), 174–175; Ben Macintyre, "Bush Warning over Weapons of Mass Destruction," *London Times*, 17 February 2001.

43. October 2002 National Intelligence Estimate, "Iraq's Continuing Programs for Weapons of Mass Destruction."

44. "Transcript: David Kay at Senate Hearing," 28 January 2004, available at http://www.cnn.com/2004/US/01/28/kay.transcript/.

45. James Graff and Bruce Crumley, "France Is Not a Pacifist Country," *Time*, 16 February 2003.

46. Blix, *Disarming Iraq*, 130.

47. Hans Blix, "The Security Council, 27 January 2003 Update on Inspections," available at http://www.un.org/Depts/unmovic/Bx27.htm; see also Fareed Zakaria's take in "'Disarming Iraq': Lack of Evidence," *New York Times*, 11 April 2004.

48. Richard Butler, "Catastrophe as the Generator of Historical Change: The Iraq Case," in *The Iraq War Reader*, ed. Micah L. Sifry and Christopher Cerf (New York: Simon and Schuster, 2003), 618.

49. Khidhir Hamza and Jeff Stein, *Saddam's Bombmaker: The Daring Escape of the Man Who Built Iraq's Secret Weapon* (New York: Scribner, 2001), 337.

50. President Clinton's Address on Operation Desert Fox, 16 December 1998.

51. Senator Edward Kennedy, Johns Hopkins School of Advanced International Studies, 27 September 2002.

52. Senator John F. Kerry, 9 October 2002, Senate vote to authorize the use of United States Armed Forces against Iraq.

53. Senator Jay Rockefeller, *Congressional Record*, 10 October 2002, S10306.

54. Representative Nancy Pelosi, *Meet the Press*, 17 November 2002.

55. Senator Carl Levin, CNN *Late Edition*, 16 December 2001.

56. Dana Priest, "Congressional Oversight of Intelligence Criticized," *Washington Post*, 27 April 2004.

57. Lisa Mages, "U.S. Armed Forces Abroad: Selected Congressional Roll Call Votes since 1982," available at www.fas.org/sgp/crs/natsec/RL31693.pdf.

58. "His Side of the Story," *Time*, 28 June 2004, available at http://www.time.com/time/magazine/article/0,9171,994507-1,00.html.

59. George Tenet, *At the Center of the Storm* (New York: HarperCollins, 2007), 331–332.

60. Ibid, 336. Colin Powell has agreed that "over a long period of time, the CIA and all of the other intelligence agencies of government had created a, a statement for all of U.S. that said, one, this is a regime that has used these kinds of weapons on the past; two, they have retained the capability of making such weapons; and three—and here's where we fell down—they have stockpiles of these weapons." *Meet the Press* interview from 10 June 2007, available at http://www.msnbc.msn.com/id/19092206/page/2/.

61. Fouad Ajami, *The Foreigner's Gift: The Americans, the Arabs, and the Iraqis in Iraq* (New York: Free Press, 2006), 54.

62. Blix, *Disarming Iraq*, 67, 107, 123, 137.

63. Ajami, *The Foreigner's Gift*, 54.

64. For the key post-Iraq intelligence reports, see *Review of Intelligence on Weapons of Mass Destruction* (the Butler Report), available at http://www.archive2.official-documents.co.uk/document/deps/hc/hc898/898.pdf; Report of the Inquiry into

Australian Intelligence Agencies (Flood Report), available at http://www.dpmc.gov.
au/publications/intelligence_inquiry/index.htm; Report of the Commission on the
Intelligence Capabilities of the United States Regarding Weapons of Mass Destruction,
31 March 2005, available at http://govinfo.library.unt.edu/wmd/about.html. For an
excellent analysis of these intelligence failures, see Robert Jervis, "Reports, Politics,
and Intelligence Failures: The Case of Iraq," *Journal of Strategic Studies* 29, no. 1
(2006): 3–52.

65. See Kupchan, *Vulnerability of Empire*.

66. Ajami, *The Foreigner's Gift*, 52.

67. Jeremi Suri, "American Grand Strategy from the Cold War's End to 9/11," *Orbis*
53, no. 4 (2009): 611–628.

68. For an excellent treatment of al Qaeda's attacks in the 1990s and the U.S.
government responses, see chapter 4 of the *The 9/11 Commission Report: Final Report
of the National Commission on Terrorist Attacks upon the United States* (New York: W. W.
Norton, 2004), 108–143; Steve Coll, *Ghost Wars: The Secret History of the CIA,
Afghanistan, and bin Laden, from the Soviet Invasion to 10 September 2001* (New York:
Penguin, 2004); Richard Clarke, *Against All Enemies: Inside America's War on Terror*
(New York: Free Press, 2004).

69. Douglas Feith, *War and Decision*, 224.

70. Jeffrey Record, "Why the Bush Administration Invaded Iraq: Making Strategy
after 9/11," *Strategic Studies Quarterly* (Summer 2008): 67.

71. Daniel Benjamin and Steven Simon, *The Age of Sacred Terror: Radical Islam's
War against America* (New York: Random House, 2003), 400–401.

72. Jack Goldsmith, *The Terror Presidency: Law and Judgment inside the Bush
Administration* (New York: W. W. Norton, 2007). 72.

73. Robert Draper, *Dead Certain: The Presidency of George W. Bush* (New York: Free
Press, 2007), 167.

74. Suskind, *The One Percent Doctrine*, 7–8.

75. Vice President Cheney interview, *Meet the Press*, 14 September 2003; http://
www.msnbc.msn.com/id/3080244/. Fouad Ajami also submits that "September 11, it
would seem, altered Cheney's thinking" about whether to try to remake the Middle
East. Though opposed before 9/11, he was nearly fixated thereafter. Ajami, *The
Foreigner's Gift*, 53.

76. Robert O. Keohane, "The Globalization of Informal Violence, Theories of
World Politics, and the 'Liberalism of Fear,'" in *Power and Governance in a Partially
Globalized World* (London: Routledge, 2002), 275.

77. John Lewis Gaddis, *Surprise, Security, and the American Experience* (Cambridge,
MA: Harvard University Press, 2004), 13.

78. Lustick, *Trapped in the War on Terror*, 2.

79. Quoted in "Analysis: Experts Disagree on Whether Containment Would Work
in Iraq," National Public Radio, 12 February 2003, available at http://www.npr.org/
programs/morning/transcripts/2003/feb/030212.shuster.html.

80. Bob Woodward, *Plan of Attack* (New York: Simon and Schuster, 2004), 27.

81. *Meet the Press* interview with Colin Powell, 10 June 2007.

82. President Bush's 2002 commencement speech at West Point lays out the foundations of the nascent Bush Doctrine, which includes the idea of preventive or preemptive attack on emerging threats. See speech at http://georgewbush-whitehouse.

archives.gov/news/releases/2002/06/20020601-3.html. Freedman makes a similar point that "the attacks changed the terms of the security debate by establishing the notion that potential threats had to be dealt with before they became actual." See Freedman, "Selling the Threat," 38.

83. For more on this mind-set, see *The 9/11 Commission Report*, 334–336.

84. State of the Union address, 29 January 2002, available at http://www.pbs.org/newshour/bb/white_house/sotu2002/sotu_text.html.

85. President Bush's introduction to the 2002 National Security Strategy, 17 September 2002, available at http://www.globalsecurity.org/military/library/policy/national/nss-020920.htm.

86. President Bush speech, "President Says Saddam Hussein Must Leave Iraq within 48 Hours," 17 March 2003, http://georgewbush-whitehouse.archives.gov/news/releases/2003/03/20030317-7.html.

87. Cheney, *Meet the Press*, 14 September 2003. Draper (*Dead Certain*, 175) refers to the post-9/11 logic this way: "If you wait for intelligence to drive policy, you will have waited too long."

88. "Iraq's Continuing Programs for Weapons of Mass Destruction," National Intelligence Estimate of 2002 October 5.

89. Ibid.

90. George Tenet's letter to Senator Bob Graham on 7 October 2002 is available at http://www.fas.org/irp/news/2002/10/dci100702.html; Senator Bob Graham of Florida had requested that information from the NIE either be further clarified or declassified. Tenet's letter responded to these queries and is available at http://www.fas.org/irp/news/2002/10/dci100702.html. See also Michael R. Gordon, "U.S. Aides Split on Assessment of Iraq's Plans," *New York Times*, 10 October 2002.

91. Representative Jane Harman's 16 January 2004 speech to the Los Angeles World Affairs Council, "Harmon Calls on President to Restore Faith in Intelligence Community in State of the Union Address," available at http://www.lawac.org/speech/pre%20sept%2004%20speeches/harman%202004.htm.

92. In *Fiasco*, 52, Ricks concludes that "the effect of this NIE can't be underestimated." Paul Pillar, who contributed to those two estimates, indicates that these estimates "spoke directly to the instability, conflict, and black hole for blood and treasure that over the past four years we have come to know as Iraq" in *The National Interest*, 6 June 2007.

93. "The Last Judgment," *Economist*, 27 June 2009.

94. National Security 2002 Strategy 6.

95. Quoted in Howard LaFranchi, "U.S. Seeks Global Aid for Iraq," *Christian Science Monitor*, 21 January 2004. See also Robert Lieber, *The American Era* (Cambridge: Cambridge University Press, 2005), 47–48.

96. President Bush, 12 September 2002 speech to the United Nations.

97. Remarks by the president on the UN Security Council 1441 Resolution 8 November 2002.

98. Brian Knowlton, "Signals Seem to Show Delay in War with Iraq," *International Herald Tribune*, 14 January 2003.

99. Julian Borger and Ewen MacAskill, "A Case for War? Yes, Say US and Britain. No, Say the Majority," *Guardian*, 15 February 2003.

100. James Fallows, *Blind into Baghdad: America's War in Iraq* (New York: Vintage, 2006), 1.

101. Author's interview with former Deputy National Security Advisor for Iraq and Afghanistan Meghan O'Sullivan, Cambridge, MA, 2 June 2008.

102. Record, "Why the Bush Administration Invaded Iraq," 72.

103. Richard Haass, Director of Policy Planning in the Bush Administration, interview with National Public Radio, 13 May 2009.

104. Michael Gordon and Bernard E. Trainor, *Cobra II: The Inside Story of the Invasion and Occupation of Iraq* (New York: Pantheon, 2006), 498.

105. Ibid.

106. Stephen Biddle, *Military Power: Explaining Victory and Defeat in Modern Battle* (Princeton, NJ: Princeton University Press, 2004), 134.

107. Anthony Cordesman, "Iraq War Note: Iraq's Missing Air Force and Army Aviation," *Center for Strategic and International Studies*, 31 March 2003; Sharon Otterman, "Iraq: Iraq's Prewar Military Capabilities," *Council on Foreign Relations*, 24 (April 2003).

108. Michael Eisenstadt, "Iraq's Military Capabilities: An Assessment," Washington Institute for Near East Policy, Policy Watch #130, 14 October 1994.

109. Bryan Bender, "Fallen Chalabi Has Few Fans Left," *Boston Globe*, 21 May 2004. As late as 2005, some Pentagon officials maintained that while the United States had not ultimately been greeted with flowers, "they [the Iraqis] had flowers in their minds" but were too intimidated to admit those thoughts because of years of Baathist oppression. See Jeffrey Goldberg, "A Little Learning," *New Yorker*, 9 May 2005, available at http://www.newyorker.com/fact/content/articles/050509fa_fact.

110. Fred Kaplan, "Does the UN U-Turn Signal a Comeback for Colin Powell," *Slate*, 4 September 2003.

111. For more on this source, see Bob Drogin, *Curveball* (New York: Random House, 2007), 231, 268, 282.

112. Author's interview with General David Petraeus, 23 April 2010, Ithaca, NY.

113. Woodward, *Plan of Attack*, 41.

114. Fallows, *Blind into Baghdad*, 74–75.

115. Gordon and Trainor, *Cobra II*, 61.

116. Kenneth Adelman, "Cakewalk in Iraq," *Washington Post*, 13 February 2002; for a critique of the "cakewalk theory," see Hendrik Hertzberg, "Cakewalk," *New Yorker*, 14 April 2003.

117. Woodward, *Plan of Attack*, 325–326.

118. Vice President Richard Cheney interview on *Meet the Press*, 16 March 2003.

119. Conrad C. Crane and W. Andrew Terrill, *Reconstructing Iraq: Insights, Challenges, and Missions for Military Forces in a Post-Conflict Scenario* (Carlisle, PA: Strategic Studies Institute, 2003).

120. Gordon and Trainor, *Cobra II*, 50, 67, 79.

121. Ibid., 29.

122. "Rumsfeld Foresees Swift Iraq War," *BBC News*, 7 February 2003.

123. Author's correspondence with Colonel Isaiah Wilson, military planner for Iraq War at CENTCOM and later a social science professor at the United States Military Academy, 20 February 2007.

124. See "Top Secret Polo Step," Tab K, Slide 10; these slides show earlier iterations of planning that called for a larger invasion force. Later iterations reduced the
number to the approximately 145,000 troops that eventually invaded in March
2003.

125. "Iraq Invasion Plan 'Delusional,'" *BBC News*, 15 February 2007.

126. Michael Gordon, "A Prewar Slide Show Cast Iraq in Rosy Hues," *New York
Times*, 15 February 2007.

127. Elisabeth Bumiller, "White House Cuts Estimate of Cost of War with Iraq,"
New York Times, 31 December 2002.

128. Eric Schmitt, "Pentagon Contradicts General on Iraq Occupation Force's
Size," *New York Times*, 28 February 2003.

129. Dana Milbank and Robin Wright, "Off the Mark on Cost of War, Reception by
Iraqis," *Washington Post*, 19 March 2004.

130. This is the phrase Paul Wolfowitz had used to describe higher estimates of
the number of troops needed to police postwar Iraq, but it is the lower estimates that
proved to be wildly off the mark. See Eric Schmitt, "Pentagon Contradicts General on
Iraq Occupation Force's Size," *New York Times*, 28 February 2003.

131. See the testimony of Cofer Black, former chief, CIA Counterterrorism Center,
to the Joint Investigation into September 11th: Fifth Public Hearing, 26 September
2002—Joint House/Senate Intelligence Committee Hearing.

132. Jane Mayer, "Outsourcing Torture: The Secret History of America's
'Extraordinary Rendition' Program," *New Yorker*, 14 February 2005.

133. John Yoo discusses how the imperative of self-defense colored all post-9/11
legal briefs in *War by Other Means: An Insider's Account of the War on Terror* (New York:
Atlantic Monthly Press, 2006), 10–12.

134. U.S. Department of Defense e-mail circulated after 9/11; author's experience
while on active duty in the U.S. Air Force.

135. Jane Mayer, "Outsourcing Torture," *New Yorker*, 14 February 2005.

136. In addition to the two memos of 2002, see Barton Gellman and Jo Becker,
"Pushing the Envelope on Presidential Power," *Washington Post*, 25 June 2007.

137. Richard Clarke, *Against All Enemies* (New York: Free Press, 2004). Separately,
Bush was quoted as arguing with lawyers who advised him against calling Saddam a
terrorist, saying, "Lawyers, they're dreadful." See Woodward, *Plan of Attack*, 407.

138. *Inquiry into the Treatment of Detainees in U.S. Custody, Report of the Committee
on Armed Services*, United States Senate, 20 November 2008, xii.

139. See "Application of Treaties and Laws to al Qaeda and Taliban Detainees,"
available at the National Security Archive at www.gwu.edu/~nsarchiv/NSAEBB/
NSAEBB127/02.01.25.pdf. President Bush signed it on 7 February 2002.

140. Memo from President Bush to his national security advisors concerning the
application of Geneva Conventions to prisoners; 7 February 2002, subject "Humane
Treatment of al Qaeda and Taliban Detainees."

141. For example, see *Lakhdar Boumediene v. George W. Bush*, 12 June 2008. This
case, which concluded that the detainees had the right of due process, ran counter to
the assertions of the Justice Department in 2002.

142. Memo from Department of Justice's Office of Legal Counsel to White House
Counsel regarding Standards of Conduct for Interrogation, 1 August 2002.

143. Ibid.

144. For a summary of these opinions, see Joseph Margulies (lead counsel, *Rasul v. Bush*), *Guantanamo and the Abuse of Presidential Power* (New York: Simon and Schuster, 2007), 90–95.

145. Department of Defense memorandum, 11 October 2002: Memo for Commander, Joint Task Force 170, "Counter Resistance Strategies," available at http://www.gwu.edu/~nsarchiv/NSAEBB/NSAEBB127/02.10.11.pdf.

146. Jane Mayer, *The Dark Side: The Inside Story of How the War on Terror Turned into a War on American Ideals* (New York: Doubleday, 2008).

147. "Authorization for Use of Military Force," S.J.23 Res 14 September 2001.

148. This caution was part of a "Parade of Horribles" memo of 15 October 2002. See Feith, *War and Decision*, 334.

149. White House's official Coalition of the Willing list, available at http://georgewbush-whitehouse.archives.gov/news/releases/2003/03/20030327-10.html.

150. For more on multilateralism as a screening and legitimation function, see Thompson, "Coercion through IOs."

151. Author's interview with Meghan O'Sullivan, Cambridge, MA, 2 June 2008.

152. Gordon and Trainor, *Cobra II*, 10. See also "Who to Call in Washington," editorial in *Financial Times*, 16 March 2001.

153. Gallup Poll, 30 January 1991–15 March 2003.

154. See "Conflict with Iraq—General Attitudes toward Iraq," Program on International Policy Attitudes, available at http://www.americans-world.org/digest/regional_issues/Conflict_Iraq/genAtt.cfm.

155. "The View before 9/11: America's Place in the World," Pew Research Center for the People and the Press, 18 October 2001.

156. Gallup Poll, 19 February 2002.

157. *Chicago Tribune*–WGN poll of Americans, 13 December 2002.

158. CNN/*USA Today*/Gallup Poll, 5 February 2003.

159. *Washington Post* poll, "Saddam Hussein and the Sept 11 Attacks," *Washington Post*, 6 September 2003.

160. Pollack, *The Threatening* Storm, 107–108.

161. Gallup Poll, 21–22 September 2001; George Horace Gallup, *The Gallup Poll: Public Opinion 2003* (Lanham, MD: Rowman and Littlefield, 2004), 31–32.

162. Chaim Kauffmann, "Threat Inflation and the Failure of the Marketplace of Ideas," *International Security* 29, no. 1 (2004): 31; Jon Western, "The War over Iraq: Selling War to the American Public," *Security Studies* 14, no. 1 (2005): 109.

163. Bob Kerrey, "Finish the War. Liberate Iraq," *Wall Street Journal*, 12 September 2002.

164. Dana Milbank and Claudia Deane, "Hussein Link to 9/11 Lingers in Many Minds," *Washington Post*, 6 September 2003.

165. Pew Research, 25 March 2003. "Public Confidence in War Effort Falters, but Support for War Holds Steady." For prewar study on Americans' support for war, see "Public Wants Proof of Iraqi Weapons Programs: Majority Says Bush Has Yet to Make the Case," 16 January 2003.

166. This February 2003 poll number of 38 percent rose from 26 percent in January, suggesting an increasing degree of support for unilateral action. "U.S. Needs More International Backing; Post-Blix: Public Favors Force in Iraq," 20 February 2003.

167. Chicago Council on Foreign Relations, "Worldviews 2002: American Public Opinion & Foreign Policy," October 2002.

168. CBS/*New York Times* News poll: "The U.S. needs to act now, even without the support of allies, or the U.S. needs to wait for its allies before taking any action against Iraq."

169. Program on Policy Attitudes, "Americans on Iraq and the UN Inspections II," 21 2003 February 9.

170. "Americans Concerned about Rift with Europe: Want Allied Backing for Iraq War," Council on Foreign Relations, 20 February 2003.

171. PIPA/Knowledge Networks Poll, "Americans on Iraq and the UN Inspections II," 15.

172. "Public Confidence in War Effort Falters but Support for War Holds Steady," 18 March 2003.

173. "U.S. Needs More International Backing," Pew Research Center for the People and the Press, 20 February 2003.

174. PIPA/Knowledge Networks Poll, "Americans on Iraq and the UN Inspections II," 15.

175. For time series data on the degree to which Americans supported the Iraq war with/without the UN and with/without allies, see Philip Everts and Pierangelo Isernia, "The War in Iraq," *Public Opinion Quarterly* 69, no. 2 (2005): 299–301. Everts and Isernia also detail a host of other public opinion polling surrounding the Iraq war.

176. The U.S. roll call vote to authorize the Iraq war is available at http://www.senate.gov/legislative/LIS/roll_call_lists/roll_call_vote_cfm.cfm?congress=107&session=2&vote=00237.

177. Kaufmann, "Threat Inflation and the Failure of the Marketplace of Ideas," 31.

178. See Authorization to Use Military Force against Iraq, available at http://www.c-span.org/Content/PDF/hjres114.pdf.

179. For a discussion on how national security strength became the dominant narrative after 9/11, see Ronald R. Krebs and Jennifer K. Lobasz, "Fixing the Meaning of 9/11: Hegemony, Coercion, and the Road to 9/11," *Security Studies* 16, no. 3 (2007): 409–451.

180. David Usborne, "Bush Remains on Path to War Despite Protests," *Independent*, 19 February 2003.

181. President Bush, quoted in William G. Howell and Jon Pevehouse, *While Dangers Gather: Congressional Checks on Presidential War Powers* (Princeton, NJ: Princeton University Press, 2007), 219.

182. Draper, *Dead Certain*, 179.

183. Woodward, *Bush at War*, 346.

184. Feith, *War and Decision*, 340.

185. Bob Woodward, "Cheney Was Unwavering in Desire to Go to War," *Washington Post*, 20 April 2004.

186. Quentin Peel, Robert Graham, James Harding, and Judy Dempsey, "War in Iraq: How the Die Was Cast before Transatlantic Diplomacy Failed," *Financial Times*, 27 May 2003.

187. Woodward, *Plan of Attack*, 357.

188. Draper, *Dead Certain*, 177.

189. See Bob Woodward, *Plan of Attack*, 162, 183.

190. Ibid., 177–178.

191. David Cracknell and Nicholas Rufford, "You Need UN, Blair Tells Bush," *Sunday Times (London)*, 2 September 2002.

192. Mark Danner, "The Secret Way to War," *New York Review of Books* 52, no. 10 (2005): 71.

193. "Get UN Backing, Blair Tells Bush," *Herald Sun (Melbourne, Australia)*, 2 September 2002, 25; Malone, *The International Struggle over Iraq*, 191-192.

194. Andrei Shleifer and Daniel Treisman document how U.S. elite consensus coalesced around the impression that Russia was a collapsed state without the ability to influence global or regional affairs, in spite of its relative economic normalcy. See "A Normal Country," *Foreign Affairs* 83, no. 2 (2004): 20-38. On military spending trends from the 1990s, see *The Military Balance 2000-2001* (London: International Institute for Strategic Studies, 2000).

195. For planning documents that included Turkey's participation, see the National Security Archives, http://www.gwu.edu/~nsarchiv/NSAEBB/NSAEBB214/Tab%20A.pdf.

196. Harry de Quetteville, "U.S. Troops Pack Up and Go as Turkey Refuses Any Help," *Daily Telegraph*, 24 March 2003.

197. Daniel Williams, "Kurds Set for War, but Not with Iraq," *Washington Post*, 8 March 2003.

198. See Robert Burns, "U.S. Bseefs Up Air Base in Qatar," *Christian Science Monitor*, 2 July 2002.

199. Author's correspondence with Colonel John Agoglia, then CENTCOM planner, now counterinsurgency director, Afghanistan, 18 July 2009.

200. "Turkish Parliament Rejects Basing 62,000 U.S. Troops," *Associated Press*, 1 March 2003.

201. Gordon and Trainor, *Cobra II*, 116; Colonel Agoglia, 18 July 2009; Robert Ingrassia, "After Long Turkey Trot, 4th Infantry's in Kuwait," *Daily News*, 28 March 2003.

202. Woodward, *Plan of Attack*, 369.

203. Private permission to use these bases came in exchange for promises that the United States would then remove its forces after the war. John Bradley, "US Troops Pouring into Saudi Arabia," *Daily Telegraph*, 7 March 2003; "Saudis Will Offer U.S. Warplanes Support," *Birmingham Post*, 30 December 2002; John R. Bradley, "Royal Rules' Private Backing Prevails over Public Doubts," *Sydney Morning Herald*, 15 March 2003.

204. Even the U.S. "unilateral" plan required basing support from Kuwait, Qatar, and Oman according to Operation Polo Step slides.

205. Michael R. Gordon, "U.S. Is Preparing Base in Gulf State to Run Iraq War," *New York Times*, 1 December 2002; Thomas M. DeFrank, "Saudis OK U.S. Use of Air Bases," *New York Daily News*, 29 December 2002.

206. Peter W. Galbraith, *The End of Iraq: How American Incompetence Created a War without End* (New York: Simon and Schuster, 2006), 13-16.

207. William Choong, "Mixed Blessings," Singapore Straits Times, April 2003.

208. Ajami, *The Foreigner's Gift*, 107.

209. Warren P. Strobel, "US Makes Cautious Contact with Iran," *Philadelphia Inquirer*, 28 November 2002; "US Approaches 'Evil' Iran," *Daily Telegraph (Sydney)*, 27 November 2002.

210. "Rafsanjani Reiterates Iran's Neutrality in Event of US Strike on Iraq," BBC translation of IRNA News Agency, 14 October 2002; "Foreign Minister Says Iran Will Remain Neutral in Event of Iraq War," BBC, 7 February 2003.

211. "Turkish Leader Arrives in Saudi Arabia for Talks on Iraq Crisis," *New York Times*, 12 January 2003.

212. This self-defeating behavior is consistent with the expectations outlined by Kupchan, *Vulnerability of Empire*.

213. John Yoo offers what he suggests is legal justification for the intervention, citing Resolution 687, which ended the 1991 Iraq War and required Iraq to disarm, as well as Resolution 1441, which found Iraq in "material breach" of WMD violations and warranted the use of force to enforce Iraqi compliance with 1441. Ultimately, he argues that the UN Charter's provision for self-defense also justified U.S. use of force against Iraq. Yoo's whole exercise is designed to justify the Iraq War in politically legitimate terms, using legal channels to do so, but ultimately makes a weak case. See "International Law and the War in Iraq," *American Journal of International Law* 97 (July 2003): 563–576.

214. Bob Woodward captures this as Vice President Dick Cheney's view in *Bush at War*, 345–346.

215. Woodward, *State of Denial*, 177–178; Suzanne Goldenberg, "Blair Refused Three Offiers to Stay Out of Iraq," *Guardian*, 19 April 2004.

CHAPTER 8

1. David Ignatius, "New World Disorder," *Washington Post*, 4 May 2007.

2. Charles Krauthammer, "The New Unilateralism," *Washington Post*, 11 June 2001.

3. Moises Naim, "Minilateralism: The Magic Number to Get Real International Action," *Foreign Policy*, no. 173 (22 June 2009): 135–136.

4. Inis Claude, "Collective Legitimization as a Political Function of the United Nations," *International Organization* 20, no. 3 (1966): 367–379; Ian Hurd, *After Anarchy: Legitimacy and Power in the United Nations Security Council* (Princeton, NJ: Princeton University Press, 2007); Alexander Thompson, "Coercion through IOs: The Security Council and the Logic of Information Transmission," *International Organization* 60 (2006): 1–34; Erik Voeten, "The Political Origins of the UN Security Council's Ability to Legitimize the Use of Force," *International Organization* 59 (2005): 527–557.

5. Henry Kissinger, *A World Restored: Metternich, Castlereagh and the Problems of Peace, 1812-22* (Boston: Houghton Mifflin, 1957), 17, 21, 321.

6. Daniel Benjamin and Steven Simon, *The Age of Sacred Terror: Radical Islam's War against America* (New York: Random House, 2003), 400–401.

7. Martha Finnemore, *The Purpose of Intervention: Changing Beliefs about the Use of Force* (Ithaca, NY: Cornell University Press, 2003), 80–82.

8. Daniel Zolo, *Cosmopolis: Prospects for World Government* (Cambridge, MA: Polity, 1997), 164.

9. Director of the Combined Planning Group at CENTCOM, Colonel Michael Greer, was helpful in identifying some of these "accommodation strategies" in a phone interview on 4 June 2007.

10. Author's interview with Colonel Dave Greco, CENTCOM, Tampa, FL, 20 April 2007.

11. Author's interview with Douglas Feith, Washington, DC, 18 December 2006.

12. Author's interview with Colonel Dave Greco, who directed the Coalition Coordination Center at CENTCOM, 20 April 2007; for more on the Coalition Coordination Center, see also http://www.defenselink.mil/news/newsarticle.aspx?id=32480.

13. Alexander Thompson also makes this argument in "Coercion through IOs," 17: "Security Council endorsement was a key variable in determining [allied] reactions to the policy" in the Gulf.

14. Author's interview with Lt. Col. Stephen Sklenka, marine fellow at the Center for Strategic and International Studies, Washington, DC, 30 November 2006.

15. In other words, many states in a coalition are there for symbolic purposes rather than the material contributions they bring. Author's correspondence with Colonel Michael D. Greer, Baghdad, 20 April 2007.

16. Martha Finnemore would refer to this as "hypocrisy," of which "judicious use" can be useful but "unrestrained hypocrisy" a challenge to the leader's authority. The line between those is unclear from the analysis, but it is safe to say that U.S. actions are often divorced and more self-interested than the value-laden rhetoric would suggest. See Finnemore, "Legitimacy, Hypocrisy, and the Social Structure of Unipolarity: Why Being a Unipole Isn't All It's Cracked Up to Be," *World Politics* 61, no. 1 (January 2009): 62–63.

17. James Fearon, "Domestic Politics, Foreign Policy, and Theories of International Relations," *Annual Review of Political Science* (1998): 291.

18. James Clark, "Poised to Strike as Never Before," *Sunday Times*, 23 September 2001.

19. See BBC coverage on the French deployment: "French Army Widens Ivory Coast Mission," 13 December 2002, and "UN Intervention Urged for Ivory Coast," 20 December 2002.

20. UN Mission in Cote d'Ivoire data sheet, available at http://www.un.org/Depts/dpko/missions/minuci/index.html.

21. Masako Toki, "Japan's Evolving Security Policies: Along Came North Korea's Threats," Nuclear Threat Initiative, 4 June 2009.

22. Horst Albach, *Culture and Technical Innovation: A Cross-Cultural Analysis and Policy Recommendations* (New York: Walter de Gruyter, 1993), 183. Other studies have shown that Confucian societies (minus Hong Kong) tend to have long time horizons, whereas Anglo cultures are more likely to have short time horizons. Robert House, Paul Hanges, Mansour Javidan, Peter Dorfman, and Vipin Gupta, *Culture, Leadership, and Organizations: The GLOBE Study of 62 Societies* (Newbury Park, CA: Sage, 2004), 289.

23. I thank Peter Katzenstein and Chris Anderson for drawing this point to my attention.

24. Strobe Talbott, "Unilateralism: Anatomy of a Foreign Policy Disaster," *International Herald Tribune*, 21 February 2007.

25. Sarah Kreps, "Shifting Currents: Changes in National Intelligence Estimates on the Iran Nuclear Threat," *Intelligence and National Security* 23, no. 5 (2008): 608–628, 623.

26. Robert Wohlstetter, *Pearl Harbor: Warning and Decision* (Palo Alto, CA: Stanford University Press, 1962), 1.

27. Robert Jervis, "Reports, Politics, and Intelligence Failures: The Case of Iraq," *Journal of Strategic Studies* 29, no. 1 (2006): 12.

28. Ibid.

29. Bruce Nardulli, Walter L. Perry, Bruce R. Pirnie, John Gordon IV, and John G. McGinn, *Disjointed War: Military Operations in Kosovo, 1999* (Arlington, VA: RAND, 2002).

30. Amy Belasco, The Cost of Iraq, Afghanistan, and Other Global War on Terror Operations since 9/11, CRS Report 33110, 14 July 2008.

31. Isaiah Wilson, *Thinking beyond War: Civil-Military Relations and Why America Fails to Win the Peace* (New York: Palgrave Macmillan, 2007).

32. Stephen Van Evera, *Causes of War* (Ithaca, NY: Cornell University Press, 2001), 14.

33. Geoffrey Blainey, *Causes of War* (New York: Free Press, 1988), 51.

34. Van Evera, *Causes of War*, 17.

35. Wilson, *Thinking beyond War*.

36. John Ikenberry, "Is American Multilateralism in Decline?" *Perspectives on Politics* 1, no. 3 (2003): 533–550; David Skidmore, "Understanding the Unilateralist Turn in U.S. Foreign Policy," *Foreign Policy Analysis* 1, no. 2 (2005): 207–228; David Malone, *The International Struggle over Iraq: Politics in the UN Security Council 1980–2005* (Oxford: Oxford University Press, 2006), 13–14.

37. As discussed earlier, this conclusion is similar to that of Ikenberry but arrives at it differently. Since coalitions are more shifting than the form of multilateralism he discusses, "lock in" effects and constraints are less operative, which actually means there are more reasons to engage in international cooperation than he might expect. The choice, though, depends more on the security context of the decision to intervene than on an institutional bargain that is made once at time *t* and expected to endure.

38. "Multilateralism for a Global Era," by Ambassador Richard N. Haass, Director, Policy Planning Staff, U.S. Department of State, Carnegie Endowment for International Peace Conference: "After September 11: American Foreign Policy and the Multilateral Agenda," 14 November 2001, available at http://www.state.gov/s/p/rem/6134.htm.

39. Karen A. Mingst and Margaret P. Karns, *The United Nations in the 21st Century* (Boulder, CO: Westview, 2006). For trend data on international political preferences, see Erik Voeten, "Resisting the Lonely Superpower: Responses of States in the United Nations to U.S. Dominance," *Journal of Politics* 66, no. 3 (2004): 742.

40. See Daniel Drezner, "Regime Proliferation and the Tragedy of the Global Institutional Commons," available at http://fletcher.tufts.edu/FILA/pdf/FILADiscussionPaperNo0109.pdf, 9.

41. Author's interview with Jamie Shea, Director of Policy Planning at NATO Headquarters, 23 May 2007.

42. Josef Joffe, "Gulliver Unbound: Can America Rule the World," John Bonython Lecture, Sydney Australia, 5 August 2003. Available at http://www.aicgs.org/documents/csi.pdf.; Richard N. Haass, "The Age of Nonpolarity," *Foreign Affairs* (May–June 2008): 56.

43. Barry Posen, "Command of the Commons: The Military Foundations of U.S. Hegemony," *International Security* 28, no. 1 (2003): 44.

44. Arthur Stein interview with Foreign Affairs and International Trade Canada, 5 December 2008, available at http://www.dfait-maeci.gc.ca/cip-pic/discussions/non-proliferation/video/stein.aspx?lang=eng.

45. Dennis Ross, *Statecraft, and How to Restore America's Standing in the World* (New York: Farrar, Straus, and Giroux, 2007), 335–339.

Index

Martha
    Finnemore
Kissinger
Classical realist
    A World Restored

Evangelista